WHITE MAGIC
WHITE MAGI
WHITE MAG
WHITEMA
WHITEM

WHITE MAG IC

ESSAYS

ELISSA WASHUTA

TIN HOUSE Portland, Oregon

Published by Tin House, Portland, Oregon

Distributed by W. W. Norton & Company

Library of Congress Cataloging-in-Publication Data

Names: Washuta, Elissa, author.
Title: White magic : essays / Elissa Washuta.
Description: Portland, Oregon : Tin House, [2021] | Includes
  bibliographical references.
Identifiers: LCCN 2020043847 | ISBN 9781951142391 (hardcover) |
  ISBN 9781953534019 (paperback) | ISBN 9781951142407 (ebook)
Subjects: LCSH: Washuta, Elissa.—Psychology. | Witchcraft. | Witches—
  United States—Psychology. | Indians of North America—Psychology.
Classification: LCC BF1598.W37 A3 2021 | DDC 133.4/30973—dc23
LC record available at https://lccn.loc.gov/2020043847

First US Paperback Edition 2022
Printed in the USA
Interior design by Jakob Vala

www.tinhouse.com

CONTENTS

This book
is dedicated
to WES

WHITE WITCHERY

An Introduction

HEADLINE: Man with land acknowledgment in his
Tinder bio declared "too woke to die"

*[Image of half-smiling white man with vest, ACAB button,
white button-down shirt, and coffee mug, in a café]*

TEXT OVERLAY: "before I ghost you, I'd like to acknowledge that this date is taking place on stolen land"

—@decolonial.meme.queens,
via Instagram

I'll stop writing abt my body's danger
when one of those goes away

—Tommy Pico, *Junk*

SOME GIRL AT SCHOOL ONCE had a mood ring. We girls were quiet about it the way we were quiet about the rolled waistbands of our uniform skirts, which we concealed with the loose overhangs of tucked-in polos. Both were kinds of witchcraft the nuns forbade: spells done with sacred tools, the conjuring power of our hips.

I bought a mood ring at the mall. On my finger, it turned from black to green and sometimes to orange when my hands filled with hot desire. A witch brings change to the seen world using unseen forces; a witch gestures through the veil between worlds. Wearing the ring, I saw my thoughts on my hand. This is how I learned I wanted witchcraft: by paying for something cheap.

Now thirty-three, I have crystals scavenged from places unknown and unimaginable after the rocks are tumbled, polished, and turned into tiny vessels to hold wishes and dread. The stones, I know, belonged to somebody's homeland. I worried about my crystals long before I read Emily Atkin's piece for the *New Republic*, which asks the reader, "Do You Know Where Your Healing Crystals Come From?" In the article, business owner Julie Abouzelof says crystal sourcing is unclear in part because of "the deep, psychological construct of the mining industry, where everything is a little bit hidden."

I know about hidden things: gathering locations, fishing spots. What happens in some ceremonies. Once, I went with my aunties to pick huckleberries on the mountain where aunties have picked since the beginning of time, but we got nearly nothing, because we were late in the season and the white people were early.

If you let whiteness in, it takes you for everything you've got.

○

Not long ago, the witches got upset on the internet. Sephora was going to sell a "starter witch kit"—tarot cards, sage, rose quartz, perfume—and the witches thought it was wrong for the makeup store to peddle spiritual tools alongside pore refiners. As a Native woman and an occult enthusiast, I had an opinion. I had an opinion about a Macklemore video interview in which a non-Native astrologer teaches him to burn white sage, a traditional medicine for California Native peoples; in the wild, it's threatened by non-Native overharvesting. I had an opinion when I saw an Instagram promoted post featuring a pentagram dream catcher beside the text of a "Good Luck Spell" and tagged #witch, #wicca, and anything close.

I kept those opinions to myself. Better to leave the critiques to people who don't buy candles from stores where non-Native people sell sage bundles, I thought. The first time I browsed a magic store, I saw shelves of sage and cedar shrink-wrapped against abalone shells, and even though I recoiled, I still exchanged my money for a divination deck. I've been looking the other way ever since.

As a child, I read picture books about girl witches. As a preteen, hoping to find a way to make magic in isolation, I took to the still-adolescent World Wide Web, where glimmering

Angelfire websites warned me I had better not try anything without a coven. In my heavily Catholic forest-and-farmland slice of New Jersey, I never did find one. The authors of those prescriptions were Wiccans, and there was no way into their closed world, even through hyperlinks.

Nearly four years ago, in early 2015, chronically drunk and desperate for relief in the Seattle suburbs, I decided the white Wiccans of the web were wrong: I could go it alone and access the power. I needed to believe things happened for a reason. I had witch friends. Even my therapist seemed witch-adjacent. Witchcraft is sold as self-help, and occultist aesthetics inspire Starbucks drinks; hardly anyone talks about covens or "rules." A witch needs only the right look, the right stuff, the right feelings. I look the part: like a Hollywood witch, dark-haired and pale-skinned (because of my European ancestry). And I'm into the Instagram-witch lifestyle: black dresses, lavender baths, affirmations about being worthy of things. But I don't like calling myself a witch. I don't want to be seen as following a fad, and I don't want the white witches I resemble to take my presence in their spaces as permission for theft. Really, I just want a version of the occult that isn't built on plunder, but I suspect that if we could excise the stolen pieces, there would be nothing left.

I've executed successful bindings against men I feared. I've cast spells I probably shouldn't have with hair and spit. I play fast and loose, sifting through websites for formulas but rarely willing to follow the steps. Even when the spells work, I feel like an amateur and an interloper. But the white women who dominate the online esoteric marketplace cannot hoard this power. When I was thirteen and first desperate for magic, I hadn't yet read Leslie Marmon Silko's *Storyteller*: "The world was already complete / even without white people. / There was everything / including witchery."

O

I am Cowlitz. My people are indigenous to what is currently southwestern Washington. I was born in New Jersey, lived in Washington (in Coast Salish territory, to the north of my ancestral homeland) from 2007 to 2017, and now live in Ohio. In Washington, I was introduced to Native spiritual practices I will not describe here. Know only that my physical husk was wilting around my incapacitated spirit. I had been reading tarot and trying out spells for a few months, but the occult was not enough. Native friends taught me to maintain relationships with place spirits and ancestors. In April 2015, at age thirty, I stopped drinking the alcohol that made my insides bleed. Something was lodged in there, clawing. Today, I feel it holding my lungs in its fists, and I can't sob hard enough to cry it out.

When I felt myself shredded, I used to wade into Lake Washington, stand on a ledge of land overlooking the bay, or walk through the strip of urban forest where cedars shaded salal. The land put me back together. In Ohio, the land and I talk like strangers. I'm running out of medicines, down to two dwindling bundles of sage, a couple of sweetgrass braids, and a charred bit of juniper that won't light. I know who gathered these. Magic stores sell sage, but even when they make their sourcing clear, I don't like the idea of paying non-Natives for these medicines.

Witches of the internet photograph sage against bright white backgrounds and market it as space-clearing incense. To me, the medicines have nothing to do with witchcraft, except that I use both to speak to spirits. I am not a medicine woman or a healer. I am a person with an internet connection and a credit card I can use to buy candles and charmed oils to cast the kind of spell that might rip a little hole in the world, the kind I might wish I could take back once it's done, the only kind I believe in. If I don't follow the spells as written, am I really a witch? The truth is I'm not a witch, exactly: I'm a person with prayers, a person who believes in spirits and plays with fire.

I am still alive and ambulatory after having been raped more times than I can recall, threatened with a knife and a gun, smothered, choked, held down, and stalked, over the course of several years and at the hands of more than several men. I've wrapped my arms around men who told me I should fear them or told me I had nothing to fear. I've been alone, certain no good man would waste his life with the rotting apple core of me.

Even when I listen to my sobriety-sharpened intuition about the men I choose, I'm not safe from strangers: the man who grabbed my thigh on the sidewalk, the guys who followed me in and out of every restaurant I speed-walked into to try to lose them, the man working on my house who pointed to my drill and growled, "I love a woman with her own tools."

Witches say, *Trust the universe, trust the divine.* But that's hard when I'm at the gym, lifting weights under a television that can't be turned off or muted, forced either to listen to today's American rape takes or leave and quit making myself strong. I am subject to the wants of a country conjured up by invaders who raped, maimed, and killed until they could settle their dream like a film over the land that held the treasure they wanted. Every day, the universe reminds me that, yes, I am safe now, but I am in America. I could be gouged out again.

I live under the tyrannical rule of my PTSD triggers. My worst panic comes by way of quiet and calm, because it's always quiet before the palm covers my mouth or the hand grabs my thigh or the footsteps begin to trail me. Placidity is a cavity that wants to be filled.

I cannot control this world. I shut my eyes, try to cry or not cry, and ask benevolent spirits for intercession. I make my body solid so the spirits will know I believe it's worth protecting, even if I'm not sure that's true.

In *As We Have Always Done: Indigenous Freedom through Radical Resistance*, Leanne Betasamosake Simpson writes that when the colonizers—white men without available white women—first encroached upon what they later called North America, they saw Indigenous women as sexual outlets. Indigenous women's sexual autonomy was thus considered threatening. This isn't over yet: "Colonizers want land, but Indigenous bodies forming nations are in the way because they have a strong attachment to land and because they replicate Indigeneity," and the colonizers "see Indigenous women's and girls' bodies as the bodies that reproduce nations." The results are embedded in so many of us: "The attack on our bodies, minds, and spirits, and the intimate trauma this encodes is how dispossession is maintained."

O

I tried to find an Ohio therapist soon after moving but gave up after a half dozen responded that they weren't accepting new patients. Years of weekly therapy had made me feel solid enough that I decided to wait. Ten months later, when my PTSD episodes returned, I made more inquiries; I got on a waitlist for a therapist, and two months after that, on another waitlist. In early September, I finally had an appointment and was asked to complete a behavioral health questionnaire: *Have you ever believed that someone was reading your mind or could hear your thoughts, or that you could actually read someone's mind or hear what another person was thinking?* Yes. In the office, I spent an hour trying to rush through the recounting of every bad thing.

"Do you ever hear or see or feel things that aren't real?" the therapist asked. I hedged—what is *real*, anyway?—but she pushed. I told her that sometimes when I'm trying to fall asleep I feel fingers in my hair. I didn't tell her I've assumed this is either a ghost or an astral projection. In her pause, I realized I'd just told her I was first raped after being startled from sleep; years later, I woke up in the middle of the night to find my then-boyfriend's hands pressing my nose and mouth shut.

"You've experienced an incredible amount of trauma," the therapist said. Too much for her. She found me someone else, whose first available appointment was a month out. I'm still waiting. Today I cried so hard I thought the capillaries around my eyes might burst again, like a baby's, like they have before. In the mirror, only my dead old face.

○

For my moods, I've tried Lexapro, Seroquel, lithium, Lamictal, Wellbutrin, Zoloft, Celexa, Ativan, Klonopin, and Abilify. For my night fear, I've tried L-theanine, melatonin, tryptophan, magnesium, Benadryl, and herbs. Ten years of antipsychotics, prescribed by a psychiatrist who diagnosed me with bipolar disorder, didn't work. Even whiskey didn't always work, unless I drank so much of it that the physical terrors grabbed all my attention and I ended up with my chin hooked onto the inner rim of the toilet bowl.

In late 2015, after a few months of sobriety, an addiction-focused psychiatrist changed my diagnosis to alcohol use disorder in full sustained remission and post-traumatic stress disorder. He told me it was unlikely I'd ever been bipolar. My medications didn't fit my new diagnosis, so he helped me taper off them.

The PTSD diagnosis scared me. My triggers and traumas had been allowed to multiply unchecked, making for a hefty pile of kindling that would catch fire from the smallest sparks: a boyfriend's irritated silence, a stranger's shouting from down the street. My challenge would be to learn through therapy to function in a world full of reminders that I would probably be harmed again.

Simpson writes:

I don't necessarily want to "heal," because I am not damaged, or diseased, or unhealthy. My response to the inter-generational trauma of settler colonial violence is correct and strong and vital . . . I want to have processed hurt and pain to the point where I can speak back to those words and harness the power of fear, hatred, and love into sustained mobilization—to the point where they don't control me, but they are experiences I can draw on when it is useful to do so.

When I choose, anoint, and burn a candle with my prayers scratched into the wax, when I make my prayers material, I convince myself I can grab on to a power that will carry me through this life. I know how to show the spirits I'm here through the light of my fire, because we have always used fire to smoke fish, conduct ceremony, burn cedar boughs, turn prairie brush to ash so the camas or huckleberries can grow stronger.

I choose witchcraft; I choose to cast spells.

Because I have given up my ability to touch a western red cedar on a daily basis. Because I have seen my binding work on a dangerous man. Because I am alone and low on hope sometimes.

○

Today, sludgy with dread, I'm going to get my weekly allergy shot. I realize I've forgotten to take the pill meant to reduce the risk of anaphylaxis. Two months ago I also forgot to take the pill: after the allergen injection, my face got hot, the oxygen supply to my brain decreased, and I felt faint. That's when I ate a fruit leather, in case I was hungry; it didn't help, so I looked up anaphylaxis on WebMD. My arms felt nearly too weighed-down to use the phone, so I told the receptionist, "Nurse." Then I was in a reclining chair, nurses and doctors all around me, blood pressure cuff on one arm, pulse-taker on a finger, EpiPen in my thigh. They say you're supposed to sense doom when anaphylaxis hits, but I always sense doom; when my body reacted, I felt

ELISSA WASHUTA

only wonder that it could reroute its energy and keep me alive. My body pulled blood from the limbs and head, quaked with uterine cramps as though I was menstruating, and sent little bolts of lightning to the soles of my feet. I felt so hot and alive in the inches of space from death.

Today, I find myself thinking I wouldn't mind it happening again.

This is a bad thought. I call the therapist's office to ask for an earlier appointment. No luck. I ask the scheduler, "I guess there's no, like, urgent care for mental health, right?"

"The emergency room," she says.

I go up to my magic place in the attic and wipe down my altar—maybe it's an altar, maybe it's just the surface where I lay my candles and my shells full of smoldering sage, maybe it's a wooden toy oven I found in the garage of my last Seattle apartment building, abandoned by some child who outgrew it. I want to outgrow something. I want to ungrow back into the child who truly believed in magic. I google spells to take the PTSD out of me. But is that what I want? To stop my brain from thrashing against the wickedness America stuffed inside?

I need to get better and I'm out of ideas. I arrange the candles, and I pray.

○

Tonight, I'm at a magic store I visited for the first time yesterday, when I needed a small stone to hold in my shaking hand. The woman who helped me said to come back the next day for a women's spiritual circle. Suggested donation: three dollars. I

12

found exactly that in my wallet today. This store, a tight space with a busy back room, feels so far from Instagram's crystal glitter. These women, not all of whom are white, haven't called themselves witches tonight.

In the circle, we speak into a bucket and cough out our fears, and then a bundle of plants—nothing I recognize—is lit. I've been told smudging is more than just the touching of flame to dried plants and getting close to the smoke; it's a piece of a cosmology, not teachable through a YouTube video. I don't know where these plants lived. I don't know who harvested them or whether those people gave anything to the land in return. I don't know what I can do to reciprocate the healing the plants are offering tonight. All I can do is promise these plants that if I get well, I will try to figure it out.

I speak every fear into the bucket: That I am not safe. That I am too wounded to be anything but a burden. That the best of me has been taken, the rest of me left to grope for a calm that might never be anything but potential space for danger. That the spirits are indifferent to me or don't exist at all. I speak until I'm through, then cough from the base of my body. I'm not healed, but I feel better.

It's dark when I walk to my car. A white man approaches me, silent and high. When I pass him, he turns and follows. My ninth-grade writing teacher taught me that when I was afraid, I could make my aura grow so everyone would stay away. A psychic once told me my aura was dark. Like a mood ring on a corpse. I have nothing now but my big aura, my fistful of keys, and my throat that still knows how to scream because no man has succeeded in closing it. If I am going to die, I want to fight.

I've been fighting the colonizers' whispers that I'm not wanted here, not worthy of protection, nothing but a body to be pummeled and played with and threatened into submission. I have not died yet. My whole body is a fire, lit back when the world was complete, never extinguished by anybody.

O

I was born just before the dawning of the Age of Aquarius, or maybe a couple of decades after it, or maybe it hasn't even dawned, and anyway, I didn't know what that meant until I looked it up on Wikipedia. We crystal witches of the internet think what we're about is not *New Age*, but it surrounds us like water surrounds a fish. I'm learning from Wikipedia that it's exactly what we're about, only we get our horoscopes as tweets and find our psychics on Yelp. We want the divine. We want to be healed and we want to fix. Most of all, we seek what we can't locate in the vast universe of the internet: reassurance that it will be okay.

New Age eats the ancient, trying to digest old systems. It's a collage of angels, magic numbers, incantations, and stolen beliefs. A collage is made not just of what's there, but also of the absence of the material from which the pieces are cut. I got good at working gaps in essays, but not in life. Instead of fearing silence and disrupting stillness, I want to be ready to set down my cards, close the JPEG of my natal chart, and ask the quiet to tell me what this life should be.

O

I'm inclined to now list the things I know about the occult. This seems like the place to talk about witch picture books that introduced me to written words, episodes of *Sabrina the Teenage Witch* that wormed into my brain as backdrop to my homework, and haunted houses across the ghost-obsessed pocket of rural New Jersey where I spent my first eighteen years. I've been reading about witchcraft and spiritualism and Carl Jung and all kinds of mysteries, and I feel I should introduce a literature review here to show that I know the history of the dark arts, but I actually don't. The purpose would only be to convince you I'm not stupid.

I couldn't convince any of my boyfriends, so I doubt I could convince someone looking at me through the thick veil of this page. Anyway, I don't care about Crowley or Salem, only about my own conjuring. I haven't memorized the entries in the catalog of demons. I don't even know the name of the one inside me.

O

Before I was born, I chose this body. I read that on the internet. My soul needed flesh and slipped into this case knowing my skin would feel like a body bag and my organs would refuse to handle what I fed them. I chose it knowing I would want to starve it and sun-singe it. I chose a pretty body, an elastic body that would swell and shrink, a little-boned body I would push to every edge because I knew I could get so close to snapping it. This would mean I chose the body knowing it would be raped. Did I? Does that mean I let it happen? I don't like that. The internet says that before I was born, I made soul contracts with everyone who would bring me change. It sounds like another way to say I was asking for it. I don't know what could've made my soul ask for violation.

Before I was incarnated, I chose my mother and the moment I would tear out of her, and so I chose my natal chart, a cosmic map. I chose every planet's position in the heavens. One of the first things I learned about astrology was that my natal sun is in the eighth-house; my therapist had generated my natal chart, and she told me this house is about sex, death, and transformation. Mysteries, shared power, the depths, psychic knowing. The eighth-house sun breaks us and makes us mend. Maybe this is why I've sought, over and over, to dissolve myself into boys and men. This underworld sun lit me with the lumens that would transfix them, pull them toward my pretty face, and break us both.

I was a child with outsize wants for boys who weren't ready to be wanted. I was a little girl afraid of the dark, depressed by the light. I wanted Halloween all the time. I wanted the pit of death buried inside life: when a woman on TV stripped off her clothes and dropped the straps of her bra, I thought, *Okay, here it is, we're gonna see her bones.* When my teen body began to rupture physically, starting with a shoulder tear, I asked for the medical images of my insides. I was a teenager afflicted by night terrors: visible blue shapes by my bed, the feeling of being watched even under the covers. In my parents' midcentury ranch house, I ran from ghosts I felt but never saw. Like most of my boyfriends have said, I'm stupid and I'll believe anything, including that dead people are out to get me, or that my thoughts are so loud they'll betray my silence if someone listens hard enough.

At first the thoughts I tried to guard were the ones that came to me in the back of Dad's extended-cab pickup, riding through the forest into town: *I'm ugly I'm awkward I'll never be wanted I'm wrong I'm just not right I'm sad I could die in these woods and I'm with the only three people who would notice I'm gone.* In the Age of Aquarius, it is said to be normal for us to hate ourselves and want out; I've read that this is why we need to raise the whole world's vibrations with our meditation and orgasms. Maybe things would've been different if I'd believed I could effect any change in the world that drove boys to throw basketballs at my head and pin me between the high school theater stage wall and the thick velvet curtain, feeling for my soft parts and gaps. Maybe I wouldn't have ended up under a college boy who showed me that my *no* was not enough, whose wall-hammering, shoulder-pressing hands had more power than my pulpy fear.

Nobody ever told me about *intuition.* They told me to count my drinks and plan my routes home but never that the sensation of gut muscles constricting tight as snakes around rodents was really the way my body screams when it knows something that hasn't happened yet. I hid the rape pain in my hips, denying it for a year, until I took up fencing and the demands on my joints forced the pain to erupt into my flesh. I cried every day. I hid in the woods. I roamed campus at night like a ghost in a graveyard. I found a doctor who called it *depression* and then *bipolar disorder* but never *fear of what happened and what might happen,* never *post-traumatic stress disorder,* never *the brain's storage of the worst violence its flesh knows,* never anything but unmendable defects.

I was told I'd be bipolar until death. Back made of bottles, pills for ribs. My medications would be with me forever: lithium to pull the mood poles together, antipsychotics for the brain screams, anticonvulsants to dull the effects of the antipsychotics, antidepressants to make me want to live. My body was slowly replaced by a new one: resurfaced, welt-speckled face; silvering hair; waterlogged cells bloating to pad bones. The kidneys were overtaxed, then the liver, too.

Because I had to drink. I smoked weed and swallowed Vicodin and Ativan. If I wasn't drunk or high, I would pay too much attention to my smart body's warnings. I once went to the ER bleeding from the inside.

I have no choice but to live among men. I used toxins to try to kill the part of me that could tell me the truth about this world: that I am going to want to open myself to all of it, and that this is probably how I am going to die.

O

I may have learned from *The Wizard of Oz* that *white magic* is supposedly good and *black magic* wicked. When I googled for spells to get the things I wanted, I turned up warnings that playing with black magic was a bad idea. I figured I was safe: I never cut anybody to get their blood, dug up cadavers, or hexed my enemies.

The internet cannot agree on definitions for black and white magic, but there is some consensus around the notion that white magic is used for good, for healing, and for selfless purposes; it is a high-vibration activity, the white witches say, and it is natural. Plants and candles and things. Black magic, they say, is selfish, malicious, and chaotic; it's for getting the bad things your heart wants; it is disruption. Blood, potions, sorcery. Of course, this is consumptive anti-Blackness and anti-Indigeneity. Some white witches say spiritual practices with African and African diasporic origins are *low vibrational, practiced by unhappy people.* Others buy and sell candles depicting orishas they don't even know.

White occultists' fascination with caricatures of Indigeneity turns up in so many corners of New Age, metaphysical, and occult practice. It always has. In the late 1800s, white people asked long-haired Indian spirit maidens to visit séance tables and tell them how to live. In the 1940s, white people visiting a Manitoba residential school offered candy to starving Indigenous children to secure their participation in a study about whether they could, using Indian senses, read researchers' minds.

I don't know what a vibration is. I know that for thousands of years, my people have had an agreement with the salmon that they will allow us to eat them, and every year, in honor of this relationship, we take a fish from the river, kill it, cook it the way we always have, and eat the flesh. This is not magic, black or white: it's tending and care.

I do use magic to get what my selfish heart wants: sometimes money, mostly love. If white magic brings light and black magic brings pain, I can see where my incantations fall. Love is exquisitely painful. I want it more than anything, and I will tear open the world to get it.

O

If there is nothing greater than sad flesh and what it touches, I need a magician to build an illusion to distract me from anguish. I was born to be sawed in half. Pulled apart in front of a crowd. Put back together. Plunged into a water tank, forced to free myself from a knotted rope. Disappeared into the divot in my mattress for days, reemerging in sunlight. Summoned from the other world. Before I was born, I chose to walk along the river that will take me to the underworld in this perishable body.

The underworld sun tells me to lodge a man's body inside me, to be cleaved, to seek a love to consume us. I set my intention to build a cult of two. If I mean it when I ask to be broken by desire, the universe will break me.

The internet says I will not release my karma across lifetimes until I learn my lesson. I am ready for this to be my last life. I do not want to come back. I'm bound by a pattern, like a ghost that haunts until—what? Or a tarot card that keeps appearing until I understand. A transit of one planet to another that opens a wound every time it circles around. Over and over, another boyfriend hurts me and leaves me.

There is something I'm missing. Without it, I can't exit the time loops teaching me through pain. Seeking out another man never works; instead, I'll open my wounds and dig out what men left. When I pull the ten swords from my back, when I die to myself, when I am transformed—I think I will feel the snap of this riddle's answer, and I'm close.

THE FIREMAN: I will tell you three things. If I tell them to you and they come true, then will you believe me?

DALE COOPER: Who's that?

THE FIREMAN: Think of me as a friend.

DALE COOPER: Where do you come from?

THE FIREMAN: The question is, *Where have you gone?* The three things are:

(*Twin Peaks*)

ACT I.

ACE OF CUPS.

A hand emerges from a cloud, holding a chalice. Waters cascade from the cup into the pool full of lily pads below. A dove descends to place a Communion host in the cup.

THE DEVIL.

The horned, winged beast-man perches with harpy feet on a block in a black room, torch in his hand, pentagram on his head. A man and woman stand small and naked below, loose chains around their necks attached to the beast's block. They have horns and tails, his made of fire, hers a berry, and he offers her his hand.

DEATH.

A skeleton in black armor rides a white horse among fallen people. Across a river and above a cliff, the sun rises or sets between towers.

A NARRATIVE HAS A BEGINNING, middle, and end. It could start with the protagonist in crisis. With a hook, maybe. A violent tool. It could start in the middle of the action or in a moment heavy with impending calamity. It should not start in a morning bed, waking from a dream. People only like dreams of their own.

A narrative could start with calm, the kind that can't last. The reader needs to wonder what's going to happen. It should start with someone wanting something so bad they'll do anything, or, at least, they'll do something. Maybe they know what they want. Maybe they don't, or have the wrong idea.

There must be trouble. A protagonist in danger. She should be thrust by high stakes into her journey and shoved off by an inciting incident. A satisfying narrative takes its shape from story structures readers recognize in their bones. The writing should teach the reader how to read it. I don't know what that means, but it's true.

Fiction writers make plot; in nonfiction, writers make insights. We shape the recollected by how the remembering changes us. The mind wants to understand what's done but not settled.

The past is boring because it's over. There is another way. You can make up plot points in nonfiction, and you can do it without lying. You just have to make your life a book. I can't recommend it. I was trapped, stuck in a hole. I was bored by what I wanted; I decided to follow my curiosity about what I *desired*. I'm best as a protagonist. I can make anything meaningful. Look at all these motifs I made for you, this rejection pain I transformed into epic heartbreak. See what a powerful witch I am?

Plot is a cause-and-effect sequence of arranged events in a created work. Narrative, same. I checked a craft book to confirm: the index said, "Plot. *See* Conflict." I thought I was anti-plot until I realized my thinking is mostly building sequence and imposing consequence. I make narratives to make sense of what happened to me.

But then I began adding plot points. I like the real: essays about life. Realer still, I figured: life about essay. It's cliché to explain that the word *essay* comes from the Middle French verb *essaier*, meaning "to try, to attempt." Now I've gone and said it. But what about this: what about essaying not just to try to think through a thing, but to force life to become a string of plot points. To make calamity from calm.

Years ago, I built a book from looping failure cycles. In every essay, I turned over the same things, asking new angles for answers. But understanding was not enough to make me whole. The book did not end with resolution. This one has to. I think what follows would be called *stand-alone essays*. Fine. Or you could think of this as a dossier, the evidence of my attempts. If I don't exit these time loops, these men echoing men, their cause, my effect, I'll meet my tragic end. I'm saying a man might kill me if I keep choosing wrong. The protagonist's stakes are what might be lost or gained when she takes a risk. I could write a book about what happened and what it all meant, attaching stakes to understanding it all. Or I could raise them. I could gain a life I can't imagine if I find my way out.

LITTLE LIES

All my life,
since I was ten,
I've been waiting
to be in
this hell here
with you;
all I've ever
wanted, and
still do.

—Alice Notley

If a man was never to lie to me. *Never lie me.*
I swear I would never leave him.

—Louise Erdrich, "The Strange People"[1]

---

1. So many epigraphs! Are you wondering whether I'm going to do this with every essay? How does that make you feel?
   a. Do you love epigraphs? If so, skip the rest of this footnote.
   b. Do you hate epigraphs? Do they make you mad? Do they bore you? Did you absorb what you just read? Are the epigraphs for you or are the epigraphs for me? Is that a leading question?

I TEXT MY BROTHER, NATE, *tell me again what you remember from the D.A.R.E. video.* He doesn't respond right away because he has a full life. He has a girlfriend and a puppy. He exercises and he goes to the beach. I just have this phone with a big screen to help me see my ex-boyfriend Carl's Instagram better. His *X-Files* stills, Perpetua-filtered amps, impossible lips, deep shelf of frown over eyes that used to meet mine sometimes. I google alone:

> *D.A.R.E. video phil collins fleetwood mac*

No.

> *Teen 80s drunk driving D.A.R.E. video in the air tonight phil collins little lies fleetwood mac*

No.

The only good thing about the internet's omniscience is that if I crack the search-term code, I'll finally find this video the nuns and cops made us watch.

Google turns up PSAs in which young people enjoy life, get into cars, and die. "If you don't stop your friend from drinking and driving, you're as good as dead," a God-voice says while a kid in a varsity jacket starts a car. With the sound of thunder and a bolt of lightning, the passengers turn into skeletons. Cut to a black screen: a fleshy hand and a skeleton hand reach for each other under the words

DRINKING AND DRIVING
CAN KILL A FRIENDSHIP

But I don't find what I'm looking for.
Nate texts me back:

These kids lied to their parents about where they were going

And they instead went to some party and i think did coke

And i remember little lies playing

And i remember them getting into an accident and being under a sheet

And phil collins was playing

Which is what I remember, too, and I feel like I'm never going to find this video, so I get up to get a can of water. When I get frustrated, I get thirsty.

○

The lyrics for "In the Air Tonight," Phil Collins's 1981 hit from one of the literally countless records featuring his face, are the subject of enough speculation that the song has a Snopes.com page. Most of the song's origin stories are lies, or, as Snopes.com says, "apocryphal." It's believed that Phil Collins witnessed a man drowning and didn't help him because the man was either a rapist or was sleeping with Phil Collins's wife. Or that Phil Collins witnessed a man drowning but was too drunk to save him. Or it wasn't Phil Collins who saw the man drown, but a camp counselor haunted by his failure to save a camper. Here's the Snopes-debunked claim I like best: "I heard that Phil Collins when he [was] small, witnessed an individual drowning another individual. Apparently that individual looked up and spotted Phil. To this day, at every concert, Phil starts out singing this song as an accusation aimed at this individual."

According to Snopes.com, the song "In the Air Tonight" is about a failed romance.

○

I haven't been on a date in three months, and that's assuming I was on a date with Carl when we went out for deviled eggs this summer for a goodbye visit a few days before I moved from Seattle to Ohio. I would say it was a date because I had sex with him. Until that point, whether we were on a date was unclear, even as I pressed my knees against his skinny black jeans and he spoke haltingly, as if he were translating the words of a ghost.

Lately, I don't date and the money I save goes toward making sure I always have at least a hundred cans of sparkling water. As soon as I stopped drinking alcohol two and a half years ago, I began carrying bricks of canned water into my apartment. I filled my mouth with carbonated jabs through every recovery meeting while people talked about drinking enough whiskey to drown a pancreas and I thought, *God, that would really hit the spot.* Now, canned water molecules form replacements for my dead, sloughed-off cells.

O

Washington State is a squatter polity knifed out from my ancestral homeland. I'm enrolled in the Cowlitz Indian Tribe, and I also have ancestry from the Cascade people, whose descendants belong to various tribes, including Yakama, Warm Springs, and Grand Ronde. In 1856, a year after my Cascade great-great-great-grandfather Tumulth signed a treaty through which he and other leaders ceded their Columbia River valley land to the United States, an ongoing war over settlers' treaty violations came to the Cascades of the Columbia River.[2] Yakamas and Klickitats attacked the Americans who occupied an important fishing site in order to guard an overland portage around the rapids. Some Cascade Indian men joined the fighting, but many, including Tumulth, did not.

Lawrence Coe, an American, recounted, "They did not attack us at night, but on the second morning commenced again

---

2. The river has names—like wimahl and nči-wána—given to it by the peoples who have lived in relationship with it forever. Columbia, a name assigned by white people as a tribute to the first ship they took up the river, is currently widely used among Native peoples still in relationship with it, including my family, and it's the name by which I know the river.

as lively as ever. We had no water, but did have about two dozen of ale [*sic*] and a few bottles of whiskey. These gave out during the day."

This past summer, in that parched land, wildfires spread so quickly it seemed they might devour every living and dead thing. I can't picture Tumulth with the executioner's rope around his neck when the US government murdered him at the end of that battle, but I can picture those bottles and feel the shudder of astringent-soaked organs on a hot day, no water anywhere, liquor mummifying the corpse even while it jangles its arms. That's just day drinking.

Sometimes, when I'm gulping soda water, a date will ask, *Do you ever miss it?*

○

A student enters D.A.R.E. (Drug Abuse Resistance Education) by signing an oath to be drug-free. Not until I transferred to public school for eighth grade did D.A.R.E. introduce the drunk goggles and the box of fake drugs. In Catholic school, we had the cop and the video. I called the school years later to ask whether they had the VHS. They said to call the cop. But Google doesn't know where he is.

The video, Nate and I determined, was birthed sometime between 1987 and 1991. Plot points include teen drunk driving, a car crash, and a funeral. The soundtrack is the strongest of any film ever made: when I hear "In the Air Tonight," I still imagine the hush after the crash, viscera ripped by metal mangled into claws, and I feel I might die, too. "Little Lies," we think, played while the teens pregamed in a kitchen before their lives changed forever, which is to say they died. If there weren't menace ahead, there would be no video. In real life, without soundtrack cues, we have to find other ways of marking plot points if we want to believe this existence means anything.

O

The internet forgot that when I was a high school freshman, my friend Lacey's crush, a popular kid with a porcelain-blond bowl cut, died. My recollection—unconfirmed, because even the newspaper archive searches turn up nothing—is that he died in a car wreck. Lacey, a liar, used to talk about the times they went to the club and got super fucked up, but I suspect they'd never spoken. The yearbook "In Memory" page is hardly helpful. A poem about heaven accompanies quotes from his friends:

"I will never forget him."

"I will always remember the things we did together as long as I live."

"His smile and laugh will be remembered and the memories that have been shared will last a lifetime."

I only learn that we share a birthday and that he really was handsome enough for a sad teen to want to build an imaginary life with.

O

Fleetwood Mac's "Little Lies" is not about underage drinking: it's about a failed romance.

O

In the 1850s, in order to grab land along the coast and the Columbia River, the US government whipped up a batch of treaties built from stock language. The one Tumulth signed reads:

> In order to prevent the evils of intemperance among said Indians, it is hereby provided that any one of them who shall drink liquor, or procure it for other Indians to drink, may have his or her proportion of the annuities withheld from him or her for such time as the President may determine.

One year after treaty signing, the white people had ales and whiskey in the blockhouse where they hunkered down during the skirmish at the Cascades; when they ran out, men axed down the saloon door in their haste to grab English porter, brandy, whiskey, wine, and oyster crackers. "We failed to get water," wrote Sgt. Robert Williams, "but the articles mentioned satisfied every requirement except surgical aid until we would get relief, which we knew was close at hand by hearing the report of gallant Phil Sheridan's guns firing upon the enemy at the Lower Cascades."

Fifty-four years later, photographer Edward Curtis reported that Tumulth's daughter Virginia told him, "The Indians, after the disturbance of 1855–56, were dying off in great numbers through the use of whiskey—so called—whole canoe-loads drowning."

One hundred and five years after that, in the traditional territory of people who came to the river to trade with us, I woke with a man—not Carl, another one I met a year before meeting Carl—asleep in my bed, stinking cups on the nightstand, and my skin a husk that couldn't stop my innards from evaporating. In the mirror, I saw I was dying.

In recovery, I was expected to tell my story over and over. At first, I didn't know what to say, except that in the weeks prior, my underarms stank of what seemed like liver fumes. My face was papier-mâché over a balloon. No DUI, no court order, no intervention, just the swollen skull-case in the mirror. I could hardly see a story there because I was living out the dénouement.

O

"Little Lies" is a Christine McVie concoction. I'm enchanted only because of the D.A.R.E. video: I'm your typical Stevie Nicks witch. Christine, a homebody without an addiction crisis and redemptive journey, rarely even stars in her own profiles. Most of them focus on Stevie, who says, "All of us were drug addicts, but there was a point where I was the worst drug addict. I was a girl, I was fragile, and I was doing a lot of coke. And I had that hole in my nose." This hole sounds like figurative kin to the metaphorical hole in my heart that, a sponsor used to tell me, I'd tried filling with whiskey, but Stevie's was literally a hole, gouged by liquid aspirin and a million dollars' worth of cocaine.

I know about Stevie's nose because I like the celebrity gossip site updates on aged rock stars. That's how I learned about Phil Collins's recovery from alcoholism. In his tell-all, he recounts an addiction that can be developed on the cheap: the inciting incident is a divorce during a career lull, the rising action is a love affair with whiskey and vodka, the climax is a pool of blood and teeth marks on tile. I imagine Phil Collins sitting in a recovery meeting room folding chair, addressing his story to his clasped hands while I stick my tongue into an aluminum can across the room.

But it wasn't alcoholism, he says: "I think it was just filling the hole."

○

I never fell, never bled (except from the inside, during the weeks when I pissed red). I was a careful drunk, sleeping on the floor next to the toilet, mouth to ground. During my first months sober, I was ashamed I'd never almost died because I kept hearing I was supposed to have hit bottom.

The more I told my story in rooms full of drying-out people, the more my narrative arc shaped itself into that of a rock star's rise and fall. Details became significant when they elicited gasps. I realized I was blessed with a garbage life full of narrative gems shinier than the diamonds studding the cocaine bottles that hung around Stevie Nicks's neck. "You're lucky your liver made it through that," someone said after learning I used to chase cherry NyQuil and Gatorade with caffeine pills before homeroom. "And the Everclear. Girl, you weren't fucking around."

○

In high school, I was a little witch with Scotch tape binding spells, a rhinestone-studded reflective silver dress, platform sneakers, and wig-black dyed hair. Unless you count the day I accepted a bottle of Pepsi and vodka on the way to class, I didn't drink until sophomore year of college. The NyQuil didn't count because, except for the members of TREND (Turning Recreational Energies in New Directions), everyone Robotripped.

O

Native Americans aren't genetically predisposed to alcoholism and drink about as much as whites. According to John W. Frank, MD, et al., in "Historical and Cultural Roots of Drinking Problems among American Indians," whites brought hard-drinking habits with them as they settled, and depravity was facilitated by perceived freedom from the law (although the whites were encroaching upon lands where Indigenous legal systems were in place):

> Our view is that the rise of native drinking cultures, which have obviously evolved further in the ensuing years, cannot be understood without reference to the extraordinary barrage of inducements to drink heavily in the early years after European contact. The harmful drinking patterns established during those years have largely persisted, despite many attempts by government and voluntary agencies to address the problem. In contrast to other explanatory factors, the role of history seems to have been underemphasized in the voluminous literature attempting to explain the phenomenon of problem drinking among Native Americans.

Binge drinking then developed in Native communities. From whites, Natives learned to drink, and whole canoe-loads learned to drown.

I, too, learned how to drink from white people, their desire and freedom preserved on magnetic tape, their readiness to die young written into every gesture. I tell writing students a good ending's seed is in the essay's opening. Those teens' demise was sketched into every gesture: the lean against the counter, the gleeful opening of the passenger door, the hurtling down a dark road. I learned from D.A.R.E. to drink like I was dying.

○

On my dad's side of the family, generations of men mined anthracite coal. Every workday, caked in the black dust that would kill them, men took elevators out of the earth and stepped into the sunshine before leaving it behind for dark bars. My great-grandfather, a Polish immigrant, died at fifty-one from, according to the death certificate, *general anasarca*, extreme edema caused by liver failure. His last day outside was like most others: he went to the mines, then to the bar, then home. He wobbled, steered by the little boy who would become my grandpa, toward the house where he'd spend the last few days of his life.

My grandpa didn't teach his children to drink that way. Throughout his career as a pilot, he bought duty-free liquor that he stuffed into cabinets, never to be opened. When I was a teenager, my dad held on to four bottles from a six-pack for years after buying beer for a guest. My parents asked me, after I came of age, whether beer goes bad. I had no idea. I drank everything in the house and brought in more.

O

According to a 2016 interview I found via Genius.com, Phil Collins said of "In the Air Tonight," "The more people say to me what it's about, I just say, I can promise you it isn't about whatever you think it is, 'cause I don't know what it's about."

O

For the purposes of this essay, the D.A.R.E. video will be the source of the thrill-seeking that sent me to the basement where I joined a circle around a bottle ready to spin, the living room where I stared at switchblades on a coffee table while white boys with oven mitts inhaled opium smoke off a butter knife, the hotel-adjacent bar where I met a man I hoped wouldn't kill me, the rug-mold-stinking apartment littered with both kinds of roaches where I'd been tasked with picking something up for a guy I was dating—he'd get me back but see the thing was he wasn't driving right then—and after I emerged, a man drove up and asked me how much money he had to give me to get me in.

None of that seems as alarming as the drunk times.

The time a near stranger called me *bitch* and told me what I was going to do and I did it before running out of his apartment, my bladder emptying itself onto the sidewalk, trying to empty me.

The time a man I was dating pulled a knife on me while my ex-boyfriend pounded on my apartment window, yelling that he knew I wasn't alone.

The time a man slipped something into my drink after I decided to stay at the bar for one more beer after my friend left, and I locked myself in my car, covered myself in Goodwill-bound clothes, and passed out.

The time a man my friend thought I'd hit it off with opened my legs on the couch while I kept saying not to.

The time, the last night I ever drank alcohol, a man choked me, like I knew he would, even after I said, *You're going to leave a mark*, and he told me he loved me.

The other times. Don't bother trying to keep track of these men. They're not even characters. They're just plot points within the falling action—or the rising action, I can't remember—populating scenes that come before the point of no return, or after.

O

A wrecked car appeared on my high school's front lawn one day. People left class and returned dressed like the grim reaper. They wouldn't speak. I felt left out. I wanted to walk around dead, too, but nobody invited me. I realized I might be dead already.

O

The veil is getting thinner, says an Instagram witch. Samhain is approaching. Halloween is the witches' new year. October is the season of black clothes making more sense than they did in the everything-combusting Ohio summer sun. Fake skeletons are propped up among the real ones walking around with skin on.

Around this time six years ago, I realized my unseen body parts were dying. I went to the emergency room with stomach pain so intense my vision went gray. Waiting in the bed, I thought about whether I was a healthy person. Then the doctor mentioned morphine, and I thought about that instead. I turned down Dilaudid, feeling as if I should say no but wanting it more than anything. That possibility of dripping viscous bliss into my veins and replacing my dread with uncomplicated warmth still feels like the one that got away.

The doctors couldn't figure out what was wrong with me, but when I saw my general practitioner the next day, she said, "You *will* stop your drinking. Now."

I would not.

O

In 1831, physician James Gregory presented the postmortem examination of a coal miner who had died at age fifty-nine:

> When cut into, both lungs presented one uniform black carbonaceous colour, pervading every part of their substance. The right lung was much disorganized, and exhibited in its upper and middle lobes, several large irregular cavities, communicating with one another and traversed by numerous bands of pulmonary substance and vessels. These cavities contained a good deal of fluid, which, as well as the walls of the cavities, partook of the same black colour.

In the 1870s, journalist Henry Sheafer wrote of coal miners, "The wonder is not that men die of clogged-up lungs, but that they manage to exist so long in an atmosphere which seems to contain at least fifty per cent of solid matter."

In 1881, Dr. H. A. Lemen presented a paper on the chronic health problems of coal miners. A patient was known to cough up more than a pint of "decidedly inky" black liquid per day. "The sentence I am reading," Lemen said, "was written with this fluid. The pen used has never been in ink."

Miners would drink rock-candy-sweetened, herb-laced whiskey elixirs to stimulate morning coughing. After work, they took shots of whiskey with beer backs to bring up dust. In the early 1900s, autopsied lung sections of career miners in Pennsylvania were found to sink in water. Normal lungs float.

Until the 1950s, black lung wasn't understood as deadly. I collect digital images of death certificates for the coal miners who came before me. Cause of death, over and over, is listed as *arteriosclerosis*, the arteries hardening, no mention of the lungs. The men were drowned deep underneath dry land.

O

What did I need to get away from that brought me to that ER bed, anyway? I was in a long-term relationship with my best drinking buddy, Kevin. We were drowning and would not lend each other a hand. When we split bottles of Crown Royal, he wobbled on long legs, threaded cigarette smoke through pursing lips, narrowed eyes that looked as empty as the alley we ashed into from his balcony late at night. I tried to get drunk enough to dissolve the barrier between my mouth and the ugliest thing my heart housed. *You don't love me enough*, I said, but that was hardly his problem because nobody could.

Four months into drying out, I dated a man who'd gone to rehab to save his marriage, which folded, but sobriety suited him. He'd talk about powerlessness over alcohol and repeat stories about things he did to lose his wife and things he did to get his life back. That man wanted a housewife; I wanted to stare at the death I'd just pulled from my body in the greatest magic trick of my life.

He said he was most likely going to die from alcoholism because, really, we're all just one drink away from that death. Actually, I am most likely going to die by choking on a magnesium tablet in my kitchen. I've had three close calls: the first two happened during that first year sober; the last time, here in Ohio, I had to slam my body into the counter to knock the tablet loose from my throat. I did give up the narrative menace of a possible death from drowning in my own vomit. Life was easier when I had an escape hatch, a way to die in a fire I set.

○

In Pennsylvania mining towns, Grandma tells me, there was a bar and a church on every corner. In the bars, I've read, there were men with dust ground into their skin. In the men, there was liquid they called "rotgut." As soon as I read the word, I felt I loved this liquid more than I would ever love anyone or anything.

The men were sooty ghouls, spirits left in the underworld, and alcohol seemed to be the only thing animating their dust-stuffed bodies.

Drinking was paid for through a practice called the "knockdown": a mine worker would reserve a portion of his paycheck for his own spending and conceal this from his wife or mother. Women were house bosses. Girls were selected for their toughness as early as age thirteen and arranged into marriages. By twenty, they looked old, broken by work and birth. My great-grandmother Anna worked for a wealthy family in Pittsburgh until her brother insisted she return to her hometown to marry Michael Washuta. She did, but she didn't want to.

After Michael died in 1929, she took on boarders. Grandpa, still a child, worked in a bootleg mine and picked huckleberries in the hills. On Anna's death certificate—congestive heart failure, 1962—her occupation is listed as *housewife*.

When I look for myself in this family, I see my image moving from body to body like a restless spirit. I am the woman who does what she does not want to do. I am the man drowning himself in liquor faster than his lungs can drown in dust. I am the child who knows what a body looks like when it's wounded from the inside out.

O

For a while, threatening my own safety worked to show me I was resilient enough to take the obliteration. A year after the emergency room visit that resulted in the doctor's order to stop drinking, I began pissing blood. Two doctors sat with me and begged me to stop drinking, to repeat after them: *My life is worth saving*. Even their tears didn't stop me from drinking for two and a half more years. I broke up with Kevin. I dried out and saturated myself again. I dated a man who baked me a rum cake with rum sauce and served it to me for breakfast the morning after he choked me. Sometimes, men were nothing but alcohol-delivery devices, glass to a Guinness, ever present because you're a drunk only if you do it alone. Alcohol, a friend told me, is called *spirits* for a reason. It will possess you if you let it.

The final, climactic battle didn't look like much. I stared at the gray girl in the mirror and smelled the carcass stench. I took a taxi to the car I'd left across town. I went for a walk with a friend I'd gotten absolutely trashed with before she'd gotten sober. I made a decision. I drove to a Catholic school gymnasium, joined the old men sitting around a card table, and said I didn't know how to go on. They did not seem to find my pain profound; they, for my benefit, brought out stories of how they'd destroyed cars, careers, and marriages until they didn't. At home, I poured out the rum and whiskey. I broke up with the choking man. I never drank again.

O

I still don't know what to make of the hands around my neck. I feel guilty for even bringing it up. The choking was not, I feel certain, meant to harm me. But he never asked what I wanted before he tightened his grip on my neck while an old fear woke inside me: my breathing cut off by a man's hands years before; somewhere in my cells, maybe, Tumulth's neck in the ligature, the shove of the hangman, the drop, his own body tightening the noose.

I lied to myself, decided I liked it. That was easier than telling him not just to go lighter, not just to avoid leaving bruises, but to stop. I'd been experimenting with "moderation," but I went back to getting so drunk and high I could slip into the void where I didn't care whether I lived or died, and so, in a blackout, might say *yes* or say *more* or say nothing. Did I ask for more? I may, in those moments I abandoned myself into memory gaps, have asked for more.

O

Stevie Nicks believes in ghosts. In a 1981 *Rolling Stone* profile, she describes herself as "very sensitive." She recounts a recent visit from a furniture-upending ghost. I keep trying to make sense of the opening:

> It is said that the door to the other side of this existence, to the Spirit Corridor and the Plain of Souls, has no knob on it and can only be opened from the outside. You, on this side of the door, must answer the spectral knock with a beckoning, for the Darkness cannot cross your threshold unless it is invited in.

Which side of the door am I on?

O

In my first weeks sober, I learned the term *drunkalogue* and that I was going to want to build one. Nobody wanted to know about my job. My only identity, beyond the observable, was my narrative. The drunkalogue resists gaps and subtext; it is chronological, linear, and causation-driven; a good one packs the rise, climax, and fall of Freytag's Pyramid into one riveting minute. It is meant to be spoken. I say none of this to dismiss or reduce: I've heard stories in meetings that I recognized as what I'd wanted God to say back when I prayed.

Nobody sets out to craft a story of this kind—it's not The Moth—but after a person speaks in enough meetings about what drinking was like and why it had to end, the narrative makes itself. Mine went like this: I had my first drink in high school; I drank NyQuil sometimes but stopped for a few years, started drinking hard and often partway through college, drank a lot, got sick, realized it, stopped. Alcoholism was said to be a sickness: a spiritual one, the program literature said, or a medical one, as my psychiatrist told me.

When I reconstructed the narrative of my drinking, I kept getting stuck on the inciting incident. Drinking NyQuil was part of a timeline, but not the beginning of a story, because there was no question, no stakes. The plot point that set me on my true course came years later, my sophomore year of college: rape.

I wanted my drinking story to be one I could tell without talking about rape. I couldn't bring it up in meetings, so I said I'd been born thirsty, and the more I said it, the truer it seemed.

I told myself it was my wanting that had gotten me perforated and bloody inside, my driving obsession to be loved. Alcohol doesn't make these things happen; men do. Alcohol weakens the paper shield I hold up to stop these things from happening. It is simultaneously true that the rape was not my fault and that it wouldn't have happened if I could stand to be alone. I've found only one thing that could ever obliterate the wanting: enough whiskey to scorch my stomach lining before turning me to a near corpse on the floor. Now I sit in my yearning, alone with my crystals, turning over tarot cards on the cold wood floor of my rented house.

O

My great-great-grandmother Mary (or Kalliah), horseback carrier of federal mail, daughter of Tumulth, had an allotment on the Yakama Reservation, but she gave it up and returned to the river. Some white people tried to steal her land, because Native people couldn't legally own land in Washington then; in 1893, President Grover Cleveland signed a bill to hold Mary's land in trust so claim jumpers couldn't force her from it.

She had three husbands, as far as I know. With Louis, a Cowlitz and Frenchman, she gave birth to my great-grandmother Abbie. Abbie's first husband, Morris, my great-grandfather, was white. He died a young man in his thirties after a few days at home with a brief and powerful illness. Years later, Abbie remarried.

I have no husbands. No land. If my ancestors are watching me, what do they see?

O

I feel like an old maid. My body is young but my heart is a crone's. I think of Carl but won't text him because I don't like waiting days for his response. I'd rather petrify on my couch than go on another first date with a man who wants to explain IPAs to me, and anyway, I'm not exactly emotionally available. I spend most nights in my creaking house Google Image searching Stevie Nicks and her large sleeves. I save images while weeping and listening to "Silver Springs," the song Stevie wrote and loved and could not get onto *Rumours* because that decision wasn't hers to make. Mick Fleetwood shuttled the song into B-side obscurity. The band included the song in *The Dance*, its 1997 live greatest hits record, the video for which was omnipresent on VH1 the year I began looking up love spells on Ask Jeeves.

It's not until pining over Carl, my own brooding, curly-haired guitarist who keeps getting away and returning, that I see what was happening onstage during the performance of "Silver Springs" for *The Dance*: Stevie, in her characteristic wing-sleeved black dress, her hand on her neck, turns to Lindsey Buckingham and sings, *I'll follow you down 'til the sound of my voice will haunt you / You'll never get away from the sound of the woman that loves you*. The whites of his eyes are moons against the dark backdrop as he sings back and along. *Never get away*. She grips the mic with ringed sorcerer fingers. *Never get away*. Her eyes are ritual blades. *Never get away*. Her mouth casts a circle around them both. He never will. I watch to imitate.

The *looks* between Stevie and Lindsey during "Silver Springs" supposedly didn't happen during rehearsals for the taping of *The Dance*, but after they were exchanged onstage, they never went away. In every YouTube-available live performance of "Silver Springs" following that resurrection, Stevie turns to Lindsey at the same moment. Every time, the energy feels real. In 2009, Stevie told MTV News, "He's married, he's happy, he has three beautiful children that I love. You know, he's found a good, happy, calm, safe place—but who Lindsey and I are to each other will never change."

In 2013, Lindsey told *Rolling Stone*, "For me, getting married and having children was a positive outcome. I wonder sometimes how Stevie feels about the choices she made, because she doesn't really have a relationship—she has her career."

I buy a blonde wig. I am trying to be alone with myself, but I can manage to be alone only with my Instagram. I draw black lines on my eyelids and wear my gauziest black witch clothes. I braid my hair, gather it under a mesh cap, and lower the wig onto my skull. I set my phone camera on a timer and ask it to capture me, looking at it like a person I want to put my wet red mouth on. There's no one in this house but me and the ghost that recently pulled my curtains off the walls and shattered a glass bowl in the drying rack while I stood at the sink. I show the ghost the tip of my thirsty tongue between my teeth.

○

I've thought about Carl every day since I last saw him, but I hardly text him because I don't want to be needy. After my first boyfriend broke up with me, my high school friends asked, "Do you need him because you love him, or do you love him because you need him?" How was I supposed to know?

Nearly a year before our maybe-date, Carl broke up with me. *You have to let him go,* my friends said. *This is toxic.* But our astrological compatibility looked so strong. I've examined the lines crossing the chart wheel until dawn some nights, trying to see our narrative there, trying to find some meaning.

Alone in my apartment in the days after our breakup, I began to smell the hot tang of his summer body. I saw his owl eyes mirrored in my own sockets. My gut was split by the lightning bolt of white streaking a dark curl at his forehead. Even after I put all this land between us, I've felt him sitting on the foot of my bed. I cast every spell I could find to sever the energetic cord, but his energy clings. A residue of his spirit nests inside my skin. He's a living ghost haunting my house.

O

In Middle English, to *intoxicate* was "to poison."

Poison, in Middle English, came from the Old French *poison*, meaning "magic potion," related to the classical Latin *potare*, meaning "to drink."

O

In astrology, the natal chart locates the planetary positions at the time of birth. It tells a story about a lifetime of wants and weaknesses, the bundle of traits that form a person, the work we're meant to do while living, and the timing of important events. Between Stevie's chart and mine, I notice only one similarity of interest: the chart location of the moon's nodes, which are points where the moon's orbit crosses the ecliptic, the path the sun appears to follow around the earth over the course of a year. The south node represents what we're pulled back to from previous lives, what we fall back on. The north node represents the work we need to stretch to in this lifetime.

For both Stevie and me, the north node is in Taurus and the first house (the house of self), and the south node is in Scorpio and the seventh house (the house of partnerships). This means we're meant to learn to love ourselves, embrace independence, trust our intuition, and let go of codependency. We look for soulmates who can never complete us, because we need to stop trying to grow through others. I don't like this. I want to grow through another by incorporating him into my being and becoming twice as large.

I have loved manboys who couldn't love me back. I've placed myself alone in strange bars, my intuition a heavy potion in my gut, because I thought I might find love there. I've struggled with sleep on nights when men lay openmouthed and cadaverish in my small bed. I'm a pretty wretch with red intention candles, heart-shielding labradorite necklaces, three dozen black dresses and no white ones, staples-and-string binding spells to immobilize the men who truly scarred me and would do it again. I keep letting myself hope that, this time, I really will be loved. But I need to work on devotion to my own swollen heart.

In light of what I've learned about my nodal destiny, I decide to buy a house. In Ohio, a house is not an abstraction. I'm driving around, compiling mental catalogs of every neighborhood bar despite myself, considering getting a house with enough space for a husband, when Carl texts me. It's been a week since I asked about a pot of soup he'd posted on Instagram. He replies with no words, just a link to a recipe. I don't open it.

○

I haven't touched a man under his clothes in so long I've reverted to my high school freshman self, interested in touching someone under his clothes but skeptical that it will ever happen. I lusted after my friend's older brother, whose face I'd seen glowing like a moon outside the school one day. Eventually, he became my first boyfriend, and when he put his tongue in my mouth in the hallway, I attained everything I'd wanted. I sent him an email about the ways I was going to touch him, but instead of replying, he asked his sister to tell me we were broken up.

The next day, I wrapped my wrists in medical gauze, dotted them with red food coloring, and went to school. He saw and walked away. I shoved nasty rectangles of folded loose-leaf into his locker, but he didn't write back. I wanted him, but I could only spit poison. I soon began drinking NyQuil on Fridays, then whenever.

It's hard to know how to make sense of this opening to my drinking history. Before I was raped, I didn't drink heavily, but before I was raped, for a short while, I did drink full bottles of cough elixir meant to be sipped from a tiny cup. Maybe the story didn't start in either place. Or maybe a causal chain will never work because multiple causes, some mostly mystery, interwound to make me need to alter reality. Even before I couldn't bear the violence of the world, I flailed against it because it wasn't enough.

O

The night of our last date, Carl slept over, but we agreed it would be friendship sleeping only. Then he changed his mind. I hold on to my modest collection of memories of that night, as though I could use them to conjure up his body:

My knees touching his knees under the empty egg plate while I asked, "Do you think, if one of us dies, the other will know?"

My fingers under the soft rag of his old T-shirt.

My thirsty tongue, wet again in his mouth.

O

In *Astrology for the Soul*, Jan Spiller says what we Taurus north node people want is to merge with another person; what we need is to stop feeding our power to another. She writes, "The first step toward self-acceptance for Taurus North Node people is to acknowledge that there is a needy person inside and to take personal responsibility for filling those needs."

It takes great effort, but I do not text Carl back about the soup.

O

In *Destiny Rules*, a documentary about the making of Fleetwood Mac's 2003 record, *Say You Will* (the occasion for their first studio reunion in fifteen years), it's clear Stevie never got over Lindsey. Maybe he didn't get over her, either, but I'm fresh out of interest in the inner workings of complicated men.

Lindsey and Stevie sit in the house rented for the recording process and talk over Lindsey's concerns about Stevie's lyrics. He's brought up tense and person disagreement, but he seems to be talking about something other than how to "strengthen the narrative." He asks, "When you say, 'Now you're going home,' who are you talking about?"

Stevie, exasperated with this man, says, "I'm talking to you!"

Earlier, speaking into the camera, Lindsey says, "It's odd sitting here singing all this stuff about myself, you know, it's, uh . . . You sort of learn to disassociate and to sort of be . . . [finger quotes] *professional* about it, but . . ." He smiles and shakes his head. "You know, it's, uh, it's pretty amazing, you know, all this time later, that there would be those subjects being dealt with in a really deep manner."

The documentary ends with the beginning of the *Say You Will* tour. Lindsey and Stevie walk out onstage holding hands. He leads; she follows. We don't see who reached for the other.

O

The official music video for "In the Air Tonight" is, for the most part, about Phil Collins's face: bright white, marked with deep shadows, it takes up the screen. It fades while the crescent moon brightens behind his eye socket. The face of Phil Collins floats disembodied in the darkness. Somehow, I hadn't seen this video until I began looking—for what will probably be the last time—for the D.A.R.E. video.

Cut to Phil Collins slumped in a chair in an empty room, looking out the window at a specter, his own white silhouette under the moon.

Cut to Phil Collins in a corridor, trying to open doors that can be opened only from the outside. He, on the other side of the door, stands and looks into the obliterating white light, as though he cannot cross the threshold until he's invited in. He fades into darkness.

This is the closest to finding the D.A.R.E. video that I might ever come.

The camera returns, repeatedly, to his face.

O

Even if I did find the D.A.R.E. video, seeing it again would only serve to puncture its sac of nighttime hanging inside my heart. Still, I suck on the thrill of the search like a plastic cup of garbage whiskey, but the promise of a drink was never going to lead to discovery or completion or the kind of ending I want: resonant, a point of arrival. Drinking was only about getting me back to the time before I knew about all there was to want and all the pain it was going to bring me. D.A.R.E. TO RESIST DRUGS AND VIOLENCE, reads a banner on the D.A.R.E. website. The program did not teach me that drugs and violence were holding hands. I learned it without cops or nuns to help.

This essay, I thought, could end with a look back at my entire drinking history and my triumphant recovery, but that's boring. Anyway, I only want to talk about Stevie, who now, sober and alone, paints angels and writes poems about *Game of Thrones* characters. She says she likes the brutality. I only want to watch every YouTube video of "Silver Springs." Even though the former lovers' turn toward each other is now clearly performative, there is truth in this fiction. Celebrity gossip sites have yet to report on the contents of the forthcoming Stevie Nicks biography, so I don't yet know that Lindsey threw her onto the floor during one argument, bent her over a car and choked her during another. Carl has never been violent, never evil, never anything but a complicated man who doesn't know what he wants. I stay affixed to possibility because of the violence that preceded him: here is a man who seems good enough, so I should never let him get away.

If I watch all the "Silver Springs" live videos, I believe I will find the end of the story about my need. I watch Stevie turn to Lindsey, her shoulders pulled up tight like the arched back of a black cat, her eyebrows a bolt from a witch's finger, her mouth straining with a howl, *Time cast a spell on you, but you won't forget me*, while the camera watches Lindsey's ringed finger choke the strings his right hand drives past, over and over, boot slamming stage floor, carotid bulging as he growls that you'll never get away, growls that you will be haunted, and the chains draped from Stevie's mic stand quake. Lindsey told the *Dallas Morning News* in 1993, "It's pivotal between being sad about things that have basically died for you and being able to move forward and find other things that are alive for you." It sounds like the little lies that come to me and ask to be called epiphanies. When I see Stevie and Lindsey turn away from each other as the song dwindles toward its end, I rewind to the moment before she turns to him, and I watch them in that pivot, climbing into the hole in front of all of us, climbing out while the camera pans so far out that she and her black shroud disappear in the darkness.

THE SPIRIT CORRIDOR

All my life,
since I was ten,
I've been waiting
to be in
this hell here
with you;
all I've ever
wanted, and
still do.

—Alice Notley

If a man was never to lie to me. *Never lie me.*
I swear I would never leave him.

—Louise Erdrich, "The Strange People"[3]

---

3. And how does this make you feel?
    a. Indifferent? Curious? Skip the rest of this footnote.
    b. Uneasy? Are you wondering what I'm trying to do here? Do you think I made an error? Did you flip back to the previous epigraphs? Do you worry you're missing my meaning? Do you like my epigraphs? Have you ever been to church? Have you ever cast a spell? How do you feel about being asked a question? A rhetorical question? A hypothetical question? An intrusive question? Have you ever played devil's advocate? If you don't like my epigraphs, let me play devil's advocate: What if you don't actually know what an epigraph is for? Or, at least, not here, where I am the center.

HERE'S A RIDDLE:

You're standing in front of two doors. One leads to heaven, the other to hell. A guardian stands in front of each. One guardian always tells the truth. The other always lies. You don't know which is which. You want the door to heaven, but you can ask only a single question to one guardian.

What is the question?

I don't know and I don't care. I've been looking for a different door.

○

FRONT DOOR OF CARL'S HOUSE

We were new at each other, together every untied minute. On a late spring night, he opened the door and stood before me as a dim shape against lamplit white walls. The image of his V-necked clavicles was seared into me that night, like the small vision hole seared into the retina of someone who stares into the solar eclipse. "Wow," he whispered. "You weren't here. And now you're here."

I looked into his eyes, which were my eyes copied into a different skull. When one of us was made, the maker started with the eyes, accidentally made duplicate pairs, and built two different humans around the eyeballs.

He was right. I was *there*, alone, then *here*, poised at the threshold between lawn and living room. Unreal.

THE FOUR DOORS OF THE LITTLE HOUSE

The primary setting of my first Ohio winter is a seven-hundred-square-foot brick rental house built sometime before 1900. People have asked whether it's haunted. I used to say it wasn't, and I would know. I salted the corners and doorways before I unloaded my car. Despite the tightness of the space, the outside sounds of football revelry and garbage collection, the broken window, and the brick walls' tiny holes that let subzero air flow inside, I like the little house and its secret-garden yard, and I wouldn't mind staying a while. But I learned that my new city, Columbus, was on the short list of possible locations for Amazon's second headquarters, so I've started looking for my forever house before it's too late. I feel myself pulling away from the little house, trying not to love it.

The bathroom door's cracked antique knob is accompanied by a keyhole without a key. The bedroom door has a modern knob, the kind with a button that can lock it from the inside but no place for the insertion of a key. There's no need for a locked interior door here. Everyone is in the bedroom: me, my crystals, and the ghost who runs fingers through my hair as I try to get tired in bed. Inside the bedroom there's a door to the murder basement with thousands of tiny blue nuggets of rat poison clustered on the dirt floor.

I'd been in the little house for a few weeks when I tried to come inside after gardening, but the storm door shut me out: the knob turned while the latch stayed put. I turned the knob until my hands were blistered. I wanted to try going in through the bedroom window, but when I began to lift the screen, the storm window slammed shut on my forearm, cutting a bloody line, and would not budge open. I returned to the door and turned its knob until my blisters ruptured. *This house is testing me*, I thought. *If I can figure out the answer, I can open the door.*

The answer was that I needed to ask for help. I am loath to, ever, because it's only when I've needed something from somebody that I've been let down. But when a stranger walked by, I asked him to help me.

He looked at the door. He turned the knob. He said, "If this were a movie, we'd use a credit card." He wished me good luck and walked on. I wedged my garden spade into the space between door and frame, and the door opened.

How do you make a house happy? How do you appease it when it never tells you what it wants? When I started house shopping, the storm window began to rattle with every gust. A streak as dark as dried blood appeared, cutting a diagonal across the exposed brick of my bedroom wall. The gate ceased to latch and now slams shut and open all night in the wind. I think of boyfriend after boyfriend who told me, after we split, *I didn't realize how awesome you were. I took you for granted.* All of them but Carl, who went into the underworld after he left me, and who emerged only once to fuck me before disappearing again. He has never been in this house, but I've filled it with him.

The house is a boyfriend. Or the house is me. Or the house is a person with its own plan.

BEFORE ASKING A QUESTION, REMEMBER

A riddle is different from a joke. Both rely on double meanings represented through language, but a riddle is meant to be worked on in pursuit of a solution, while a joke's punch line should do most of the work. I hate punch lines. I distrust humor. I'm not comfortable with the notion that I have all the information I need, because I've never known that to be true.

DOOR WITHOUT KNOB

According to astrology internet, Venus has disappeared from the night sky and now travels through the underworld. When she is in this place, we are alone. Before she gets out, we will lose something. *Lose* isn't the right word—it will be a sacrifice.

FAKE MARK TWAIN'S INDEX-O-VATOR

The Claymation film *The Adventures of Mark Twain* was made to delight strange adults, but I felt it had been crafted for my childhood alone. The premise, as presented in the film's text preface: Halley's comet returned in 1835, as it does every seventy-five years. That year, Mark Twain was born, so he believed he and the comet shared a destiny. He wrote, "The Almighty has said, no doubt, 'There go those two unaccountable freaks; they came in together, they must go out together.'" Twain noted the comet's return in 1910, wrote that "It is the final chapter," and died.

That's pretty close to reality; the film that follows is fantasy. The white-suited Twain takes off in his airship to meet Halley's comet and die. It's a film with more strangeness than plot: Twain's black-suited doppelgänger haunts the airship, mourning; the Index-O-Vator, a doorway-turned-portal, offers passage to other decks and worlds pulled from Twain's body of work. Mostly, this film is about death, the only certainty we're born into and the only adventure we're all assured.

Looking for the facts, I go down the Google rabbit hole and end up at a website that claims that the death of Twain's wife, Olivia, in 1904, compounded by the death of their daughter Jean in 1909, led him to die of a broken heart in 1910, and that he was able to predict he'd go out with the comet because those deaths made his own inevitable. The source article has unintentional font changes and broken image links, so I have to wonder about it. There may be a fact-checked book in the library that would put an end to my speculation, but it's cold outside and I'm curious right now and I've got this portal right here that can tell me anything I could want to know.

I didn't come in with a comet. I know of no astrological significance to being born in a year when a comet makes itself known to those on earth. I was born close to a total solar eclipse. Astrologers say eclipses mark beginnings and endings: they bring people into our world and lives, and they take people out. Lunar and solar eclipses generally occur in pairs (sometimes triads), the lunar eclipse at the full moon and the solar at the new, but only when the moon is near one of its nodes. Eclipse pairs arrive twice a year. When will I die? That's the wrong question. I can't predict the year. But I have a feeling I'm going out between eclipses.

I think I began demanding repeat screenings of *The Adventures of Mark Twain* at four, the age I remember becoming a person. In that golden time, I could get up in the dead of night to play, unencumbered by the nonsense of a schedule. Sometimes little children know more than a human should. Sometimes children are psychic, according to paranormal internet. Actually, some of the internet says *all* children are psychic, until they're taught that normal people don't see visions or hear thoughts, so they suppress their abilities until they're gone. I don't remember what I heard or saw, only what I felt: sheer panic. At the grocery store, I screamed. At day care, I lost a doll's hand and threatened to suffocate myself with a sheet at nap time. Home—place of books, cats, parents, and tree canopy—was a refuge. I was bad. A "little divil," in the loving parlance of the coal region. Why not? The devils knew as much as the angels, so, almost everything. I didn't know as much as an angel or a devil but I knew something everyone else seemed not to: something horrible was going to happen to me.

The Adventures of Mark Twain is best known for the Satan scene. Through the door-portal of the Index-O-Vator, the children depart from Twain to enter a starless void-world a chipper voice introduces as "The Mysterious Stranger," which is the title of one of Twain's books. Out of the pink clay earth rises a red-armor-clad, headless, person-shaped being. A flat white mask on a stick appears in the being's hand.

"Hello," the being says, its voice metallic, stilted, and ominous.

"Who are you?" Becky asks.

The mask becomes human-featured, the color of Twain's flesh, with holes remaining where eyes might go if this were a person, which it almost is, but persons have heads. "An angel." Its name is Satan.

While Satan talks, the mask changes, first turning wizened, then furred with mustache and brows like Twain's as the being invites the children into the void. The face becomes placid and smooth again when they enter. Satan is welcoming at first, a magician making fruit appear in their hands. Is this hell? It's not heaven. Satan makes a little castle and builds life around it, then destroys everything while the mask turns flushed and horned.

The children aren't having fun anymore. While Satan tells the children that people are of no consequence, the mask's eyes widen to skull-sockets and the fleshy smoothness gives way to the sharpness of bone before turning to a skull by the time the children run back through the portal. The Index-O-Vator disappears into the earth and the being stands alone in the meadow.

"Life itself is only a vision, a dream," Satan tells us. With the wave of a hand, the plants wilt and the ground breaks into rocks. "Nothing exists save empty space and you, and you are but a thought." The rocks fall away, the stranger's shape disappears into the void, and only the mask remains as a speck in Twain's eye as his face fades in.

This may have been how I met Satan. All my religious picture books concerned unfallen angels and child saints. The priests' homilies were celebratory and practical, telling us how to be good. I liked clay Satan and wanted to play with it. God the Father was the one to fear: he had all the rules and expectations. Both heaven and hell terrified me because they were forever. The only difference I could see was that hell was hot. It would be easier to get comfortable in hell than to succeed in striving for heaven. Once I began school, I sketched courses through hell's tortures: magma moats, poisoned spikes, skin-shredding blades, fire meadows. I wasn't afraid of pain. I was afraid of the omnipotent one's pressure, because I knew it.

CRYING ROOM DOOR

I liked church because of the mysteries: joyful, sorrowful, glorious. I liked that my dad called one of God's three persons *the Holy Ghost*, like a character in a book of scary stories.

In Catholic school, I learned that some supernatural truths could not be accessed through human reason. I took this to mean that God kept secrets, like I did. My secrets were that I wanted to kiss the Ninja Turtles, I had a twin brother nobody could see, and I peed in the closet. God's secrets were about other worlds.

In the New Testament, though, *mysterion* (μυστήριον) doesn't mean *mystery*, something impossible or difficult to understand; it refers to what is *mystical*, with a spiritual meaning inaccessible without initiation. The priests said we could never understand how God impregnated Mary, how Jesus rose from the dead, or how Mary was pulled to heaven. But I was instructed in assumption before gravity, resurrection before biological death, and immaculate conception before reproduction. The problem with *mystery* is that I have always understood completely. I never fully cultivated a sense of reason in which what's called *supernatural* would be anything but natural.

The church was dark, built from wood beams and black pillars. Off to the side, in the crying room, there was a statue of the Virgin. I wanted to be secreted inside with her. I cried through masses, hoping Mom would take Nate and me to that hiding place so I could watch the porcelain woman, in case she might weep with me.

FORBIDDEN DOOR

Before I was born, I was halved. New Age internet says many of us are this way, half-hearts looking for completion. I've been looking for my lost parts forever, so I am never not serious in love. It could be anyone, I used to think. I just had to find him and lock myself into him. I tried so hard to force the fit that sometimes I barely noticed that the force had broken me.

Something was different with Carl: I could listen to his thoughts and speak them back to him. We stared into each other's eyes, making a psychic rope. We knew we had to keep our bodies together as much as possible. Otherwise, our halves might pull apart again. I had never felt this way before; until a year earlier, I had never felt much at all for very long because I could mostly submerge myself through intoxication.

This meeting was fated. This was my other half. The intensity of my desire made me believe the divine had paired us, and I told him so. It had never been safe to tell a man I believed in something greater than myself—greater than him. It takes safety to dream: to play house in my mind, to build us a little life in the future, to believe we are living in magic and can use it to make us happy.

I had to go away for a week, and soon after, Carl had to go away for three. We never returned to each other, not really. Every day, I change my mind about whether he's my missing half or whether I just want him to be.

DREAM DOOR

Mark Twain was drawn to the British Society for Psychical Research, an organization seeking to reckon with paranormal concepts countering contemporary scientific principles, because of a dream. Twenty-four years earlier, Samuel Clemens dreamed of his younger brother's body in a coffin balanced across two chairs, the body covered by a bunch of white roses and one red one. Days later, in Samuel's waking world, a steamboat boiler explosion killed his brother. When Samuel approached the casket, he saw it balanced across two chairs. A nurse approached to adorn it with roses, mostly white, one red.

In 1891, after working with the society for several years, Twain published an essay in *Harper's* on what he called "mental telegraphy," known to most as telepathy, offering anecdotal evidence of correspondents sending "crossed letters" to each another (equivalent to today's text that arrives as the recipient is texting the sender), writers and inventors coming upon ideas simultaneously and separately, and Twain's knowledge that he would run into a friend on the street before doing so. Over distances, he wrote, one mind develops an idea and another receives it. "We are always mentioning people, and in that very instant they appear before us. We laugh, and say, 'Speak of the devil,' and so forth, and there we drop it, considering it an 'accident.' It is a cheap and convenient way of disposing of a grave and very puzzling mystery. The fact is it does seem to happen too often to be an accident."

I don't remember the first time I found myself thinking a full sentence, out of nowhere, seconds before the person in front of me said that exact sentence. I do remember the moment, sitting in the back of my dad's truck, driving through our woods at night, I began to fear that my family could hear my thoughts. I thought I could hear other people's, which seemed like something the nuns would have called the work of Satan. I tried to close my mind-ears.

DOOR IN MY MOTHER

Eclipses occur when the sun, moon, and earth align. During a total solar eclipse, like the one happening around the time I was born, the moon passes between the earth and the sun, completely covering the sun when observed from a narrow strip of earth known as the path of totality.

By the time I was born, the bodies had moved out of alignment, but astrologically, the eclipse's effects were still in place to shape the life ahead of me. Eclipses energize events. Days later, the effect would be less potent, but I was likely affected by energy that lingered.

According to astrologer Charles Jayne, solar eclipses near the time of a person's birth "can be expected to inflate one's individuality, purpose, and drive." Bill Meridian, a student of Jayne's, adds, "While these individuals possess these strong qualities, they also shared a burden. They proved to be part of collective destinies. Their fate was beyond their control. They could not control or deflect the events in their lives . . . These folks are swept up in the collective energy of the eclipse."

On my birthday, another three-body alignment was in effect: a conjunction of the moon, Venus, and Jupiter. After the sun, these are the three brightest celestial bodies in our sky. They are known as *benefics*, having favorable influence. Their meeting in a natal chart is a blessing.

At the time of my birth, no planets were stationed retrograde. Most of the time—92 percent, actually—at least one planet appears to travel backward through the sky. For those of us born with all planets direct, the world feels fast, unpredictable, and intensified, and we are driven to conquer it.

None of this is nearly as rare as a comet's visit, but I choose to believe it to be auspicious. It is significant because it is mine.

A DOOR IS A SYMBOL

Astrology, tarot, and witchcraft are symbol-heavy systems, with archetypes foundational to the divine communication and understanding they facilitate. Carl Jung wrote, "The archetype is a disposition to produce over and over again the same, or similar mythic conceptions" and identified archetypal images like the witch, hero, and magician that exist as patterns or motifs within the collective unconscious. The images take form through repetition across individual psyches.

Astrology is based on a belief that planets have archetypal significance, a place in cosmic and mythic narratives that influences individual lives. Much of our astrological understanding comes from stories of the deities for whom the planets are named.

I came to tarot before astrology, maybe because the clarity of the archetypes was a way in, and as a literary person, I was predisposed to think in motifs. The major arcana features a series of archetypal figures, layered with symbolic resonance: THE MAGICIAN. THE DEVIL. DEATH.

Astrology Twitter introduced me to the Sabian Symbols, a long list of phrases (mostly images), one for each zodiac degree. They were recorded in 1925 by astrologer Marc Edmund Jones and clairvoyant Elsie Wheeler, who collected visions that came to her as Jones offered 360 face-down cards from a shuffled stack, each marked with a zodiac sign and number. Jones thought Wheeler had a psychic connection to an ancient Mesopotamian alchemist. Why he wanted to conduct this "experiment," I don't know.

Some of the symbols resonate with me: a drowning man rescued; a serpent coiling near a man and a woman; the gate to the garden of desire; a canoe approaching safety through dangerous waters; miners emerging from a mine; a conversation by telepathy; the Great Stone Face. Others are strange: rabbits dressed in clothes and on parade; a man formally dressed and a deer with its horns folded; a rabbit metamorphosed into a fairy; a triangle with wings. Nine symbols feature "Indians": an Indian chief demanding recognition; an Indian woman pleading to the chief for the lives of her children; Indians rowing a canoe and dancing a war dance.

Symbols are problems when they reduce what shouldn't be reduced, placing significance not in what something is, but in what it brings up beyond itself. Some things are actual, though. Symbols are flat, without dimensions or depth, glimpsed on the way to finding meaning. Maybe there is danger in the reduction. But the mystery is so much bigger than me, like a constellation, every piece of it rendered to a speck I can connect with invisible lines.

BEFORE ASKING A QUESTION, REMEMBER

The thesaurus says *enigma* is considered to be a synonym for *riddle*, but an enigma is not a riddle. An enigma is something baffling, difficult to explain, or a mystery. It cannot be solved. The Latin *aenigma* comes from the Greek αἴνιγμα, which is from αἰνίσσεσθαι, "to speak in riddles." I make problems when I hold the mystery in my hands and think it's asking to be solved instead of the opposite.

DOORS AT THE BOTTOM OF THE RABBIT HOLE

My Catholic picture books made me think heaven was a town built on a layer of stratocumulus clouds, which disappointed me, because I wanted a heaven like the garden on the other side of the door in Alice's wonderland. I considered myself the true owner of the library's copy of Disney's *Alice in Wonderland*, nesting in its puffy white VHS case until I could bring it home again.

I studied Alice as she crept through the black woods and sat in disoriented defeat among the mome raths. I watched her shrink and grow. I was looking for the garden, too. Our lawn violets never spoke. There had to be a door somewhere, but I couldn't even find a rabbit hole to fall down. In the woods, I turned over rocks, looking for the underworld, always fearing I'd find a nest of snakes instead.

Once I could read, I worked through the book enough times to memorize parts. Maybe my woods were already wonderland. Maybe my cat would dissolve into a hanging grin. At school, when boys played games that ended with the loser having to kiss me without my invitation, I understood I was stuck somewhere, like Alice: "There were doors all round the hall, but they were all locked; and when Alice had been all the way down one side and up the other, trying every door, she walked sadly down the middle, wondering how she was ever to get out again."

In the Disney adaptation, Alice faces only one door. It is locked, and has a talking face. "You did give me quite a turn!" the door puns, and makes sure we get the joke: "Rather good, what? Doorknob, turn?" Alice peers through the keyhole mouth at the garden. In my recollection of the movie, the viewer sees what she sees. I can picture it: fountains, hedges, rosebushes, topiaries.

But I imagined the image. Alice doesn't look through a door-portal until the film is nearly over. She's been crying in the woods, singing to the creatures gathered to gawk at her pain, saying to herself, "It would be so nice if something would make sense for a change!" when the Cheshire Cat, a puff of purple around a crescent moon of teeth, tells her there's a way out. He makes a door appear in a tree trunk. Alice steps in to meet the tyrant queen in her garden. I should have seen this as a cautionary tale: the girl thinks she's looking for something that makes sense, but the deeper she pushes, the closer she gets to the seat of senseless violence in the world.

DOOR IN MY MOTHER

Early colonizers of the Americas believed the devil lived here, having been banished from Europe through religious effort. Europeans believed Native peoples worshipped gods that served Satan. Sixteenth-century Spanish colonizers executed a Guachichil woman whose people resisted conquest. She lived in a place occupied by Tlaxcalan and Tarascan converts to Christianity, and she tried to persuade them to rebel against Spanish rule by threatening them with black magic. The Spanish, fearing a loss of control, charged her with witchcraft and killed her immediately. Alison Games recounts this in *Witchcraft in Early North America*, writing that "witches were not only rebels against godly order (as they were throughout Europe), but also armed rebels bent on overthrowing established governments." Revolts were blamed on the devil. The settlers became obsessed with witches.

But I didn't know about any of this when I was four, as my parents read to me from my favorite picture books, Patricia Coombs's Dorrie the Little Witch series. Every book begins the same: "This is Dorrie. She is a witch. A little witch." Some arrangement of introductory details follows: her room is messy, her socks mismatched. She has a cat named Gink and a mother known as the Big Witch. Dorrie strives and fails to be good; the Big Witch is important and busy. Left alone to figure out how to behave, Dorrie often ends up in the secret room where her mother makes magic.

She fumbles with spells, coming up with her own elixirs after failing to find them in the Big Witch's book of magic.

I don't know whether I understood that world to be pretend. My mother was a big witch, too: important, a role model, and a healer, in a way, a nurse with national recognition and local renown. But I was left alone only when I wanted to be. It was my mother and father who read me the books.

I mixed every liquid hair product in my parents' bathroom cabinet, hoping to come up with the spell Dorrie sought to ease the constriction of adult reality's force upon the glittering cloud of childhood. I held out hope for finding a book of magic that might have what I needed.

My schoolbooks held only dead ends: a rule for every known thing, and every thing was a known thing, except for the things the church knew to be unknown, like the mechanism God uses to turn bread into his body or what that even means since the Communion host doesn't seem like anything but an unusual cracker melting on the tongue.

But there was something existing in my house—not a being like God or Satan, but something potent and present as a gas. In the hallway, surrounded by the bedroom and bathroom doors, I felt I wasn't alone. Belief in ghosts seemed to fall under superstition, which was sinful as a subcategory of idolatry, so I didn't let myself think of the women in the large old photo hanging in our house's hallway as anything but ink on framed paper. The standing woman smiled and the sitting woman did not. Their hair was gathered tight behind their heads and their skin was cloaked in black cloth. My mom said they were my great-grandmother and great-great-grandmother, granddaughter and daughter of

Tumulth, but this was impossible. I had never smiled at anyone as if my eyes were jaws and I had never sat with my sadness as if it were a second nervous system. They wore black, like witches, but they couldn't be, because all witches were white.

They knew something, though.

I decided to read every book in the library, looking for instructions I could use. The books I found weren't about witches—they were about otherworld travelers. In *The Castle in the Attic* by Elizabeth Winthrop, a boy uses a magic token to turn people into miniatures who can pass through a toy castle into another world. Lynne Reid Banks wrote about similar magic five years earlier in *The Indian in the Cupboard*, but I didn't take to that book, probably not because it features a white boy who plays God with a tiny Iroquois man—I was used to that—but because I wanted to travel to the otherworlds, not have their residents come to me.

In Anne Lindbergh's *Travel Far, Pay No Fare*, two children use a magic bookmark to go into the worlds of books. Inside one, a woman says, "Houses aren't the only things with windows. Time and space may well have them too." I collected library bookmarks and tried every one, hoping to travel across the threshold of the page. I even made my own, carefully lettered with the words from the book: *Travel far, / Pay no fare, / Let a story / Take you there!*

I couldn't get it to work, so I reread the book periodically, looking for a missed step in the instructions. I found my answer in *A Wrinkle in Time* by Madeleine L'Engle. The journey between worlds was a *tesseract*, travel in the fifth dimension, possible only by the thoroughly initiated, which I was not. "Playing with time and space is a dangerous game," says the protagonist's father. "It's a frightening as well as an exciting thing to discover that matter and energy *are* the same thing, that size is an illusion, and that time is a material substance. We can know this, but it's far more than we can understand with our puny little brains."

All these books illuminated small pieces of the same set of principles. There were too many connections for the magic not to be real. The books never taught me to travel to other worlds, so I began to wonder whether I could manipulate this one.

DREAM DOOR

I think dreams are riddles because they need to be solved. I am sure dreams are enigmas because they really can't be. After I read *The Battle for the Castle*, Winthrop's sequel to *The Castle in the Attic*, in which the hero and his friend defend their castle from attack by large rats, I began dreaming I was in a besieged castle. I never dream I'm naked, flying, or falling. In my nightmares, I don't have long before the people outside the walls come to kill me.

ELEPHANT HOUSE DOOR

I was prepared to see books as riddles long before high school teachers taught me the mode of literary study I'd have to unlearn, searching texts for the single correct interpretation coded in symbols and subtext. In one of my favorite childhood books, there really was a solution. *The Eleventh Hour: A Curious Mystery* is a picture book by Graeme Base in which an elephant named Horace throws a party for his eleventh birthday. He invites ten animal friends to his house, plans eleven games, and prepares a feast to be served at eleven o'clock. But the guests arrive to the banquet hall to find the food already eaten. Readers are tasked with identifying the thief using "a little close observation and some simple deduction." The solution is in a sealed section at the book's end, following a warning: "Do not turn this page until you have tried your hardest to unravel the Mystery—*for the getting of wisdom is no match for the thrill of the chase, and those who choose the longer road shall reap their reward!*"

Clues are encoded in basic cryptography in every illustration: WATCH THE CLOCKS lettered into the wrought iron of the property's entry gate, RED HERRING spelled out on fallen tennis balls, PUT NO TRUST IN HIDDEN CODES AND MESSAGES decoded from symbols substituted for letters, a verse visible when the book is held up to a mirror: *Yea, all who seek take heed forsooth—For everyone has told the truth!* Technically, that is factual. But someone is lying, of course, by omission.

The Eleventh Hour, I Spy, Where's Waldo?, Magic Eye: I wanted all books to make me feel the way these did when my whole body and brain lurched with the click of visual recognition. I still do. I want the whole world to make me feel it.

DOOR IN MY MOTHER

My uterine lining first bled out when I was twelve. The red was brighter than I'd expected, the liquid more voluminous than any that had poured from my cut flesh. I pulled up my pants, walked down the hall, and decided not to say a word about it. Everything was going to change, like the nuns said. I was carnal now and would be tempted. The devil would track me by the stink of my woman blood.

But my mother was more powerful than the devil, with more goodness than he had wickedness. Mom had made me buttered macaroni—my favorite, but I could hardly eat. "Sweetums," she said, "did you get your period?"

CAVE DOOR

I memorized the hell facts the nuns told me I'd need to know for the test:

Hell is an underworld where sinner souls sink into punishment.

It may be a cave, a pit, an abyss, or a lake of fire and sulfur.

It may be darkness.

Nobody knows where it is.

Hell is the hole the wicked fall into forever.

If hell was darkness, I wanted hell. As a girl tearing photos of rock stars from magazines and folding the pages into rectangles I carried in my backpack, imagining the breath-balmy nights of my adulthood, I was more afraid of heaven, a place devoid of the tingle of temptation, a place where the lights never go off.

Hell sounded like Crystal Cave, near where my dad grew up, a deep, pool-dappled cavern blooming with calcite crystals and dripping with stalactites; the lowest point is called the Devil's Den. At the gift shop, I bought a box of crystals so I could start growing a cave in my room. In a photo of the first wedding performed in Crystal Cave in 1919, the groom's black suit blends into the void. With her white gown and hard eyes, the bride is a medium ready for a séance. White bouquets burst around them like tongues of the hottest flame.

I wanted a love that would rouse the dead. Maybe the devil, then, was the beloved I'd been looking for.

DOOR TO HELL

Despite my eight years of Catholic school, I have only a vague sense of who Satan is. I know he is a bad angel. The Bible says:

> War broke out in heaven; Michael and his angels battled against the dragon. The dragon and its angels fought back, but they did not prevail and there was no longer any place for them in heaven. The huge dragon, the ancient serpent, who is called the Devil and Satan, who deceived the whole world, was thrown down to earth, and its angels were thrown down with it. (Revelation 12:7–9)

The Catholic Encyclopedia asks, "And in the first place what was the nature of the sin of the rebel angels?" but I can't answer. Apparently, neither can many theologians, though they think it must have been that Lucifer wanted to be equal to God. Wanting to be like God is not a sin on its own; the sin came when Lucifer wanted the same miracle-making supernatural power of the divine. *The Catholic Encyclopedia* calls this "a species of spiritual lust."

What is spirituality if not lust? Spirit is a kind of vigor, lust nothing more than potent want. I lived without spiritual lust for a long time, believing life was nothing more than the reality I could easily access—workweeks, overdrafts, men pushing their dicks into my mouth, liquor to rinse. But then I saw a small rip in the cloth of the real. I wanted to go through that rip, a portal. *Go toward the light of the Lord*, the nuns said. The only light I knew was hot, just like my lust, and anyway, how could such pure, potent want be evil? The nuns said Satan came in through our fear. I was not afraid of my lust.

Lucifer, in Latin, means "light bringer." *Lucifer* is the Latin word for the planet Venus in its appearance as the morning star. *Lucifer* made its way to the devil through translations and interpretations of the Bible. Now, the name Lucifer is attached to the angel whose luminescence led to his fall. Why go toward the light when you're made of it?

Trying to understand where Satan was coming from isn't exactly a good look, but I feel driven to understand how an angel who only wanted more could be the highest tempter, the source of all evil. Into a verse in the Book of Wisdom is tucked this aside: "by the envy of the devil, death entered the world." I can't follow the maze of theological corridors to an understanding of sin, evil, and the motivation to tempt. I leave that in my childhood.

He gets in through temptation, the nuns said. *Temptation and doubt.*

Maybe I want him to, I thought but didn't say.

FAKE MARK TWAIN'S INDEX-O-VATOR

The first clay sequence animators crafted when beginning work on *The Adventures of Mark Twain* was "The Diary of Adam and Eve," based on Twain's short stories. I knew the story of Adam and Eve from an illustrated book about their loss of paradise, but I liked them better in clay because animated Adam and Eve forgot about their absent God. Among trees spangled with heart-shaped leaves, bulbous mounds of otherworldly flora, and rainbow jungle thick enough to obscure the world beyond Eden, Adam and Eve regard each other. Adam resents the intrusion; Eve yearns to know this strange creature evading her.

She's such a bother that he decides to escape, but she finds him. When Eve builds a house abutting his, he erects a fence between their yards. She takes it out. He restores it. Over and over, they do this until Adam storms into his house. When he slams the door, she turns, and we see her sad face.

Sitting in front of a stream, Eve looks at her reflection.

I go to the water when I need someone to talk to. It is a good friend to me and my only one. It talks when I talk. It is sad when I am sad. And it comforts me with sympathy.

Later, she serves tea to a cluster of beasts.

He is avoiding me and seems to wish I would not talk to him. So I made friends with the animals.

I've watched this sequence so many times I have to remind myself the memory is made of clay, not of my own past. I have never been to Eden.

"The Mysterious Stranger" appears in a break in the Adam and Eve story. In the immediately preceding segment, a snake in sunglasses tempts Eve to eat the apple. Paradise darkens. The pond dries to reveal a fish skeleton, a parrot becomes a crow, the animals bare their teeth, trees die, and a beast swallows the unicorn Adam loves.

At this rupture point, the children meet Satan. This placement makes sense: I had forgotten, somehow, that Satan is the snake, and that in the Bible version, after Eve eats the apple, God tells her, "I will intensify your toil in childbearing; in pain you shall bring forth children. Yet your urge shall be for your husband, and he shall rule over you." This part of Genesis didn't make it to Claymation.

I never understood why Adam and Eve were forbidden from eating the apple. If the snake had told me, as he tells Eve in

Genesis, "God knows well that when you eat of it your eyes will be opened and you will be like gods, who know good and evil," I would have found this credible, and I would have eaten the apple skin to core. Wanting to know what God intended as mystery, I pore over my astrological natal chart, looking for the future.

The Satan thing is long behind us by the time *The Adventures of Mark Twain* returns to the Adam and Eve story. Twain reintroduces the story by saying, "How deep a debt of gratitude we owe to Adam and Eve. They brought death into the world."

We see them in their banishment, clothed in fur. Adam has decided she's a companion and he would be lonely and depressed without her, now that Eden is gone. After she proves herself useful, discovering fire, Adam decides, "I was mistaken about her in the beginning. Perhaps it is better to live outside the garden with her than inside without her."

Eve reflects, "Why do I love him? I guess just because he is a man, and because he is mine."

BEDROOM DOOR, OPEN

Sometimes I forget about Carl, but his absence from my thinking never lasts. I wonder what *love* is and whether I've ever really felt it. In overlaying two natal charts, one can see the aspects between two people's planets; some aspects show feelings that can resemble love, like the hook of early infatuation or the vortical pull of karma. Other aspects show the potential for longevity. But only potential: a chart is like the outline of a story. I just wish ours would tell me the point of this feeling, too ugly to be love but too potent to be nothing. I can't forget him because then I'd have no occasion to even wonder about love.

LOCKED DOOR TO THE UNDERWORLD

According to some of the witches who love Lilith, she was Adam's ungovernable first wife, the woman created before Eve. Some Jewish texts depict her as a woman who left Adam after refusing to lie beneath him, the wife of Satan, destroyer of angels, and a flying demon. Witch internet wants to trace her back to the ancient Sumerian epic poem *The Descent of Inanna*, placing Lilith as Inanna's maid, but scholars have rejected this connection.

Lilith's name is applied to three items in astrology: Asteroid Lilith, located in the belt between Mars and Jupiter; Dark Moon Lilith, supposedly a second moon of the earth, though it doesn't actually seem to exist; and Black Moon Lilith (the one most commonly referred to by astrologers), not a body but a mathematical point in the space between the earth and its moon.

All the astrological Liliths have something to do with the feminine. I can't keep track. I'm more interested in Inanna, Queen of Heaven, who descended to the underworld to visit her sister Ereshkigal, Queen of the Dead. As depicted in *The Epic of Gilgamesh*, Ereshkigal's husband has died; Inanna was responsible. The underworld entrance is the point of no return, but Inanna thinks she can leave when she's ready, and she approaches wearing the finery of a queen. At every gate of the underworld, she has to remove a piece of her outfit: her turban, her necklace, the twin egg-shaped beads at her breast, her breastplate, her golden ring, her measuring rod and line, her robe. Over and over, she is told not to open her mouth against the rules of the underworld.

She arrives naked and approaches her sister's throne. The judges of the underworld give her the look of death, shout at her, and turn her into a corpse. They hang her on a hook to rot, a piece of meat.

When Inanna doesn't return to heaven after three days, her minister, with help from a deity, sends two figures to rescue Inanna's corpse and revive her. They find Ereshkigal in the pains of labor, delivering a baby whose father is dead. The figures make her feel better, and in return, she'll give them whatever they want. They want Inanna's corpse.

The demons follow Inanna out of the underworld. She can't return to heaven without making a sacrifice. Someone has to return in her place: not her loyal minister, she says, who retrieved her. Not her beautician, not her sons. But her husband, Dumuzid—Inanna sees him on his throne, lavishly dressed, entertained by girls. She gives him the look of death and tells the demons to take him.

Dumuzid's sister wants to go to the underworld instead, so Inanna lets her take his place for half the year. When he's gone, Inanna's powers fade. When he returns, so does her power.

DOOR TO HELL

The oldest known knock-knock joke appears in *Macbeth*. A hungover porter talks to himself, listening to knocks at the door, imagining himself standing at hell's gate: "Knock, knock, knock! Who's there, i' / th' name of Beelzebub?" (2.3.3–4).

Who's there, he imagines: a farmer who hoarded his crops, hoping for a famine as occasion to extort the hungry, and hanged himself when it never came; an "equivocator" who, in essence, lied in court about his Catholicism by giving vague responses to Protestant inquisitors to avoid persecution; a tailor whose offense is unclear to me, but "Here you may roast your goose" reads like a punch line. As the knocking persists, the porter drops the joke: "But this place is / too cold for hell. I'll devil-porter it no further. I had / thought to have let in some of all professions that go / the primrose way to th' everlasting bonfire" (2.3.16–19).

I would stroll to hell on a path covered in flowers. Actually, I'd stroll to hell on a path covered in used condoms, empty Crown Royal bottles, and lipstick-smeared cigarette butts. I'd stroll to hell through a puddle of my own blood, through vomit, through the pre-cum of a man I'm afraid will punch me in the face like he punched the wall if I shove him off me. Knock knock, who's there? It's him again, at my bedroom door because my room-mate let him in. Knock, knock, knock! Now it's my college ex-boyfriend at the window, drunk and earnest, but he has to leave because there's a man inside my apartment with a switchblade in his hand and a gun in his glove box. Knock, knock, knock! It's my friend at the hotel bathroom door. He's still sobbing, but he thinks he's ready to stop groping me. Knock. *Never at quiet*. I'm in hell, but when the devil approaches, I freeze.

As I've chased Satan down the internet rabbit hole, I've learned that many Satanists don't believe in Satan, except as an antiauthoritarian symbol. The Satanic Temple's FAQ says its members don't believe in evil but denounce undue suffering, defend personal sovereignty, and reject tyranny. "Ours is the literary Satan best exemplified by Milton and the Romantic Satanists, from Blake to Shelley, to Anatole France." Satanism, they claim, does what a religion should: "It provides a narrative structure by which we contextualize our lives and works."

My Satan is a cinematic Satan, an as-told-to Satan I kept alive in my religion class notebook, a Google-fed Satan. I'm told

Milton made Satan familiar, but I wouldn't know. The only part of *Paradise Lost* I remember is the one about

> Rocks, Caves, Lakes, Fens, Bogs, Dens, and shades of
>   death,
> A Universe of death, which God by curse
> Created evil, for evil only good,
> Where all life dies, death lives, and Nature breeds,
> Perverse, all monstrous, all prodigious things,
> Abominable, inutterable, and worse
> Than Fables yet have feign'd, or fear conceiv'd,

because I grew up in a place of rocks, caves, lakes, fens, bogs, and dens, a five-minute drive from Shades of Death Road. That place remains an intact heaven in my memory, a moss-covered land of the living where three-inch mushrooms spring up overnight. I don't need to die to reach it, don't need to choose a door I can never step back through; I only need to drive across Pennsylvania, through mountain tunnels and across river bridges, over a mangled crust. When I drive alone, I remember the things I don't think about when I manage to find distraction in anything else, and I realize I don't need Milton's Satan because I've met the guy myself.

FORBIDDEN DOOR

I didn't think I was looking for the devil, but nothing has ever looked as exquisite as Claymation Satan, seen through a doorway, standing in the blossoms he made. In my twenties, far away from home and unprotected, I thought I was looking for a boyfriend, but goodness can be so hard to discern. God and Satan seem similar: temperamental, powerful, invisible, everywhere. I didn't want to be looking for a man to rule me, but I'd been taught to strive to be close to God, so at twenty-four, I began dating a man who soon put the fear of God into me. I met Henry at a bar. He was an electric car engineer, boat owner, and board sports enthusiast; we had nothing in common, but I don't remember caring. He didn't seem to like me, but he did want me around. I don't know whether I liked him. That wouldn't have mattered to me. Our relationship was exciting at first, scary later, feelings that are not so different in the gut, which I never listened to anyway.

Henry and I had been dating for a year when I had my tarot read for the first time. My friend Elissa (same name, same sign, same life's work) pulled three cards: past, present, future. I gasped when she flipped over the card for my present: THE DEVIL.

"It's not as bad as it looks," she said.

The card features a beast with the body of a man, feet of a harpy, horns of a ram, and wings of a bat. He scowls. His hairy legs are spread. They looked like Henry's always did when we were in his bed and he was about to grab the back of my head and push my face down onto his dick.

I said, "It just looks familiar, is all."

DOOR TO HELL

In a 2014 issue of the Jehovah's Witnesses' magazine *The Watchtower*, an unnamed author begins the article "Should We Fear Satan?" with this:

> It is very hard to detect. Colorless and odorless, it may catch its victims unawares. Perhaps over half of all deaths

by poisoning worldwide may be traced to this single culprit: carbon monoxide. However, there is no need to panic. There are ways to detect that gas and to protect yourself. Many people wisely install warning monitors and then carefully heed any alarms.

Like carbon monoxide, Satan is invisible, very hard for humans to detect, and extremely dangerous. But God has not left us without help.

The article says we can choose God or Satan. I think it's a trick. I refuse to make a choice. I will not go through a door. I know exactly where hell is, because the nuns always told me hell is not a faraway place: hell is everywhere.

FORBIDDEN DOOR

I'm told I should try to avoid abusive men by making a list of the qualities I seek in a potential partner. I once made such a list, but a man that good isn't real, and anyway, I'm looking for a portal to another world. Henry stood at the door to hell, and I never asked him a question. Early on, he asked me one: "Are you afraid of me?" I wasn't. "You should be," he said. This was fine. I remembered God saying the same thing.

Two months after my tarot reading, Henry, with his roughed-up hands attached to big CrossFit arms, covered my mouth and pinched my nose while I slept. I'd known it was coming. "You were snoring," he said when I woke trying to suck air out of his palm. He sounded like a movie killer. His face was a flat white mask lit by the double moon that watched from the sky and the lake reflecting it. After that, when I stayed over, I slept in his second bedroom, in the twin bed stacked with snow pants and jackets. The night I stepped on his expensive snowboarding goggles, I thought he really would kill me. I came into this world with a lake and expected to go out with one.

I took up smoking again. Most nights, I drank until I passed out. I ate foods he told me not to eat because he wanted me skinny. I stopped going to the unaffordable CrossFit gym he pushed me to sign up for, where I'd once coughed up blood and still kept going. I made myself repulsive to him. I didn't mean to. But something inside me wanted to live. I couldn't make myself end things with him; this, I thought, was reality. There was nothing better for me.

He broke up with me weeks after the smothering. I don't remember why. I was drunk.

DREAM DOOR

In a book of spells, I read that the best way to protect oneself from psychic sleep attack is to keep a jar of water on the nightstand and empty it every morning. The only way I know to protect from physical sleep attack is to sleep alone, or to avoid sleep. The first time I slept next to a man, when I was twenty, I woke up under the full weight of his body and the breaching press of his dick into a space that had never seemed like an entryway.

For nearly ten years after, I slept next to men with the help of psych meds that knocked me out. Slept like the dead. Went to dreamless nowhere.

BEFORE YOU ASK A QUESTION, REMEMBER

A spell is different from a riddle. A spell is a set of words meant to invoke magical power; a riddle is a set of words meant to evoke intellectual power. A riddle relies upon veiled meaning; a spell pierces the veil between worlds.

DOOR TO THE UNDERWORLD

Inanna was the goddess of the planet Venus, and the story of her descent into the underworld and back to heaven is tied to Venus's setting in the west and rising in the east. When Inanna disappears into the underworld, so does Venus, before coming back to the sky as the morning or evening star. When she travels through the underworld, so do we, over and over losing our protection in the land of the dead, over and over being hung on a hook to rot.

On its way through the underworld, Venus makes seven conjunctions with the moon; on its way out, seven more. Each marks a gate. When Venus is in the underworld, stripped of all our protections, we are sacrificed. I read about the Venus cycle on astrology internet and became fascinated: Venus went into the underworld a few days after I met Carl and came out the day he broke up with me.

That cycle is over and a new one is underway. Morning star Venus is descending. Soon, she will return to the underworld. And then, somehow, I will be hung on a meat hook, a corpse. But first, on the way down, I see what pulls me into the ground: every loss, every inheritance, every fear in my blood.

GATE 1, AT WHICH INANNA SURRENDERS HER TURBAN

A half hour's drive from my dad's hometown, a coal mine fire has burned for fifty-five years in Centralia. The fire started in 1962 as an intentional aboveground burning at the landfill.

Improperly extinguished, it spread underground through abandoned mines. For years, the fire raged, largely ignored. In 1981, a boy fell into a sinkhole in his backyard; he was pulled out, but a hole remained, with a hot, toxic, smokelike cloud of carbon monoxide rising from it. Miners knew this as *white damp*, a gas that could kill them without warning.

Eventually, residents were paid to move. Evictions of remaining residents began in 2009. A former resident told the website Cracked, "Every once in a while, you would come across a deer sticking out vertically with steam billowing out. They looked like they were crawling out. The poor deer had fallen into a sinkhole and had either starved to death or suffocated to death from the fumes. My friends would claim to see smoke coming out of its mouth, as if it had been burnt alive, but it was just the way the smoke came out."

In his book about the Centralia fire, David DeKok writes, "This was a world where no human could live, hotter than the planet Mercury, its atmosphere as poisonous as Saturn's." Even as pits opened in town, people wanted to stay, and seven still do. After they die, the government will take their property.

Most of the town has disappeared under government-sown forest. The zip code has been erased. The fire will burn for hundreds of years.

GATE 2, AT WHICH INANNA REMOVES HER NECKLACE

Growing up, when Dad played outside in some parts of town, anthracite dusted his skin. Boys' sooty exhales clouded the air. Coal ash, not salt, was spread on slick winter roads pressed into gutted land. The coal veins had names like "Mammoth" and "Primrose," and "veins" weren't just vessels under the flesh: they ran under the earth in solid streams of shining gems whose beauty was in the eyes of those who beheld how hot they burned.

A long time before Dad was born in the small Pennsylvania region defined by the presence of three-quarters of the earth's anthracite, trees covered the hills and fish swam in luminous waters. Folklorist and Schuylkill County Historical Society member William H. Newell wrote in 1912, "When the early settlers looked beyond the Blue Mountains and saw a great wilderness of forests, mountains, swamps, and streams, they unanimously decided this was a realm of Satan and solemnly consigned Schuylkill County to the devil."

It's said that Native people taught whites to ignite the glinting black rock studding hillsides. White men then stripped those hills of trees, gouged out the land, and cut hells into the earth's crust. They sent other men down to make the deep, weeping lacerations. Rivers turned sulfur-yellow, coal-black, and shit-murky. Fish died. Creeks dried. The surface of the earth caved in.

By the early 1950s, when Dad was born, the veins were tapped out. Strip-mining machines—"We called them *walkers*," he said—tore into the earth.

"It looked like the dark side of the moon," he said. "Nothing could live there."

But five generations of my family did. I come from men with gleaming silver faces and women who kept the world in order while knowing that every man—and some of the boys—they loved might not come home from work: they might be buried alive under a crumbled mine ceiling, obliterated by an explosion of gas or powder, bone-crushed in the coal breaker, or run over by three carted tons of rolling coal. The expectation of a dead man could become habitual. In the pursuit of glimmering rocks burned to fight cold and darkness, the mines took all the men they were offered.

GATE 3, AT WHICH INANNA SURRENDERS THE TWIN EGG-SHAPED BEADS AT HER BREAST

An anthracite miner would wake before dawn, step into a cage, and descend into the earth. The mines stunk of rotting wood beams, noxious gases, sulfuric acid drainage from disturbed earth, and the shit and piss of miners and coal-moving beasts. Small lamps barely lit the fungus-crusted rock walls. Miners ate lunch with muck-coated hands and often worked while sick with parasite infestations, colds, pneumonia, tuberculosis, and typhoid fever. The men would die young, if not from accidents, explosions, and roof cave-ins, then from black lung. In testimony to the Anthracite Strike Commission, a miner said, "Of course I was hurt in the mines . . . I haven't a safe bone in my body, only my neck. My back was hurt too, and I have a leg no better than a wooden leg, my ribs are broke, I have only one eye, and my skull is fractured."

No wonder the miners carried amulets and charms. Some talked to witches and bargained with the rats they believed had an otherworldly ability to sense impending cave-ins. They cast spells, even if they wouldn't have called them that—they called it *powwowing*, their word for an old way of healing. To cure a toothache, for example, as folklorist George Korson described: "Stir the sore tooth with a needle until it shows blood; soak a thread in this blood. Then mix vinegar and flour well to form a paste, then spread it on a rag. Wrap the rag around the root of an apple tree, and tie it tightly with the blood-soaked thread, and cover up the root with earth."

This is how they maintained a sense of control in a place where corpses were dumped on porches and in kitchens after the mines took another body. The difference between hell and the mines is that in hell, you know you're already dead. In the mines, they knew this was the rest of their short lives.

GATE 4, AT WHICH INANNA SURRENDERS HER BREASTPLATE

My grandpa, whom I never saw drink alcohol, watched the polkas on TV. From the living room in a house not even an hour from my dad's hometown of St. Clair, a place we never, not once, visited, I would hear,

In heaven there is no beer.
That's why we drink it here (right here!)
and when we're gone from here,
our friends will be drinking all the beer!

Years later, I liked to sing it alone in my apartment while I drank whiskey from a plastic jug. The song doesn't make any sense. If there is a heaven, it must be intoxicating. If there is a hell, we're in it, drunk so we can't feel the cold.

My grandma's father, Edmund, didn't die so young, but when he did, he left a body that had been harmed by mining: he lost a thumb in a coal car accident. His wife, Margaret, outlived him by twenty years. A woman has to be tough: I quit my Ancestry.com search because I was too confused by the dead babies' names reassigned to new children, the households combined after the death of a man, and the names of saints used over and over again: Catherine, patron against fire, ills, and sexual temptation; John, patron of love; Margaret, patron of childbirth and dying people; Joseph, patron of fathers, families, immigrants, and workers; Patrick, patron of Ireland; and Mary, patron of basically everything.

But not Barbara, patron of miners, locked in a tower like Rapunzel—not by a witch, but by her pagan father, who beheaded her. He was struck by lightning and burned to death.

Never Paula, patron of widows, a rich woman who fasted herself to death.

And never Bernadette, patron of the sick, whose asthma-inflamed lungs brought her constant suffering; who saw a dazzling figure rising from the flowers in a cave-grotto; who died in pain at thirty-five; whose liver remained soft and whole decades after her death; who said, "The Virgin used me as a broom to remove the dust. When the work is done, the broom is put behind the door again."

To be canonized, a potential saint must have performed, after death, miracles in response to prayers. A miracle is a God-wrought event defying the known order of things.

A spell is a set of words meant to make magic by calling upon a deity, spirit, demon, or other supernatural power. The spell is the request; the magic is the miracle.

A spell, then, must be the same as a prayer.

GATE 5, AT WHICH INANNA REMOVES THE GOLDEN RING FROM HER HAND

The way Henry handled me didn't seem that bad. So many men have shown me they'd do what they wanted. Sometimes the want is hidden so deep under the mantle of a man it seems he'll never be satisfied enough to back off. Henry wanted no drama, no baggage, just like the rest of them. He would never let his deep desires slip out through the hole in his face. His want could encompass anything. When I slept next to him I'd catalog the edges of his *anything*: to hold me down and squeeze every pimple on my back, neck, and screaming face until I was covered in tiny open wounds; to fuck me in the hole I begged him to leave alone; to make me understand I was an idiot, I was too fat, I had a fucked-up gouged-out face. He could not love me. He did not emote. I learned to mirror his lack.

Seven years later, I'm standing inside my little rental house in Ohio. The furnace breathes in the basement. Outside, a chill, and also men. I could go to the bedroom, alone. I could go outside. I'm standing in front of each door, always telling myself the truth as I understand it, always lying to myself, but I can stay here as long as I want. I am more alone than I have ever been, sharing no walls or rooms in this house, and in this safety, all my fear and suppressed memory burst from hiding places between bones.

GATE 6, AT WHICH INANNA SURRENDERS HER MEASURING ROD AND LINE

Last year, I visited St. Clair for the first time. When the mines were active, the town thrived, but the anthracite mining industry collapsed, earthmoving machines knocked out the sides of mountains, and St. Clair became depressed, full of shuttered businesses. Though, on the way into town, a convenience store seemed to be doing fine. I saw at the counter a product called SEX WITH A GRUDGE (TM), Made in the USA. Two pills were affixed to packaging printed with two sets of stick figures. In one set, a faceless stick figure with a hard dick stands over a faceless stick figure with breasts, poised on all fours, a cloud of smoke rising from between her stick legs. Below, it says, "1 To Hurt It." In the other set, a stick figure with a hard dick, flexed biceps, and a wicked grin stands over a stick figure with breasts sprawled faceup. There's a fire between her stick legs, a smile on her circle face, and white X's where her eyes should be. Below, it says, "2 To Kill It."

Sometimes I think I'm near the end of my energy for living. I plot to travel to another world because this one seems too decimated by the white men who wanted money and skin, too dangerous to navigate because of the sentinels still roaming, raping, and gouging out the earth to maintain power. In St. Clair, the sulfur creek still coats the rocks on its banks with orange film. The churches still operate. The bars are closed, mostly, and outside a few houses, I saw garbage cans filled to the brim with empty Yuengling's cans. In front of Saint Mary's Orthodox Church, a white-lettered sign reads:

CHRIST IS IN OUR MIDST!
HE IS AND EVER WILL BE!

GATE 7, AT WHICH INANNA REMOVES HER ROYAL ROBE AND SURRENDERS HER LIFE FORCE

In the movies, men like Henry are charming sometimes. He was only cruel and quiet. I try to make sense of how this happened and why I stayed, but maybe there's just no sense. Maybe there's nothing. Like my decade of dreamless sleep.

THE UNDERWORLD

In Coast Salish and Columbia Plateau cosmologies, there is no Satan. Our stories tell us there are *dangerous beings*. In 1929, settler anthropologist Melville Jacobs wrote that other anthropologists "translate the idea as monster; the Sahaptin natives do not seem to think the word monster gives an adequate rendition in English of the frightening, powerful, charged with magic power, dangerous being that a k'wa·li is; k'wa·li may be large, small, or any size; it is the evil power in a being that makes it a k'wa·li."

In our stories, the dangerous beings sleep on riverbanks, make mountain camps, walk trails, pick camas on prairies, and come for villages. They look like people. They can't be devils because they don't live in hell. There is no hell, but there is an underworld where ghosts live. Healers can visit. In the land of the dead, everything happens in reverse: rivers, tides, day, and night. All the earthworld's springs flow from its river.

All I know about the land of the dead comes from Coast Salish and Columbia River Plateau stories about Blue Jay's visits. I've heard and read many versions, and this is my recollection of the one that has stayed with me:

Blue Jay's sister wants to marry a dead man. She goes down to the land of the dead with her dead man and stays there.

In the land of the dead, there is a river belonging to ghosts. Blue Jay goes to the river, and his sister sends her husband by canoe to meet him. The canoe is full of bones and has a hole in the middle: it's a burial canoe. Blue Jay throws out the bones, and he can hear his sister scolding him, because he's thrown her husband overboard. She retrieves the bones, and, again, she sends her husband. Again Blue Jay sees a pile of bones. His sister tells him to keep his eyes closed so he won't see the bones; only she can see this is her husband. He keeps his eyes closed as the canoe approaches, and the husband carries him across the river.

He arrives at a place filled with bones. This is opposite land: eyes must be shut for vision, ghosts hear yawns but not speech. When Blue Jay closes his eyes, he sees flesh on the bones, fish in the river. But he wants to keep his eyes open. He throws out bones that are actually people who live down there, and so his sister throws him out, sending him home with five water buckets of different sizes. He can't go home until he puts out the fires that spread across the prairies. The dead people tell him to use the smallest bucket on the first prairie, the second-smallest bucket on the second prairie, and so on.

He first comes to a small prairie, burning, and he dumps the water from the largest bucket onto it. He passes through safely. He comes to another prairie, this one burning, too, and he dumps the water from the second-largest bucket onto it. He passes through safely. He comes to a bigger prairie, scorched by higher flames, and he dumps the next largest bucket onto it. He barely has enough water, but he passes through safely. He comes to a big, blazing prairie, and he dumps the fourth-largest bucket onto it. He's half-burned, but he passes through. He comes to the fifth prairie, bigger than all the others and burning, and he dumps the water from the smallest bucket onto it. He can't get halfway across before the flames consume him. He burns to death on a prairie that, to the dead, seems to be carpeted with flowers.

The dead people are expecting him. Blue Jay sees the bones have people on them now, even when his eyes are open; he is their kind.

Blue Jay says, "It's so nice here now!"

Blue Jay's sister says, "That's because you're dead!"

DOWN HERE, MORE DOORS

How can I choose between two doors when I see so many left unguarded? Behind her mother's door, Dorrie knows she'll find a cauldron and a spellbook. Behind the doors in the wonderland hall, Alice sees a garden. There may be as many otherworlds as there are doors.

I first heard Blue Jay's story from an elder who told me, "We go to the land of the dead all the time. We go in dreams."

DOWN HERE, DREAMS

Stuck in subterranean limbo, Alice says, "I almost wish I hadn't gone down that rabbit-hole—and yet—and yet—it's rather curious, you know, this sort of life! I do wonder what *can* have happened to me! When I used to read fairy tales, I fancied that kind of thing never happened, and now here I am in the middle of one!"

But everything gets worse. Alice is put on trial. The queen wants to behead her. At the moment of crisis, Alice wakes up.

Lewis Carroll wrote in his diary:

Query: when we are dreaming and, as often happens, have a dim consciousness of the fact and try to wake, do we not say and do things which in waking life would be insane? May we not then sometimes define insanity as an inability to distinguish which is the waking and which the sleeping life? We often dream without the least suspicion of unreality: "Sleep hath its own world," and it is often as likely as the other.

Through the Looking-Glass, and What Alice Found There, Carroll's sequel to *Alice's Adventures in Wonderland*, ends with the line "Life, what is it but a dream?" A dream built from riddles, maybe. He packed them into his letters and books. "Why is a raven like a writing-desk?" appears without an answer in *Alice's Adventures in Wonderland*. He added an answer in the preface to a later edition and wrote, "The Riddle, as originally invented, had no answer at all."

The answer was, "Because it can produce a few notes, though they are *very* flat; and it is never put with the wrong end in front!" But this unsettles me, because I always thought I knew the one true answer: a raven is like a writing desk because they both have legs. Did the riddle really have no answer? Or is a riddle a hallway, with its maker's answer just one door?

DOWN HERE, A LABYRINTH

It was easy to blame Carl for our end: his attentions turned to other women. He left me after I became boring and stifling. Hardly any time had passed since the night we wished we could stitch our rib cages together; toward the end, we tried to figure out our "love languages" from an online quiz so we could reconnect, but the results were inconclusive because our only shared love language was dread.

I forgot, though. About Henry. One week after I met Carl, I saw Henry for the first time in five years. I didn't know I was afraid of him until I saw the way my fear made him smirk. He had been inside me the entire time, and he might not ever leave. Of all the things that have happened to me, he might have been the worst: the chronic exposure, the slow death. Maybe my body will never expel Henry: his dirty fingers left their spirits sealed over my mouth. I adopted Henry's methods of hating me, learned to pop my own pimples before he could. When I look at the ice-pick scars on my cheeks, I wonder, *Did he make that one? Did I? Was scarring my body our shared love language?*

Hell is not the underworld or the land of the dead. Hell is not where you go when you die. Hell is a place you get to while living. You get there through men. I kept looking for a husband, but nearly every body was a door to hell. I'm drowning in a lake of fire, barely keeping my mouth above magma.

DOWN HERE, THERE IS A WAY OUT, BUT DO YOU REMEMBER IT?

In his essay on mental telegraphy, Mark Twain wrote:

> Now one of their commonest inquiries of a dreamer or a vision-seer is, "Are you sure you were awake at the time?" If the man can't say he is sure he was awake, a doubt falls upon his tale right there. But if he is positive he was awake, and offers reasonable evidence to substantiate it, the fact counts largely for the credibility of his story . . . Now how are you to tell when you are awake? What are you to go by? People bite their fingers to find out. Why, you can do that in a dream.

I have known my whole life that magic is real. If the otherworlds of heaven and hell and the TV portal exist, there must be others, too, and I should be able to get to them. Dressed in a baggy black dress, knee socks, and pointed black ankle boots, I drip oils onto dried leaves in a black cast-iron pot sitting on my altar among crystals and a laser-printed copy of the hallway photo of my great-grandmothers. The moon is full and I am going to start a fire. Carl is avoiding me and seems to wish I would not talk to him. I cry so hard the capillaries around my eyes burst into red pinpricks. My mom texts, *Supermoon tonight.*

DOWN HERE, NOT A DOOR BUT A CANOE

Say I went down to the land of the dead to find my great-grandmothers and ask them how to live. In the land of the dead, place of opposites, I would find their stories reversed. The husbands wouldn't die young. Maybe there wouldn't be husbands at all. After a month in the little house, I was told in a dream, *Your house is the key*, but I saw no speaker and no house. No husband, either. When Carl and I met in a coffee shop to catch up four months after the breakup, I knew he had died. He sat across the table gray-faced as a cadaver, hair whitening, hands clutching a coffee mug as though it was his heart he was trying to warm. The light had left him and the springs that supplied his veins had dried. I asked him what was wrong, but he didn't know. I thought there might not be a spirit in that body at all.

I didn't know I had sacrificed him. I thought he was the one who had chosen to go. While I had been in the underworld that summer when Venus was invisible, he'd sat on a throne, entertained by girls, and I couldn't get out without sacrificing him so I could ascend to heaven.

DOOR TO HEAVEN

I love the little house, but I know it's nearing time to leave. Anyway, I don't think it wants me to stay.

In the first house my realtor shows me, a sign on a bedroom closet door reads, *3rd floor through here.* Behind the door, we see shirts hanging on a rod, but behind them, there's a secret door. The thought thrills me until I see it leads to a dark, dusty murder attic. We don't ascend.

Days later, we see another attic. This one is finished, bright, and clean. I look out the window onto the city and cry. So many stairs above the dead-bolted door to the street, at the top of a castle, I feel safe. I must be in heaven. I tell the realtor, "This feels like a book I read." I will sacrifice anything, anyone, to stay here and feel this safe forever. But I already did: my husband's cadaver is in my soul's basement. I put it there; I could only ascend to freedom alone.

I make an offer. I sign a contract. My hired home inspector finds the furnace exhaust duct broken. "This whole place is probably full of carbon monoxide," he tells me. I go outside and nearly faint. Two emergency rooms won't take me in, even though I tell them my brain is dying from carbon monoxide poisoning. I lie on the couch in the little house, taking deep, rhythmic breaths to calm myself while I die. Of course, I live, because I am not poisoned: I'm panicked, unable to cope with the thought that a house, like a man, could be dangerous in invisible ways.

Four days before my first date with Carl, I moved into an apartment building constructed at the shift from the 1920s building boom to the 1930s depressive halt. I brought him through the foyer I remember as vintage-opulent (though thinking harder reminds me it was just aged) and showed him the elevator. I called it, opened the cage, stepped inside with him, and let the metal snap shut.

Except when he went away that summer and, in some sense, never came back, we spent nearly half the nights of that partial spring and partial summer in that building. There exists an elevator in which we are always caged, kissing for the first time. There is a room with cracks near the ceiling where we have always been infatuated and hopeful.

Every morning, I woke up first and memorized him. Part of me knew he would be leaving soon. When Venus disappeared into the underworld right after we met, I was naked, dead on a hook, even though I thought I was living. Death, really, is transformation, the work I was put here to do. When Venus arrived at the first gate the day he broke up with me, she was ready to go back and collect the things she set aside. Before I could return to heaven, I had to make one more sacrifice. Before I passed through the first gate, I had to lose Carl.

Now I am in the underworld. I have to sacrifice another husband. I don't have one. But as I write the word *husband*, he texts me for the first time in ages, asking whether I'm coming home soon.

In *The Adventures of Mark Twain*, Satan's voice was created through the combined speech of a woman and a man.

I'm standing in front of two doors. A guardian stands in front of each. One guardian always tells the truth. The other always lies. I don't know which is which. I can ask only a single question.

What is the question?

As I write, I remember. I forgot about my golden birthday: four months after Henry and I began dating, I turned twenty-five on the twenty-fifth. He crocheted me a wool hat I loved so much I'd wear it even in the heat. He bought me a decadent chocolate cake and drove me in a large loop around Washington and Oregon to places I wanted to go: the *Twin Peaks* diner, a cabin near a lake, a historic hotel on the Columbia River, and a hundred-year-old Portland saloon-hotel where my recent ancestors may well have drunk. We did fight; I don't know why. I only remember I was drunk and he was mad I didn't eat the whole cake. I don't want him to have been kind, ever. I don't want to remember feeling loved. I remember the hat, folded on the passenger seat when he picked me up, and the feeling in my gut like a swim bladder buoying me, and that's when, for the next year, I black out.

The question I always ask is, *Is it real?* My memories, their love, mine, the selves they show me. But that's not the question that solves the riddle about the doors to heaven and hell. The answer is this: *What would the other person say?*

I'm coming home for work a week after Carl writes. One black morning, I leave the little house and its slushy alley; a few hours and two airplanes later, I'm across from him in a diner. There, then here, so real.

But he's distracted. We cut our food into small pieces. I've found five different ways to ask him how things are going.

"I feel like you're on the other side of a shut door," I say.

"Am I?" he says. "Maybe I am."

It's his turn to ask me a question, but he doesn't, so we stare at our plates in silence. I decide I have something to tell him: "From the moment I first met you, I've wanted to live inside your skull." I watch the door fling open: a full-face smile escapes before he can shut it in. I always tell the truth, so I don't say *I love you.* When I thought I did, I was probably just having a feeling, and without alcohol or my psychotropic blunting fuzz, all feelings came in hot. I know I am drawn to him, curious about the great riddle and what he means to it, which might be a version of love, but it's not the one I'm dead set on finding.

In the evening, his band plays a show. We stand and listen to the other bands. While he and his probably-pleasant girlfriend— how would I know, she and I don't speak to each other—stand ten feet from me, talking inaudibly and mask-smiling, I feel a man watching me from across the room. When I glance over, I swear I see Henry, short and oxen in a Gore-Tex jacket and fat skate shoes, so I remain very still until I can study him enough to know it's just some leering stranger. From the other direction, I feel the whites of Carl's eyes, and we look at each other. He leans toward me and asks if I saw someone I know. I ask him if he saw me recognize a guy. "No," he says, "but I heard you thinking."

When he tells me he and his girlfriend are going to move away from the open door that's letting in the cold, a look passes between us. His girlfriend swerves and ducks to avoid walking into it. *I'm working something out,* he tells me without words, and without words I say, *I don't like it, but I understand it.* I move closer, too, but only after he's onstage. I watch his fingers jogging up and down the neck of his guitar, his boot tapping pedals, and I keep feeling his eyes flash at me, but we can't look at each other.

Not with me down here, him up there, and between us, a long hallway between his locked heart and my fistful of broken keys. Not when he's descended, and in this black-walled, cave-like corner, I can't see him. Suddenly, it's my door that's shut, because I want him more than he wants to be free, so I must be contained. I tell him I'm leaving. He doesn't object.

I'm not standing in front of any doors. There are no guardians to question. What would the other person say? I'm tired of wondering. I want to find a way to heaven, but I'm not in a corridor at all: I'm outside in the city I left, a place so bright the moon's shine is useless.

ROCKS, CAVES, LAKES, FENS, BOGS, DENS, AND SHADES OF DEATH

All my life,
since I was ten,
I've been waiting
to be in
this hell here
with you;
all I've ever
wanted, and
still do.

—Alice Notley

If a man was never to lie to me. *Never lie me.*
I swear I would never leave him.

—Louise Erdrich, "The Strange People"[4]

---

4. When you don't understand the meaning of something you read, whose fault is it? Yours or the writer's? It has to be someone's fault. Everything does. Anyway, I just ask because this is my book. Do you think I understand everything in this book? If I don't, can you?

ROCKS

I was told that I grew up at the foot of a mountain, but Jenny Jump is just a hill. It hardly has a summit. That tree-topped bent knee rising over the lake passes for a peak in Jersey.

People say Jenny lived there a long time ago, in a small white house under a cliff with her father. She was nine, picking berries or playing atop the cliff, the day a savage Indian, or a bunch of them, supposedly came to ravage her. She called to her father, but he was far below. The Indians were coming for her. Her father cried, "Jump, Jenny, Jump!"; so Jenny jumped from the high, rocky cliff to her death.

One online account of the Jenny Jump story says her father intended to catch her. As a child, I assumed he wanted her to die rather than be kidnapped by Indians: the story could be a tidy example of the cinema trope of *the fate worse than death*, a phrase that once referred exclusively to rape, especially one that took a girl's virginity. Catholic school prepared me to spot these narrative tropes: I memorized dozens of virgin martyrs' stories, sickening accounts of girls and women whose commitment to purity for Christ never faltered, even as pagan men tortured and killed them. Agatha's breasts were amputated. Agnes's body sprouted an impenetrable hair coat to block rape, and a burning at the stake failed before a soldier beheaded her. Lucy, after an eye-gouging, wouldn't burn, either, so her head, too, was severed. Maria Goretti was stabbed fourteen times after refusing a man's advances. Cecilia bled out for days after an executioner failed to cut off her head. Dymphna was beheaded. Juliana was beheaded. Justina was beheaded. Catherine of Alexandria was strapped to a spiked wheel, which broke, so she was beheaded. Apollonia's teeth were shattered and then she was burned at the stake. Ursula was beheaded.

Jenny jumped.

Near the end of the 1992 film adaptation of *The Last of the Mohicans*, violins throb while the petite white Alice shuffles to a cliff's edge, never taking her eyes off Magua, the Huron villain who just ate a man's heart. Alice's blonde hair covers her cheeks but doesn't obscure her dying eyes. She looks left. We see the cliff's impossible face. She looks back at Magua for nine whole movie seconds. He lowers his knife, but not much, and flicks his fingers to beckon. The shot moves back to Alice's face, and her head turns, and we see Magua's hand wait as she shifts her body forward and steps off the cliff. Shot from below in slow motion, she falls, all skirts. Magua walks away.

The TV Tropes website has a listing for "No Escape but Down," but this *down* is not an escape. It is a decisive end. And *trope* is inadequate. Even *plot device* is not enough. Before I knew how to write my own name, I knew that women jump off cliffs to die. I've known Jenny's story longer than I've known what *story* means—longer than I've known the difference between history and figment.

What's currently called New Jersey was first inhabited by people around thirteen thousand years ago, after the Wisconsin Glacier melted. People moved as animals moved. About a thousand years ago, the Lenape people began making permanent villages, growing crops, trapping animals, and fishing the rivers.

Lenapehoking came to be New Jersey through forced sale and threats. In 1524, Giovanni da Verrazzano, working for the King of France, arrived uninvited on the shore. During the 1600s, Europeans brought their war and wants to this world they called new. I'd like to explain what happened, but it bores and confuses me. *Exploration, patroonship, charter, survey, mapped, municipality, transatlantic trade, laws of inheritance, loyalty to the crown, quitrents, proprietors, common law, Articles of Confederation, Great Compromise*: these words are a new world, rich with subtext. I don't know how to understand Wikipedia saying, "The Swedish and Finnish colonists generally lived in peace with their Dutch and Lenape neighbors." In fourth-grade New Jersey History class, my first schooling about Indians who were not murderers, would-be child rapists, or ghosts, I learned about the Lenni-Lenape, the first nation the United States signed a treaty with after declaring independence. Lenape place-names describe the land and what happened there before settlers tore into it. Aquashicola: the place where we fish with bush nets. Mahoning: at the mineral lick. Lopatcong: winter watering place for deer. Hokendauqua: searching for land. Settlers made new names: Liberty, Hope, Harmony, Independence. I imagine the naming was a kind of white magic, an incantation against the wickedness they believed was striated into the bedrock.

I lived in a county called Warren, as in a system of underground rabbit tunnels; I'm from Mountain Lake, the name of both a lake and the unincorporated community surrounding it.

The lake is one of many glacial pits left on worn ridges wearing the plush mantle of deciduous forest. An hour northeast, the Franklin Mineral Museum, at the site of a famous defunct zinc mine, holds a massive collection of minerals, many found nowhere else on earth. Some are fluorescent, absorbing and emitting light.

This magnetic land of glowing rocks holds more ghosts than average. New Jersey's identity story is, in part, a volume of tales of deaths, hauntings, and malingering Indian spirits. Most of the stories are unremarkable: someone sees a little girl but there is no little girl; someone hears a fife but nobody's played a fife in town for hundreds of years.

In *Haunted New Jersey: Ghosts and Strange Phenomena of the Garden State*, Patricia A. Martinelli and Charles A. Stansfield Jr. write that in the hilly Highlands region of north Jersey, early white surveyors blamed witches and bad spirits for the spinning compasses, unaware that the land was packed with magnetic iron ore. The authors wonder, "Do ghostly apparitions cause magnetic fields that can affect electricity? Or are ghosts somehow a result of magnetic fields? Or perhaps both?" They write that psychologists consider ghosts manifestations of emotional unrest and unexpressed fear, while ghost experts claim hauntings represent the trauma of a person who died tragically and experiences those final moments in a loop, unaware they're dead.

Revolutionary War stories dominate the New Jersey ghost storybooks I have on hand. I am short on sympathy for unsettled undead whites who fail to find relaxation in an afterlife following their tussle over nationhood in a land already filled with nations. Ghosts are tethered to land, unable to detach and drift to the beyond. Over the last five hundred years, shiny things have repeatedly enraptured settlers: gold, anthracite, petroleum, uranium. Settlers once so feared the forest that they'd barely venture beyond their landing spots, but they came to need so much land for villages, fields, and herds that everyone foolish enough to have been living there for thousands of years would have to move or die.

My bedroom seemed haunted by ghosts I could sense but not see; every episode of Nickelodeon's *Are You Afraid of the Dark?* convinced me a poltergeist might paint a message on my wall or that my mirror might house a spectral child. Into my teen years, I'd bolt around the empty upstairs at night, afraid to see creepy shadows or reflected death. At fourteen, I began waking up with night terrors. One morning, following a set of fluorescent visions, I wrote,

Night Terrors

Now the transparent men
come to wake me.
They plot, they discuss
how they will kill me.

I pull my blankets over me.
Under the covers,
I frantically seal myself
against the bed.

A bird beats its wings
  against my shoulders.
(Opalescent blue woman
  tightly spins translucent yarn
  around my ankles, my neck,
  binds blankets around me.)

The men tear all the leaves off,
punch the birds into the sky.
They verge upon me.

Maybe I picked up a haunting in Belvidere, the town where Mom and Dad took Nate and me to get books from the library. Belvidere was fixated on its Victorian painted ladies, life-size dream dollhouses. The library building was an old Victorian made an eyesore by too many additions. I borrowed all kinds of books, even the scary collections with the story about the girl who wore a ribbon around her neck so her head wouldn't fall off and the one about sleeping children choked by invisible ice fists.

Later, in my freshman dorm, I realized that even though this new place had no mosses, lakes, mushrooms, or glacial crags, it also had no feeling of someone at the foot of my bed. I missed my see-through night people. One dead person was better company than a hundred live ones.

CAVES

The Jenny Jump legend is not a ghost story, but my mind files it there. Her death is the end: she doesn't linger. But it's possible she haunts Shades of Death Road. A few minutes' drive from my parents' house, the road runs between Jenny Jump State Forest and the sod fields. Growing up, I was warned about hauntings, but never heard stories about Shades specifically. The internet filled me in. Those mists rising off the road, the sod, and the water of roadside Ghost Lake are the spirits of the dead: malaria casualties, residents whose throats were cut by bandits, Natives slain by early settlers. I've never seen a ghost there, but to be fair, I haven't spent much time on Shades, except for a few drives for ghost-watching and a high school party I spent playing with the WebTV until my friend and I walked out to the driveway's end looking for ghosts, wanting something supernatural to happen. We found only the same forest darkness we lived in.

I looked in the wrong places along the road. I haven't been to the Fairy Hole, a cave where Lenape arrowheads and pottery shards were supposedly found, or down Lenape Lane, an unpaved dead-end road running along Shades of Death. People have seen white orbs there at night. If the orb turns red, those who see it will die. I don't know how anybody knows this. An Indian spirit guide is said to shape-shift into a deer; if a driver doesn't slow down, an accident with a deer follows. Never mind that Jersey deer are omnipresent, Jersey drivers reckless.

In Hope, just a turn off Shades of Death, is the Land of Make Believe, the modest amusement park that opened in 1954 and thrilled me more than any collection of stomach-tossing roller coasters and upside-down rides. The park offered wholesome fantasy fun to smaller children, and I, mostly an indoors child, preferred the park's dimly lit buildings that felt as if they were underground, cool and a little musty in the Jersey sun. I liked ducking into the dark of the Enchanted Christmas Village, accessed through a fake fireplace and narrow stairs, and the Haunted Halloween House, whose bats and Dracula automatons showed me the dotted line between thrill and fear. But I couldn't enter the Jenny Jump House. Said to be the oldest structure in Warren County, it had a sign:

> Nine year old Jenny is believed to have lived in this house around 1748. While playing or picking berries on top of the rock she was chased by Indians and called for help to her father below.
> He shouted "Jump Jenny, Jump."
> . . . So she jumped.
> The entire mountain range, part of it now a State Park, is known as Jenny Jump Mountain.

The house was among wonders and amusements: Colonel Corn, the Famous Talking Scarecrow; an old-fashioned carousel; a Magic Dragon ride; and a circle of canoes emblazoned with birds and suns around a gleaming brown Indian warrior statue, one hand shading his far-searching eyes, shield in the other, quiver of arrows at his feet. This ride is called Indian River, but the canoes hover above hard-packed dirt. When children are locked in and the canoes start to rotate, the fantasy begins: we make believe we've gone back to a time before settlers set out to scrub every Lenape man, woman, and child from this land. They didn't, of course: the settlers scattered the Lenape, but their nations remain. I didn't know, in that time before internet, that the Nanticoke Lenni-Lenape Indians, Powhatan Renape Indians, and Ramapough Lenape Indian Nation were (and are) actively self-governing in New Jersey.[5] I learned about the Lenape in history class, not social studies, never in the present. I felt I might be the lone living Indian girl in New Jersey's cupboard, a trinket like the tiny plastic drums and dyed feathers in the amusement park's gift shop. The Land of Make Believe was where I belonged.

Still, at first, I was too afraid to enter the Haunted Halloween House. My dad told me, "The only thing we have to fear is fear itself." I bolted through the house so I couldn't be caught by a girl-strangling ghost, but I think part of me always knew that the menace wasn't real—it was suggested by the shack's black walls and floor, flat bat shapes at the ceiling, and eerie music pumping from speakers. At the winding hall's end, a life-size animatronic Dracula played an organ inside a glass case in the wall. I wanted to loop through again and again and again. Every time I burst out into the sun, I emerged more hardened, less afraid, more like a little skeleton, less like a flesh child.

LAKES

When retreating glaciers dragged their bodies across the land, melt collected in low points. Nate and I hauled inner tubes down the street to Mountain Lake every summer, remaining basement-bound the few days each year when posted signs warned us about

---

5. For more about these tribes and the state of New Jersey's rescinding and reaffirming of state recognition, I recommend the work of Lenape and Nanticoke journalist Lisa J. Ellwood.

weed-killing herbicide treatments. I wasn't worried about toxins. I was worried about snakes. I imagined they were eight feet long, wrist-thick, and black. Grandma Kate had told me Horsethief Lake, connected to the Columbia River, was full of snakes. Mountain Lake was not, but I believed my feet would hit a fanged mouth instead of the patches of clay I shaped into poison bowls.

Some lakes near home:

Mountain Lake, once a summer resort, which seemed impossible because why would anyone want to relax anywhere but the mall.

Lake Just-It, which Dad said got its name because it was *just it*, which made no sense because it didn't even have a dock to jump off.

Lake Hopatcong, near the car dealerships; a lake monster with the body of a snake or an elephant and the head of a dog or a deer once lived near its inlet, the River Styx.

Ghost Lake, just off Shades, made not by ancient glaciers but by men who dammed a creek between their houses. The internet says its informal name (officially, it has none) comes from the *wraithlike vapors* that rise off the water, spirits of people murdered in a cabin or ghosts seeping up from an Indian burial ground disturbed by the white men's lake. They say the sky is bright all the time there. I wouldn't know. I've been there once. The midmorning light turned lily pads to flecks of glitter. I saw no mists, no ghosts, just an egret wading through weeds.

Sand Pond, not really a lake, hardly known by its map label, secreted in a purse of private forest owned by a Boy Scout camp, called by a fake name and known by millions of people who couldn't locate Warren County on a map. Most people know Sand

Pond as Crystal Lake, a place where teens died on film for the world, whose watching eyes changed our place forever.

But I didn't know that when I lived there. As far as I knew, our place was secret, and so it was safe.

By the road circling Mountain Lake, rainwater sometimes cascades down a small rock face. As a child, I recognized it as a miniature version of Multnomah Falls, the tallest waterfall in Oregon. Those falls empty into a lake connected to the Columbia River. I went to this place in my ancestral territory as a kid but only just learned from Twitter about the "Indian legend" of the falls: a chief's daughter supposedly jumped to her death as a sacrifice to the Great Spirit to end the sickness among her people. I've never heard this story, and the only textual sources I can find are Wikipedia, a late-'90s-looking "Native American legends" website that does not appear to be Native-authored, and William P. Young's evangelical Christian novel *The Shack*. With sales of over twenty million copies, it's one of the best-selling books of all time.

According to Wikipedia, the book's title is a metaphor for "the house you build out of your own pain," and its narrative functions as a parable about trusting God's wisdom through unspeakable suffering. The "legend of the beautiful Indian maid" is introduced early: the chief's daughter, a "princess," is ready to marry "a young warrior chief" of another tribe, chosen by her father because she loves this man. Right before the wedding, a lethal sickness spreads among the men. A medicine man says that a long time ago, a similar sickness "could be stopped only if a pure and innocent daughter of a chief would willingly give up her life for her people. In order to fulfill the prophecy, she must voluntarily climb to a cliff above the Big River and from there jump to her death onto the rocks below."

The tribal council won't ask a woman to do this. Sickness keeps spreading. Even the fiancé gets sick, and so:

> The princess who loved him knew in her heart that something had to be done, and after cooling his fever and kissing him softly on the forehead, she slipped away. It took her all night and the next day to reach the place spoken of in the legend, a towering cliff overlooking the Big River and the lands beyond. After praying and giving herself to the Great Spirit, she fulfilled the prophecy by jumping without hesitation to her death on the rocks below. Back at the villages the next morning, those who had been sick arose well and strong. There was great joy and celebration until the young warrior discovered that his beloved bride was missing. As the awareness of what had happened spread rapidly among the people, many began the journey to the place where they knew they would find her. As they silently gathered around her broken body at the base of the cliff, her grief-stricken father cried out to the Great Spirit, asking that her sacrifice would always be remembered. At that moment, water began to fall from the place where she had jumped, turning into a fine mist that fell at their feet, slowly forming a beautiful pool.

The book says she's like Jesus, driven by love to make a sacrifice. I've tried to find out whether this story has any basis in our real oral tradition, but I've found nothing. I suspect this is a white fantasy. Settlers love a martyr girl. Our stories, though, are never so easy.

In particular, settlers love a girl who goes over a cliff. My Twitter timeline was overtaken one day with jokes about Cliff Wife. YouTube celebrity Shaun McBride was vacationing with his influencer family in Hawaii. (I can't say more. I don't understand.) During a hike, his wife, Jenny, slipped and fell off a cliff. Really, a small hill. A knoll. "Here's the video of Jenny falling off the cliff," he says after an introduction in which she's in tears and he's solemn, saying, "We want Jenny's near-death experience to be motivation for you guys to make every single day the best day ever and make life the best ever, 'cause it can just change, like *that*." I lost count of how many times they called it a "life-changing experience." We see her slip and tumble about twelve to sixteen feet, then see it in slow motion. She gets up unharmed. There is much more video.

Twitter took hold of the swollen melodrama of the clickbait. Some thought she took the fall as a sacrifice at the altar of You-Tube views. People threaded her into memes and rewrote song lyrics. My contribution: "You have to learn to fall off cliffs alone before you're ready to fall off a cliff with somebody else."

This never would've happened to me. I would not walk a cliff's edge. I'm afraid of heights. America would love to shove me off. No, actually, America asks me to do it myself.

FENS

Shades of Death Road runs along the sod fields, a massive expanse of hyper-lush lawn where a marshy lake was drained in the 1880s after a deadly malaria outbreak. The sod farms, neon green long after trees have given up their leaves, supply rolls of Kentucky bluegrass for faraway dirt plots. A peat company concocts clay-mound mixes used by more than a hundred pro baseball teams. The owner doesn't list the Shades of Death address on the website.

Across the fields from Shades, down Hope Road, you'll find the unincorporated community of Great Meadows, home to a general store, the Polish church I went to for eighteen years, the Ukrainian church, the tactical supply store, the strip club that was called Cannonballs for ages but is now named Stage Dolls. I assume the old name is a double entendre, its less obviously apparent meaning inspired by the Revolutionary War ammunition shaped from the hills' iron. Some nights, near Cannonballs and the fields, lights shoot across the horizon. Not ghosts, not specters, just cars racing at the dragway open to anyone with cash, a vehicle, and a license. When I lived in New Jersey, I didn't understand what the strip club and dragway were for: lighting up the limbic system when the days fail to keep life in the living.

Across the river in Pennsylvania, my second-favorite amusement park, Bushkill Park, was built in the crook of a creek that flooded the park over and over. Alongside the standard carousels, bumper cars, and skating rink were oddities like the Barl of Fun, one of America's oldest fun houses, with tilted floors, unsettling wall paintings of strange clowns and toothy faces, a moving cylinder to climb in, a shifting staircase, fun-house mirrors, and a wooden floor sloping into a slide. I can't imagine a time when the building didn't seem old. Another ride, the Haunted Pretzel, carried people in small cars on tracks through a structure's dim interior.

In 2011, the park appeared in the movie *The Fields*, a semiautobiographical thriller inspired by screenwriter Harrison Smith's childhood memories of the area. Shot and set there, the film is about a child temporarily living with his grandparents after seeing his father point a gun at his mother's head. He's warned not to venture into the cornfields around the farmhouse because some menace lurks there, but he does. Scene after scene opens with sinister rows of secret-keeping corn. The boy finds a dead woman; then, on the other side of the fields, he finds Bushkill Park. The film takes place in 1973, but we see the gutted, flooded park of the 2000s. The boy creeps through the devastated fun house, where, we later learn, a group of squatters lives, one of them homicidal.

I couldn't follow the plot or feel the menace of the cornfield's unknowns. I was hung up on the mother at the end of the gun and the grandfather who said, "I could bury your nanny in this garden and no one would ever know." I kept waiting for the funhouse mirrors I remembered. What makes a fun house fun? That what we expect doesn't match what we see. That we can feel flat reality bent under our feet.

BOGS

Adjoining my lake, three-quarters of a mile from my parents' house, are fifty-seven bog acres where the bears live. Really, black bears live everywhere in that part of Jersey, tossing garbage cans, breaking car windows to get food, entering houses. When I lived there, they strolled through our yard while we barbecued; one came up to the cellar door to look in at my cat. For thirty years, the bear hunt was outlawed in New Jersey after their population dropped under fifty; as it swelled to thousands of bears, I learned how to live among them. Stay alert in the spring, when they're hungry. If they approach, be calm, yell, raise your arms, look big, back away slowly.

Now, New Jersey's bear population is likely the densest of any US state; the human population is certainly the densest of any US state. As New Jerseyan humans push farther into bear habitat, the more inevitable it seems that people will die. In 2014, a hiker in another county *did* die by bear. Placed as crown jewels of quirky and cutesy news stories are photos of bears enacting my childhood terrors: "Brownie-Loving Bear Pokes Head in Parked Car for Snack in N.J. Neighborhood." "Massive Black Bears Brawl on Front Lawn of Man's N.J. Home." I've seen the photo of a bear my mom took from the porch and posted to Instagram; taped to my parents' basement door, there's a bumper sticker with an illustrated bear and the words, *If you really care, don't feed the bears.*

The bog is a sunken swamp that I've always considered to be none of my business: low, wet, inaccessible, a good place for bears to hide out. West Nile carrier mosquitos lived there, too. I want to say people will never live there. But it's hard to be sure what people will do in Jersey.

Like—the lady with all the tigers. In 1999, a huge Bengal tiger got loose and took a few hours' walk around a central Jersey subdivision. After eight hours of searching in yards and woods, authorities found it but couldn't tranquilize it, so they shot and killed it. The *New York Times* reported, "The day after the authorities shot and killed a 600-pound Bengal tiger that had escaped into the woods, residents awoke today to learn that a one-square-mile area here has a surprising concentration of tigers." The Division of Fish, Game, & Wildlife was aware of nine (all accounted for) at Six Flags Great Adventure and twenty-three at a private tiger compound "run by Joan Byron-Marasek, who has earned a place in local lore and among local children as the mysterious 'Tiger Lady.' But her existence was often doubted by many adults."

In 2013, I read Susan Orlean's *My Kind of Place*, and by the end of the second paragraph of her 2002 *New Yorker* essay about the tiger, I was thinking, "Oh yeah, I know that tiger." My dad was a fish biologist for the division, so there were familiar source names in the news stories. I remember imagining a gleaming lab table filled with a tiger ready for necropsy.

Byron-Marasek never admitted the escaped tiger was hers, and it couldn't be proven. According to Orlean, some people believe the tiger could have been a drug dealer's guard animal, an abandoned pet, or even a Six Flags escapee whose flight was covered up; "In the end, however, the tiger has simply been relegated to the annals of suburban oddities—a lost soul, out of his element, doomed to his unhappy end, whose provenance will never be known." I mean, same.

Orlean's essay, published the year before game wardens seized and relocated Byron-Marasek's sick and filthy tigers, ends like this:

> You really could live your life here in the most usual way and never know what extraordinary thing was afoot just a few yards away; you would dismiss the occasional whiff of something weird or a roar at midnight because the alternative was simply too strange. Everything about the story was so surreal—Marasek's personal history, the idea of collecting these creatures, the image of a tiger walking through the suburbs—that I decided I really wanted to see one of the animals, to assure myself that they really existed,

and mostly because I know that sooner or later, by the irreversible order of the New Jersey courts, these tigers will be taken away from this strange little patch in New Jersey.

Orlean is from Ohio, and her website's "About me" page doesn't list Jersey among the places she's lived, so it makes sense that she'd consider this so strange. Nearly a decade later, she wrote a brief *New Yorker* piece that begins, "A small, drowsy town in Ohio, a pile of dead Bengal tigers." The animals massacred in Zanesville, fifty-five miles down Route 70 from the house I now own, actually included seventeen lions, eight bears, three cougars, two wolves, a baboon, and a macaque, but the news of eighteen dead Bengal tigers hit people harder, there being fewer than 2,500 alive worldwide then. They were killed because Terry Thompson, owner of the Muskingum County Animal Farm, freed fifty of his animals before shooting himself. Cops killed the roaming animals, by order of the sheriff.

Some people consider the New Jersey bear hunt an annual massacre. From long before my birth until three months after I left for college, black bears could not be hunted in New Jersey, and the bear population climbed. I'm in favor of the bear hunt as a means of controlling a stressed population in a densely packed area with dwindling wilderness. I don't consider hunting inherently unethical, and I don't understand why people object to the bear hunt more than the turkey hunt or the deer hunt.

Orlean writes, "I love wild animals, but if I knew there might be a bear in my backyard, I would understand that it might need to be killed." I like wild animals. I love this picture I just saved of a black bear sitting in a patch of skunk cabbage it's going to eat.

I've eaten bear meat and I've eaten salmon cooked in skunk cabbage. I've known there was a bear in my backyard, but it didn't cross my mind that it might need to be killed; we let it know it was too close to us and should go back across the road into the thicker woods, private property stretching south, mostly unbroken, to the bog. Orlean recalls, "When I wrote about the Tiger Lady of New Jersey, I realized that every possible outcome for her tigers was sad—even sending the animals to a sanctuary that could provide them with better care. There should never have been twenty-seven tigers in suburban New Jersey to begin with."

Every probable outcome for the New Jersey black bears seems sad. They should be there, but should the people?

Our bog and our woods feel closer than most New Jersey landscapes to resembling the place that belonged to the bears before colonization. The New Jersey Natural Lands Trust website says the Mountain Lake Bog Preserve is "steeped in botanical history": beginning in the nineteenth century, naturalists and botanists visited this glacially formed wetland to document rare plants like the leathery grape fern and bog willow. The bog, home to mosses, swamp trees, beavers, and ducks, hasn't really changed. With no traffic, the drive to New York City would take about an hour and a half; to Newark, an hour. I still don't get cell service at my parents' house on cloudy days, and the nearest grocery store is a twenty-minute drive. Any number I pull from New Jersey feels impossible. A place can't be so wild and so densely built, so desolate and so populous. Living in contradictions, we learn to want the strange and nonsensical. We covet and hoard rare things—rare bogs, rare rocks, rare lakes. I blossomed toxic, emerging a person of rare traits: unusually thick skin, say nurses with needles; a remarkably movable jaw, says the dentist; a bent cervix; extreme astigmatism; a uterus that grew tinier, throttling the IUD that once fit; severe and plentiful environmental allergies—the list goes on. Maybe it's not that I'm so strange; it's just that I catalog pieces of strangeness and, through them, bring my body into focus in a way I can't when I look into the mirror.

Maybe wanting to be special is an American condition, the swamp of entitlement from which the American dream is supposed to be able to grow. Orlean sees it in Zanesville's Terry Thompson: "There will always be vain, obsessive people who want to own rare and extraordinary things whatever the cost; there will always be people for whom owning beautiful, dangerous animals brings a sense of power and magic. It must be like having a comet in your backyard, a piece of the universe that is dazzling and untouchable right outside your door."

What should happen to the bears? Am I special or what, and is it wrong to want to know? Can pain be special? What's wrong with me, really, though? All the questions I still can't answer were born in Jersey.

DENS

Technically, New Jersey black bears don't hibernate; they den. Their winter sleep, *torpor*, is shallower than true hibernation, and while a hibernating bear wouldn't be roused by activity around it, a bear in torpor is easily stirred. In Jersey, they might be up and about all winter if they find enough to eat. Usually, though, bears go dormant in autumn, making tight dens in spaces like holes, caves, leaf beds, tree hollows, or built nests. Bears like to be alone. In torpor, a bear's heart slows, its body cools, and its fat feeds it.

I was like a bear. In winter, I spent most of my time in the basement. Mom, Dad, Nate, and I made separate dens of desks and couches. I rarely ate, living instead off the internet, sometimes rising to get the wax-wrapped cheeses and baby carrots I tallied in a composition book. Sometimes, I shut myself in my bedroom with my tiny TV. While Fleetwood Mac's *The Dance* special looped on VH1, I pored over printouts from witchcraft websites, studying binding spells as dutifully as my biology textbook because before I learned about mitochondria and osmosis, I learned that the veil between worlds was thin and full of holes. The other side reached into the known world of New Jersey all the time; I decided to reach back.

Twine, an index card, the name of a boy who took me down to his basement one afternoon and held me so close our bodies nearly melded from ankles to necks. It wasn't like in a movie: we didn't kiss. Upstairs later, he wouldn't look at me. Later still, when I asked to touch him again, he taunted and derided me, asking how I could possibly think he wanted me. I couldn't figure out whether he'd changed his mind or I'd misunderstood all along; I couldn't believe both his lie and my intuition. So: an incantation. *I bind you, Spencer. I bind you from hurting yourself and others.* Trying not to think, *I am being punished because I want.* Trying to think only, *I bind you.* Wrapping him, and without meaning to, wrapping myself into a bundle, hoping nobody would see my desire ever again.

SHADES OF DEATH

I've been trying to write as if I'm an expert on Mountain Lake and the surrounding area, but that fell apart when my parents mentioned that *Friday the 13th* was filmed at a nearly identical lake seventeen miles north of our house, with some scenes filmed in Hope, the township directly northwest of mine. I thought I could have the place mostly to myself, but fandom involves claiming through an imagined sense of knowing.

Friday the 13th, an early tone-setter for the slasher-movie genre and an establisher of the concept of summer camp on film, grossed nearly $60 million at the box office. I always thought Mountain Lake looked like a movie summer camp setting, and I've described our forest as "horror movie woods." Now I realize my notions of *summer camp lake* and *horror movie woods* were built from pop depictions of scared humans in hostile natural settings, most of these stories driven by tropes made famous by a movie filmed in woods that bled into mine. As long as I've been alive, Warren County has been lodged in the national consciousness as a remote location where screams go unheard. I just didn't know that until age thirty-three.

The movie was set on already bloodied ground. Land of unhappy ghosts. Land of genocidal fairy tales. Land of white guilt mistaken for poltergeists. Land of young white men with Facebook photos of assault weapons longer than torsos, with *This is my rifle*, with unmuffled cars peeling down the drag strip between expanses of sod meant to adorn lawns in some other place. Land of hot-air balloons. Land suffering from some of the biggest environmental releases of industrial toxins in a significantly toxic state. Land whose roadside corn stands justify the *Garden State* thing. Land of iron, land of malingerers, land of pink Victorians settled into soil wicking chemical waste, land of diners at the edges of dark forests. Land of the impossible: my young body riddled with rot, doing what a body shouldn't, ovaries blooming with cysts, gallbladder dying, nasal passages twisted, teeth turning dried-blood red from the inside, skin so impervious to what D.A.R.E. and *Cosmo* told me would age it that I may have been born embalmed. Land of waters so pristine that it seems you shouldn't imagine something lurking below the lake's glassy surface: monsters, undead persons, bad molecules, snakes. New Jersey: Only the strong survive.

X

I've seen eleven horror movies, including *Friday the 13th*, which I first watched a few days ago. I don't like them. They're too real. A hallway in *The Sixth Sense* looked like my family's, a room in *The Ring* like my first bedroom. In "Recreational Terror: Postmodern Elements of the Contemporary Horror Film," Isabel Pinedo writes:

> A film promises a contained experience. Regardless of how open a film's ending may be, the film ends and in this there is a modicum of closure.
>
> A film is not only a time-bound experience, it is also an imaginary one. The screen constitutes the spatial frame on which a film is projected. It marks off a bounded reality, one that need not conform strictly to lived experience. The borders of the screen establish parameters that free the viewer to engage in fantasy.

Pinedo argues that horror pushes viewers to accept the disruption of the rational order of things, experiencing "a simulation of danger not unlike a roller coaster ride. In both, the conviction that there is nothing to fear turns stress/arousal into a pleasurable experience. Fear and pleasure commingle."

But for me there is no pleasure, only suggestions of terrors living in my woods and walls. I can't tell myself, *It's only a movie,* when the tangible stuff of my life—wood, water, darkness—convinces me it isn't.

X

In *Friday the 13th*, kids die by knife, arrows, an axe to the head. Mrs. Voorhees is beheaded. Screenwriter Victor Miller said that, until the adoption of CGI, "everybody cooperate[d] in fooling themselves." Director Sean Cunningham said of the beheading, "Now that had never been done before. Today it's just absolutely common. But the question is, how could you cut somebody's head off in the movies and not have to cut around it . . . It's the equivalent of sawing a girl in half on stage. People know you didn't saw the girl in half but they're just looking at it and they just saw her cut in half. It's doing the things that magicians do."

The kids sliced up a snake on film. This wasn't scripted or faked. Special effects artist Tom Savini came up with the idea after encountering a snake in his cabin. Harry Crosby, son of Bing, took a machete to the body of a living, writhing snake. According to IMDb, "When they filmed the scene, the snake's owner was standing off to the side and crying."

X

Two years after the release of *Friday the 13th*, in Blairstown (the filming location for the just-far-enough-from-camp fictional town), a real teenage girl's dead body was found by a gravedigger at work. The bludgeoned body could not be identified, so she is known as Princess Doe. She was named by primary investigator Lt. Eric Kranz, who, according to a fan site (but nowhere else, IMDb included), appears in *Friday the 13th* as a cop who calls to Alice from the lakeshore as she drapes herself over the side of a canoe.

Princess Doe's grave in the cemetery where her body was found reads:

> MISSING FROM HOME
> DEAD AMONG STRANGERS
> REMEMBERED BY ALL

X

Approaching the movie's climax, a cop drives the camp owner back from the Blairstown Diner (a real diner, one I've probably eaten at) to camp, saying, "Bad enough it's Friday the thirteenth, we got a full moon too. They keep statistics. We get more accidents, more rapes, more robberies, more homicides, more of everything when there's a full moon. It upsets people. Makes 'em nuts."

"You've made a science out of coincidence," the camp owner replies.

X

I just learned that in 2000, when I was in high school, MTV's *Fear*, a paranormal investigation reality show, featured Blairstown. A text overlay introduces the show:

> *The people are real.*
> *The place is real.*
> *The fear is real.*

The next screen tells us:

Five people have been
sent to a campground
23 miles from the
nearest town to
determine if it is haunted.

They're at Camp No-Be-Bo-Sco, renamed Camp Crystal Lake in *Friday the 13th*, six or seven miles from Blairstown. The reality show cabins are the movie cabins, which are the IRL cabins. The contestants watch a video informing them they're at "Camp Spirit Lake": "For forty-seven years, this site has been home to numerous missing persons and cult activity, until authorities finally closed the camp in 1976." A talking head billed as a "local hunter" says it's "a place where bodies were dumped." A "former camper" describes a body with head, hands, and feet cut off. A "local priest" says, "There certainly are cases going on today where people get involved with the occult and evil in terms of worshipping Satan himself." A "cult specialist" talks about how people "use the entrails as different Satanic offerings to the different demons and stuff like that that they're trying to conjure up."

Supposed area residents say Princess Doe was the victim of a cult sacrifice and now haunts the campground in a spot known as "The Devil's Dancing Ground." One person says she was found headless (wrong); another says she was pulled from the lake with teeth knocked out and hands cut off (wrong); the clip about entrails gets recycled.

The contestants, competing for a cash prize, must venture into the woods and around the burnt "ruins" of cabins named Lakota, Pawnee, and Hopi, "investigating extreme cult rituals that have taken place at this notoriously haunted campsite." The dares:

1. Dig up a grave and sit silently next to the bones for ten minutes.
2. Contact the dead through a black mirror.
3. Recite a chant and behead a dead chicken while a teammate paints a pentagram onto the floor.
4. Stand with head in a cage onto which rats climb.
5. Prick a finger and drip blood onto a pentagram.
6. Lie in a coffin while the others shovel dirt on.
7. Perform a ceremony to facilitate the passage of ghosts of the cult's torture victims, reciting incantations like, "Spirits, use me as a portal if they wish to speak," and asking, "Spirits, do you wish to cross over?"

Nothing scary happens. One contestant hears voices, but at the end, she says, "I didn't feel any spirits. I think I just felt memories." Contestants are certain there's *something* going on in those woods, which is not untrue, because television is going on.

All this cult stuff is make-believe. Camp No-Be-Bo-Sco has been owned and operated by the Boy Scouts of America since 1927. The only real part: the call of cicadas at night, males asking for mates, the only sound I've ever been able to sleep through.

If I saw the episode in 2000, I wouldn't have known it was filmed in Warren County. Through the window behind the TV, I would've seen woods that stretched all the way to Jenny Jump

Mountain, touching the sod farms and the Land of Make Believe and Shades. I didn't know about Princess Doe or the wicked Indian spirits supposedly clinging to Shades. I only knew about Jenny with her skull bashed at the cliff bottom. Maybe it never occurred to anyone that her spirit might haunt those woods because in death, she served her purpose, continued the trope, and could rest easy in the afterlife knowing her death scene would live forever as the looping retelling's end.

X

Two *Weird NJ* magazine readers found hundreds of Polaroids in the woods off Shades. Most are of women, none smiling, not posing, sometimes lying down, but not, it appears, sleeping or dead.

X

At the end of *Friday the 13th*, Alice, sole survivor because she wasn't distracted by fornication, floats in a canoe on a glassy lake nearly identical to mine. It can't be June 13 with leaves that fiery, but the lake is real to me, close kin to the body of water where I caught sunfish, unwrapped weeds from my ankles, and dared Nate to swim with me under the algae-scummed dock. I wasn't startled when Jason burst from the water; I'd been bracing myself for as long as I'd known the shock of cool lake under hot sun.

X

After I watched *Friday the 13th*, I tweeted at Nate, *did you know about this and not tell me*, and he said he didn't know and hadn't seen it, but he did know of a *Friday the 13th* video game whose semi-open world is a virtual version of ours, calling to mind

Pinedo's argument: "The postmodern horror genre constructs an unstable, open-ended universe in which categories collapse, violence constitutes everyday life, and the irrational prevails." I'm downloading the game. I think I should play as Jason, the one born where I was born.

But the installation isn't working. I gather my sunglasses, keys, and money and head out into my real Ohio world, a place where I have no history and my senses are still learning the blade slap of surveilling police choppers, the twitter of sunrise songbirds, the bacterial fetor of sewer that rises from the lawn. The flat horizon holds none of the mysteries that teem in ridges and thick dark places. How am I supposed to live, not knowing where the ghosts are, where my murder will happen, where my corpse will be left? I could be murdered anywhere, really, because that's where the men live, but that truth was easy to ignore when I was blithe and rosy in that made-up land where I might have been dreaming, might have been playing pretend, might have been nothing more than a man's imagining.

ACT II.

FOUR OF CUPS.

A person sits under a tree, arms crossed, legs crossed. A hand reaches from a cloud to extend a cup. The person looks down in refusal. Three cups stand upright in the grass.

TEN OF SWORDS.

A person lies facedown on the ground with ten swords plunged into their bleeding body through a red cloth. Distant blue mountains form a horizon under yellow sky that, above the clouds, becomes darkness.

THE TOWER.

Against black sky, a mountaintop tower burns, struck by the yellow arrow of a lightning bolt. A crown flies off the fire-engulfed top; two people fall upside down through the air—they may be the two depicted on the card preceding this in the major arcana, THE DEVIL, but they're clothed. Smoke billows. Flames rise from windows.

BEGINNING A NARRATIVE IS EASY. But the hook becomes distant. The middle needs rising action. The protagonist should try to solve the initial problem but just make things worse. Antagonistic forces are at work, external and internal. Things get complicated, ideally. A subplot might develop. The protagonist must grow and change to overcome new obstacles. This cannot be a comfortable time, or else the narrative will slow and sag; it must be filled with threats.

Dramatic structure seems most possible when story time is linear. In this book, time is folding, looping, told by a clock's minute hand advancing and retreating. If I stretched my life's events onto a triangle diagram of narrative tension, what would the climax be? The rising action culminates there; it has nowhere else to go. Everything has built toward this breaking point, some crisis or confrontation. Then act two should end with the protagonist at the lowest low, the worst loss, the dark night of the soul.

This book is a narrative. It has an arc. But the tension is not in what happened when I lived it; it's in what happened when I wrote it. Like I already told you, this is not just a recounted story; I am trying to make something happen and record the process and results. What about this, then: the scientific method:

1. Make an observation.
2. Ask a question.
3. Research.
4. Construct a hypothesis, or testable guess, extending beyond the available information.
5. Experiment to test the hypothesis.
6. Analyze the data.
7. Communicate the results and formed conclusions.

I recently saw a pencil pouch claim SCIENCE IS MAGIC THAT WORKS. Okay. I have an observation: my reality is pain. A question: What is *real*, anyway? Research: there is more of that to do, and my hypothesis is undetermined at this time. Science feels so limited. Can I experiment if I know too little to guess the outcome?

An experiment is a kind of narrative, a story outlined before it's written. The climax of an experiment comes at the reckoning with results. But this is not that part. I haven't even made a mess yet. This is the part where I circle the shore of a lake and walk the riverbank. Where I keep leaving and then become a dry place all my own. This part is a map, and I lose it.

WHITE CITY

All my life,
since I was ten,
I've been waiting
to be in
this hell here
with you;
all I've ever
wanted, and
still do.

—Alice Notley

If a man was never to lie to me. *Never lie me.*
I swear I would never leave him.

—Louise Erdrich, "The Strange People"[6]

---

6. Are you curious or are you scared? This is my house, I am your host, and I am offering you two options.

MADISON PARK BEACH

The first time my future self visited me—flesh, not metaphor—I was close to the part of Lake Washington where a'yahos, a serpent spirit, once lived in and above the water. I wasn't seeking anything but a bus ride home. I didn't trek into the mountains or wait for the sunrise to address me. I missed it altogether, having been up late with whiskey. I didn't burn cedar or call upon the ancestors. I slumped post-drunk in my bus seat and beseeched my liver to forgive me again while a woman passed in front of me wearing a wool cape, a medical mask, and black-framed glasses like mine.

She stepped onto the stairs, looked at me, and froze. I could see my reflection in the glass between us. I saw her see it, too: ten years separated us, but we were two variations on a single body. She stepped off the bus and onto the grass above the beach.

This was in Madison Park, where I lived from age twenty-five to thirty until escaping north to the suburbs. I first touched its beach on the evening of Seattle's hottest day in recent memory. My friends swam but I was afraid of something—maybe the display of my body, maybe leaving my keys on the shore—so I sat and looked at the night: city glitter across the lake, patterns of wakeboat disturbance, condo boxes, white bodies sailing off the high dive. I knew I could become a thriving person by throwing my body into the land the way these white people threw themselves into it, certain the land would give and they would not break. A month later, I moved to Madison Park.

SEATTLE FAULT

The Seattle Fault cuts across Puget Sound, through downtown and central Seattle, and across Lake Washington. A'yahos lived at a few places along the fault, including a spot near Madison Park. This monster would change shape from an enormous double-headed horned serpent to a deer-snake. It caused landslides and tore the earth. Not all monsters are monstrosities; some help hold the world in order. This one did. In every source I have seen, it's written about in the past tense. I'm guessing colonizers drove it out.

I am not Duwamish, so the story of this power isn't mine and I don't know how to tell it. Even within my own tribe, people from a little ways south, I'm a young person learning how to live, so I make space for silence. I never disclose everything. Most of our seen world has been colonized. While we work to regain it, we protect the unseen from encroachment, from being stolen and mangled.

Since I have no authority in telling the story of this place, I don't write this to inform. I do it for myself, to make sense of the unseen world through rumination so I might be good here.

A'yahos is already known to white people, especially after a burst of journalistic speculation about whether Seattle would be leveled by an earthquake. Kathryn Schulz's *New Yorker* article "The Really Big One" struck fear into Seattleites' hearts, with a regional FEMA administrator's quote excerpted all over Facebook: "Our operating assumption is that everything west of Interstate 5 will be toast."

I didn't pay attention to much of the article because I don't worry about death by natural disaster, but I did notice Schulz mentioned one of my all-time favorite seismological articles: "Ruth Ludwin, then a seismologist at the University of Washington, together with nine colleagues, collected and analyzed Native American reports of earthquakes and saltwater floods. Some of those reports contained enough information to estimate a date range for the events they described." This study, "Dating the 1700 Cascadia Earthquake: Great Coastal Earthquakes in Native Stories," was the site of my first textual encounter with a'yahos. It should be read alongside my *very* favorite seismological article, "Serpent Spirit-power Stories along the Seattle Fault," written by a group of coauthors whose roles and affiliations are noted at the bottom of the first page:

> R. S. Ludwin (Department of Earth and Space Sciences, University of Washington), C. P. Thrush (Program on the Environment and Department of History, University of Washington), K. James (anthropologist), D. Buerge (historian), C. Jonientz-Trisler (FEMA), J. Rasmussen (Duwamish Tribe cultural resources expert), K. Troost (Department of Earth and Space Sciences, University of Washington), and A. de los Angeles (Snoqualmie Tribe cultural resources expert and great-grandson of James Zackuse, Duwamish Indian doctor).

I could have picked up the pace by compressing the above to "Ruth Ludwin and seven colleagues," but I can't gloss over a fact I must convey before I continue: this research was a collaborative process involving the consensual sharing of Duwamish knowledge by those with the authority to do so. What I know about a'yahos comes from this citable article, meant to be accessed.

The authors write of four Seattle locations associated with a'yahos, one of which is by Lake Washington's shore near Madison Park. Around 1,100 years ago, landslides and earth-shaking struck just north of the a'yahos site along the fault. "Throughout the region, individuals sought personal spirit powers to guide their lives and bring them luck and skill. *A'yahos* was one of the most powerful of these personal spirit powers, though it was also malevolent, dangerous, and possibly fatal to encounter," and its power could be used only by certain people.

After the publication of the *New Yorker* article, other outlets responded with their own earthquake angles. David Bressan's *Forbes* article about a'yahos begins:

> Oral tradition played—and still plays—an important role in many societies. The subjects of these stories range from fantastic fairy tales to myths, tales based on real persons, places or historic events. But interestingly enough, these stories may also represent attempts to record and transfer knowledge of past geological catastrophes as a warning from generation to generation.

He writes that a'yahos "haunted" boulders in and around Seattle. Myths, hauntings, tales: this language makes me uncomfortable, corralling Indigenous knowledges into the realm of fantasy and lore, but still, the article's aim is right: settlers would've known about earthquake dangers earlier if they'd listened to Indigenous peoples. Settlers have always lived in a world shaped by forces that are known, understood, and described, just not by them.

MADISON COURT APARTMENTS

I believed that if I lived by the beach, I would be on vacation all the time, even though I knew it was wrong to think that. Mountain Lake was a resort community before I was born. Life never became a vacation there; life was hard, simply because I found it challenging to do the basic work of being a person interacting with other people and wishing to be comforted in some vague way that seemed best expressed by the songs the radio host Delilah played on her nighttime request and dedication show, everything with a dedication declaring the love the nuns at school called *agape*: unconditional, true. My parents loved me unconditionally, but my brain still screamed.

Like every other place I'd inhabited, I expected Madison Park to bring me contentment. This was why it was established. I failed to find my ease there because deep in the mystery inside me, I wanted the opposite.

MADISON PARK

The city of Seattle is situated in a violent place where land bucks against ocean, tectonic shifting sends chills across the earth's skin, and volcanoes spill lava onto glacier-bitten crust. For the past 2.5 million years, tectonics and glaciation shaped the folded, jutting, sloping land currently referred to as the Pacific Northwest. Sixteen thousand years ago, the last glacier left what's now Seattle. Then people began to live there. Duwamish creation stories tell of a world recovering from an ice age. The Changer (or

Transformer) arrived, eventually bringing warmth, allowing for the arrival of salmon and cedar. The Changer's capsizing of the world turned some beings into immortals, some into humans.

People lived in villages and camps along the rivers that drained into the sound, and these communities came together through marriage, ceremony, and other gatherings. Now, those people from the lower Duwamish River and the land that is now Seattle are known as the Duwamish people. Many were removed from their homes and relocated to the Muckleshoot and Suquamish Reservations, though some families remained on their land and maintained Duwamish self-governance and traditions. The Duwamish Tribe is not federally recognized despite its resilience through systematic destruction of communities, food-gathering places, and centers of ceremony. In 2001, at the very end of his presidency, Clinton granted recognition; not even two days later, Bush rescinded it.

White people began passing through now-Seattle in the late 1700s and began settlement in the 1850s. In 1864, Judge John J. Mc-Gilvra bought 420 acres east of the village center. He cut through the wilderness from town to his parcel, creating a straight-shot road that would become Madison Street. He eventually divided up land for cottages and developed the waterfront. His vision: a lakefront resort and amusement park. Vision executed: the Music Palace of Washington with its five turrets and seating for hundreds. Visitors drank beer and listened to John Philip Sousa marches. Opera performers threw villains off barges. An unnamed baseball team with no mascot played afternoon games. If pioneer families brought enough supplies in their wagons, they could stay all summer in the judge's "Tent City."

A world's fair came to Seattle in 1909. Madison Park got a makeover, a turreted pavilion gate, amusement rides, and a new name: White City. The carnival had a roller coaster, a Ferris wheel, sideshow oddities, and a miniature train so popular with adults that kids missed out. By 1913, White City was gone, and the long-term buzzkill of Prohibition soon set in.

LAKE WASHINGTON

I did move there for permanent vacation, but also because my boyfriend, Henry, lived south of Madison Park in a lakefront apartment with moorage for his wakeboat. We had dated for a year. I wanted to be close to him. He did terrible things to me. It's possible he'd disagree. Many people don't want to believe their bodies' wants are violent. I would not believe the liquor I loved was scouring my insides and wasting my outsides, because it was the only thing helping me forget I wasn't safe.

Colonization is not a metaphor for my body and I do not present what has happened to my body as a metaphor for colonization. But the violence done to my body was facilitated by colonization: dominance is central to the American creation story. White men's violent rule over brown bodies built this young nation. By telling stories over and over, we give them life. By enacting narratives over and over, we give them shape. A white man dominates a Native woman and keeps his world in order.

A metaphor makes an analogue of two unrelated things with shared characteristics; a metonym is a figure of speech in which something is referred to by the name of something associated with it. But neither of those fits because I can't name what Henry did. I'm still in gaps between phrases forming, stalled in sense memories I pivot from as soon as they return. The images inside me behave as boundaries in the way white people think of rivers. I come right up to the edge. In the deep place, my body is in his bed in the apartment hanging over the lake. If I let you in—what happens if I let you in?

WATERFRONT, DOWNTOWN SEATTLE

In 1854, Duwamish Chief Si'ahl (commonly known now as Chief Seattle) gave a speech shortly before white people took his people's lands. Knowledge of his speech has been maintained through Indigenous oral traditions, but his words didn't enter the non-Native record until more than thirty years later, when Henry A. Smith printed his version of the speech in the *Seattle Sunday Star*, conjured up from records and memory.

Smith said Seattle said, "The great, and I presume also good, white chief sends us word that he wants to buy our lands but is willing to allow us to reserve enough to live on comfortably. This indeed appears generous, for the red man no longer has rights that he need respect, and the offer may be wise, also, for we are no longer in need of a great country."

Smith said Seattle said, "It matters but little where we pass the remainder of our days."

Smith said Seattle said—most quotably—"And when the last red man shall have perished from the earth and his memory among white men shall have become a myth, these shores shall swarm with the invisible dead of my tribe, and when your children's children shall think themselves alone in the field, the store, the shop, upon the highway or in the silence of the woods they will not be alone. In all the earth there is no place dedicated to solitude. At night, when the streets of your cities and villages shall be silent, and you think them deserted, they will throng with the returning hosts that once filled and still love this beautiful land. The white man will never be alone."

There exists no record of Smith's notes from or presence at the speech. Seattle's words were translated from Lushootseed, eroded and warped by the passage of time, and flattened onto the page to build an imaginary world where the last living Indian gave white men permission to keep cutting.

RED ONION TAVERN

Every day for years, I sat at that dark bar, drinking pints and hoping for conversation. I wasted coins on pinball and pull tabs. Outside, I flicked spent cigarettes into coffee cans. My friends favored a couple of dives with ceilings dotted white with playing cards put there by the old, tuxedoed magician who went from bar to bar and table to table, but never to my den at the slope's bottom.

Yelp review: "It's the type of bar that lowers the property value of the neighborhood in a much needed kind of way."

Yelp review: "If you're a loner, go somewhere else. I have never eaten here so I can't comment on that."

Yelp review: "When we first walked in we were a little disappointed with there being almost no one in the bar and the decor clearly has not been updated for at least 20 years."

The space had previously housed a drugstore with a soda fountain, which is basically what the Red Onion was for me once it could offer the whiskey I took with ginger ale. I lost hours, dollars, layers of lung, and neighborhoods of brain. Some nights, I closed the place down and brought Kevin—first my drinking buddy and then, after Henry, my boyfriend—back to my place to work at collapsing the blood bag inside the wine box. Some nights, we'd go from the tavern to the playground across the street. Swings, slides, and a zip line were installed where Madison Street Park Pavilion, White City's entertainment hub, once stood. Before that, the land was covered in timber. Before that, the forest wasn't timber—it was trees.

In deep night, we swung so high I thought I'd launch into flight over the neighborhood.

LAKE WASHINGTON

Henry told me I, a lazy person who would not exercise, wasn't useful, so I asked to learn to drive the boat. I wanted to do something other than pound Rainiers while he wakeboarded. I learned well, got a license, and always drove sober, having seen his friends' boats impounded during the Seafair bacchanalia of the Microsoft set.

We were happy together only on the boat, skipping across wakes, creeping along the shoreline to study the houses and grounds of the rich, pulling bodies and boards, not talking. I never got the hang of wakeboarding. My legs were too weak to let me stand on water. Henry had magic: he made flips look easy, soaring above the wake. I liked him best upside down and impossible.

He did wipe out; everyone did. He once went down hard on his skull. He didn't come up right away, but maybe time was just stretching right then, my back rigid in the driver's seat, his friend silent and stoned. I don't remember feeling anything as the friend and I pulled him into the boat when he finally did surface, speaking nonsense. After we returned to his apartment and docked the boat, he said he was sure it was another concussion—he'd blacked out,

I think—but it wasn't a big deal. I hadn't heard about how a con-cussed brain can change—the way the trauma can turn thoughts into sinister nonsense that moves violence from unthinkable re-sponse to natural answer. We were together for three more months.

WATERFRONT, DOWNTOWN SEATTLE

Poet William Arrowsmith published a rewrite of Chief Seattle's speech in 1969. Arrowsmith said Seattle said, "When the last red man has vanished from this earth, and his memory is only a story among the whites, these shores will still swarm with the invisible dead of my people."

Arrowsmith reprinted his version in the *American Poetry Review*, prefacing it, "Beneath the dense patina of white literary rhetoric there lies a text which, in my judgment, no white man of the period could conceivably have written."

Then this white man does what he said was impossible: he writes the text. He shapes the words before him into a figurine.

LAKE WASHINGTON

Underwater sediment holds records that can be read through the extraction of core samples. Fossilized pollen can be read as mark-ers in the layers, showing disturbances to flora growing on nearby land. A core taken in Madison Park shows dramatic changes in plant life around the start of settler encroachment and in waves after as settlers logged, replaced evergreens with houses, planted leafy decorations, and changed the lake. Deep down in the old lay-ers, there is pollen from fir, hemlock, and cedar, nearly no grass. Everything after the mid-1800s presents as *post-disturbance*. The layers lie undisturbed in the lake, deep in water, holding.

MADISON PARK BEACH / MADISON VALLEY / CENTRAL DISTRICT

It was a series of visits, not visions. I thought seeing my future self would be a onetime thing, but she returned, at another stop on the 11. Still on Madison Street, but farther from the lake. This woman—by the way, I'm in the same seat as the other time—stops at the top of the stairs and waves her hands at me and says, "Hiiiii! Hiiiiiiiiii!" And I notice she's me. Except maybe fifteen years in the future. And I don't look great. I look *aged*, beyond what time does.

So this lady gets off the bus waving, and I don't speak. I'm looking through the window at her as she's standing on the curb, waving and waving and still waving when the bus pulls away.

It was a while before I saw her again.

I saw her in the Safeway on Madison, farther toward downtown in the Central District. I was in the longest ATM line of my life, looking around at people. I know it's rude, but I just like to look at people's faces and try to listen to what they're thinking, or maybe I'm looking out for men who've done unspeakable things to me, but anyway, that's when I see her: this woman, me from, let's say, twenty years in the future, standing at the customer service desk and waiting for someone to help her. And *no one does*. She's me. She doesn't look *bad*, but she looks lost. She doesn't look like the woman I want to grow up to be. She's uncomfortable in her body, which I always figured I'd grow out of. I stand in line forever. She walks away.

So I wondered, *What does it mean?* I was thinking these were warnings—that if I keep going, this is how I'll end up. Ragged. Or unsure. Or wearing some medical mask.

A friend said, "What if you met this woman at turning points—points at which you sloughed off a version of yourself? And she came to show you what you departed from."

PAHTO OR MOUNT ADAMS

Cowlitz people have access to tamanawas: spirit guides, supernatural things. Children, in the old days, worked to find them, fasting and following instructions in set-away places. Children were forbidden from telling others about the tamanawas they found, who would guide them for life. I never received instructions, but I did go to a set-away place, picking huckleberries on the mountain with my aunties nine months after I first saw the woman. They showed me how to pick fast, the way their mother taught them. At night, in darkness that felt both obliterating and world-making, I saw the Milky Way. The kinnikinnick, ferns, evergreens, and mosses had always been there; we had always gone there when it was time to pick berries; I was young and sick and knew nothing, not even how to ask tamanawas to approach.

RED ONION TAVERN

Sitting at the bar or smoking out front, I met my neighbors: the Salish sisters who lived above me; a VP of a company everybody knows; a lady with family money and no job who once biked drunk to her house to retrieve a carved Coast Salish mask I did not want to see. I knew it would upset me further; she'd just said I couldn't possibly be Native and had run her hands through my hair to investigate.

Mostly, though, I talked to the bartenders, middle-aged men I pretended didn't want to fuck me because they never came out and said so. Once, drunk, I lent my childhood copy of *The Eleventh Hour: A Curious Mystery*, to one of them, telling him it would be good to read with his daughter. I should've read it myself, but I didn't want to think about riddles, secrets, and codes. I lived a simple narrative and lacked the capacity to search beyond the apparent. The bartender never returned the book. I don't think he and his daughter ever read it. I understand: decoding is demanding work. It takes something out of a person before the answers come.

MADISON STREET

Cable cars ran along Madison Street before the 11 did. In 1927, Almira Bailey wrote in the *Seattle Post-Intelligencer* that the street now called East Madison "was just a little, moist, woodsy road through miles of forest for years. And then there was the cable car that went all the way to the lake. And now broad boulevards lead to stately homes."

A street like a knife, a crease, a rip in space and time through which my future selves step into view.

MADISON PARK BAKERY

Next door to the Onion, the baker worked at night, dipping a metal basket of dough into a hot oil vat. My bar friends told me that if I knocked, he'd let me in and give me a donut. At 2:00 AM, the bars were closed and I had nowhere to go but home, the dangerous place with no cigarettes, only thoughts. The baker gave me my first taste of marzipan. In exchange, he wanted a cigarette. "Are you a virgin?" he asked. The marzipan didn't taste like I'd imagined. I wished I'd never eaten it. But I did, and one more thing stopped being magic. Before long, I vomited it up.

LESCHI, LAKE WASHINGTON

In the deep place, my body is in his bed in the apartment hanging over the lake, guts churning to untangle the feelings: first, my brain fought itself as one part recognized violence in his hands stopping my breathing while another part denied there was malice; later, my heart panicked when he broke up with me, not because I loved him, but because he lived in my skin and I was afraid I was too porous and my spirit might leak out without his wishes filling me.

He's been in the deep place, holding me by the ankles. I was drowning myself so I wouldn't have to come ashore and look back into the water.

WATERFRONT, DOWNTOWN SEATTLE

Home, a 1972 made-for-TV movie written by Ted Perry, features another version of Chief Seattle's speech.

Perry said Seattle said, "I am a savage and I do not understand any other way. I have seen a thousand rotting buffalos on the prairie, left by the white man who shot them from a passing train. I am a savage and I do not understand how the smoking iron horse can be more important than the buffalo that we kill only to stay alive."

Perry said Seattle said, "What is man without the beasts? If all the beasts were gone, men would die from a great loneliness of spirit."

Chief Seattle may have killed a buffalo, for all I know, but it was the water beings—the cockles and salmon and clams—that kept his people alive.

LAKE WASHINGTON SHIP CANAL

The Duwamish people had been carrying boats between the lakes, or shoving them down a creek that appeared when the lake was high, forever. The white men wanted a canal. Logs, lumber, and coal would no longer be portaged; ships could pass through the wound gouged into the isthmus.

The Lake Washington Ship Canal was built to connect Lake Washington, Lake Union, and Puget Sound. When it opened in 1916, Lake Washington's water level dropped 8.8 feet. The Black River, a Duwamish River tributary into which Lake Washington emptied, disappeared. Joseph Moses (Duwamish) said, "That was quite a day for the white people at least. The waters just went down, down, until our landing and canoes stood dry and there was no Black River at all. There were pools, of course, and the struggling fish trapped in them. People came from miles around, laughing and hollering and stuffing fish into gunny sacks."

THE SPOT

Some bar friends showed me a secluded waterfront public park separated from the Broadmoor Golf Club by a chain-link fence. It was mostly secret; occasionally, it would be listed as one of Seattle's best secret waterfront access points, and teenagers knew it as a place for smoking joints. The entrance driveway, at the dead end of a road, looks like private property. The driveway leads to a path to murky water. I liked to stand alone on the dock, watching cars race across the bridge floating on the lake, listening to invisible beavers move through water.

In 2010, the golf club dredged the lake near The Spot to improve water flow for maintaining their greens. The beavers departed during dredging but returned to find their lodge intact. Quoted in the Madison Park blog, a resident said, "Some of the beavers slapped their tails right next to the dredge to say goodbye. It was quite touching."

A commenter said, "My son and I went out on the lake today May 31 2011 and saw several dead Beavers near the Broadmoor golf ranges in take pipe. Also some dead fish and a bad smell around the Lodge. We took photos of the Beavers."

WHITE CITY

In 1909, a circus elephant named Queenie wreaked havoc in the amusement park. Two little white dogs approached while she was being moved. Queenie chased them, crashed into the carousel, broke wooden horses, and stuffed her mouth with apples and oranges from the fruit stand. Then she allowed herself to be chained again.

Two ladies fainted.

Later that day, a tiger reached through the bars of its cage, grabbed a fox terrier, and tore its body to pieces.

CACTUS

I had my first and last Madison Park meals at Cactus, where I used to spend afternoons getting wasted on neon-pink cocktails. I wanted to be rich like my neighbors so I could afford double orders of brisket tacos. After I moved to the suburbs, I learned Kurt Cobain had loved Cactus. His last residence was a few minutes' drive south along the lake, but despite my teenage obsession with Nirvana, I didn't visit the park next to his house when I lived there. I kept him in myth. I avoided thinking about death in the neighborhood.

Two days before his suicide, Kurt ate dinner with friends at Cactus. They started with bananas dulce. Kurt's credit card was declined because Courtney had canceled it when he left rehab.

Cactus's owner asked him to pay by check and remembers, "It was kind of gibberish but it was still decipherable, so I accepted the check. That was the last time I ever saw him—that Sunday night. Sometimes, I wish I had held onto that check. I did try afterwards to get it back from the bank, but the check had already gone through the system and it was too late."

Stars hang from the ceiling, cow skulls from the walls. At the end of Kurt's last Cactus meal, someone saw him licking his plate.

MADISON COURT APARTMENTS / THE SPOT

I moved from Madison Park on a whim a month after ending my four-year relationship with Kevin, who liked having me around, but not enough to try to imagine our future. When escaping (from whatever) to the suburbs, I didn't clean the fireplace. I failed to repair the cabinet door that had been half ripped off when Kevin, drunk, lost his balance. I left mold on the windowsills and wine spots on the carpet. I ruined that home. The blemishes could be fixed—I mean I broke its energy. My sadness will haunt that place like a restless spirit.

Before moving, I had to complete a ceremony requiring I be in a set-away place. In waterproof boots, I went to The Spot and veered off the path into the swamp. I toe-tested bog stones, stepped on those that didn't sink, jumped over muck, and grasped tree trunks. On solid land, I completed my ceremony. I retraced my steps thinking I remembered every stone I'd tested, but I trusted one with the weight of my body and sank.

I smelled rot—dead things turned living. I felt my body sinking without resistance and without hitting bottom. I would die drowning in decomposition, my lungs filling with swamp muck.

I grabbed a sapling and muscled my way out, clawing the solid earth I realized I was desperate to stand on again. Sludge coated me to my waist and filled my boots.

If I had sunk, if I had found spirits of that place deep in the muck, they might not have recognized a living thing inside me.

Or maybe the spirits rejected me because it wasn't my time to leave.

EDMONDS, WASHINGTON

Three months later, I quit killing myself with whiskey. My great-great-aunt Virginia spoke with the photographer Edward Curtis in 1910, and from their conversation he wrote, "The Indians, after the disturbance of 1855–56, were dying off in great numbers through the use of whiskey—so called—whole canoe-loads drowning."

Removed from the city, I could hear my instructions for living. I'd never thought I'd find them on those nights I stumbled from bar back doors, smoked in alleyways at dawn, and slept with a swamp mouth dirty with traces of my insides.

I stopped seeing Future Elissa, but other people began to tell me, "I saw your doppelgänger!" Someone kept seeing her along Madison. They would ask whether it was me. I'm waiting to have the answer.

I made the long drive from my suburb to Madison Park two equinoxes and a solstice after I left. The neighborhood looked as if it had been painted over with fresh, bright coats, but only because of my new clarity, the hangover haze long departed. Nobody was going to make the neighborhood change.

I did not see the woman.

WIND RIVER

Edward Curtis reported this paraphrase of my great-great-aunt Virginia's words:

> An old man dreamed and announced that new people were coming, with new ways, and the Indians would die. He made them put coyote-skins over their shoulders and two by two, men in front and women behind, march in a circle, while he sang his song of prophecy. The old woman who told [Virginia] about this said it happened when she was a little girl. She took part in the dance, and laughed at the flapping tail of the skin on the girl in front of her, and the old man seized her by the wrist, flung her aside and said, "You will be the first to die." As it happened, she outlived all the others.

LAKE WASHINGTON

In the deep place, my body is in the apartment hanging over the lake. If I let you in, will you pull me out?

EVERY NEIGHBORHOOD

This Cowlitz story was told to ethnographer Thelma Adamson by James Cheholts in 1927:

> God sent X̣wáni the chief, here to teach people how to live. He was to teach them how to work stone and to do all the necessary work. But X̣wáni did not do as he was told; he just fooled around with the girls and never showed the people the right things to do. God once came to him and

discovered him neglecting his work. God looked around and saw that the new people had trains, steamboats, steam-donkies,—all of which X̱wǻni was supposed to have shown the people how to make. Then he threw X̱wǻni on an island where he turned into a rock. In the next world,— when the world turns over, X̱wǻni will be a [real] man.[7] I guess he is still there on the island. I hear people say that he looks like a rock in the shape of a person. He gets up at night and walks when everyone is asleep. A man once caught him in the act: X̱wǻni was walking around all over the house and seemed to be half-asleep.

THE SPOT

I emerged from the swamp with a body covered in death. The power told me I had work to do. I am meant to be porous because my instructions come in through holes I can't close or even see. They go to a deep place. I do not know what happens there. I washed my swamp skin until I gleamed all over.

---

7. Bracketed addition in original.

OREGON TRAIL II FOR WINDOWS 95/98/ME & MACINTOSH

Challenge the Unpredictable Frontier

All my life,
since I was ten,
I've been waiting
to be in
this hell here
with you;
all I've ever
wanted, and
still do.

—Alice Notley

If a man was never to lie to me. *Never lie me.*
I swear I would never leave him.

—Louise Erdrich, "The Strange People"[8]

---

8. If I tell you what I want, will you believe I know? What I want is to say it over and over and over: *If a man was never to lie to me.* Like the speaker, "I dream of the one who could really wound me." Do you have recurring dreams? I dream I'm in a fortress under siege. I can't explain dreams. I write books instead. How do you feel about repetition? Do you think a person's relationship with repetition is culturally shaped? Is that a leading question?

DOUBLE-CLICK THE CD-ROM ICON. A window will open. Click. Click. New game. Conjure up an escape route. If you want to disembark from the life you've known, there's a trail. But you can't know the expanse of what's ahead—staggering vistas, sickening width of the sky, skin stink. Your Oregon Trail exists inside a rectangular window, a finite world with three possible destinations and a handful of ways to die. Click. Go. Elissa, yes, you've made it clear you're on a quest for freedom. But limits will save your life.

You're a pharmacist who has come to Council Bluffs in 1855 for the purpose of setting off on a journey west to Oregon City. You've already bought a large farm wagon, but you still need to buy the other supplies you'll need for your journey. You're accompanied by three others:

    Kurt Cobain, age 30
    Mia Zapata, age 30
    Layne Staley, age 35
    Travel the trail!

In town, a man with a smart vest and bow tie wants to sell you a package of supplies. Exit this man. You've traveled this trail more times than he could imagine. In the dry goods and grocery store,

173

you carve into your stack of pioneer money to buy 1 axe, 200 pounds of bacon, no brandy, no banjo. You buy 3—no, make that 5 boxes of bullets, 2 butcher knives. You buy out the pickles and acquire enough oxen to drag your pickle kegs across the land. This is the best part of the journey, so much like the late-night WinCo trips you make in your "real" life outside this window, now that you've moved to the suburbs. The discount rice and bulk beans you buy aren't sustenance so much as protection from famine.

Inside the window, you change your mind and buy brandy because, here, you are a white man. In this place that is both safe and unsafe, you can have all the brandy you want. You buy no bags of beads.

You don't know what Duffy's Elixir and James Fever Powder are for, but you know whiskey and tobacco. These were abstractions when you set out on this trail twenty years ago: you weren't acquainted with the sweet, toxic astringency of spirits. You buy 3 gallons of whiskey because, outside the window, you've lost whiskey forever: you just passed the seven-months-sober mark. You're a miracle. You buy laudanum and a rifle. Morale is high. You depart.

The choice of starting date used to feel arbitrary. Whether you left in 1840, 1865, or any year in between, you traveled the same trail, albeit one with different stops and travelers. No matter when you leave, you'll pass Chimney Rock, run into heavy fog and severe thunderstorms, and shoot yourself while hunting. This time, though, you choose 1855, the year your great-great-great-grandfather and eleven other headmen signed the treaty that completed the cession of the Willamette Valley to the United States. Inside the window, you'll be one of so many settlers who strike out that summer after reading newspaper notices from Washington Territory Governor Isaac Stevens declaring the land open and available.

Your adventure begins at a river.

Check the river conditions: the Missouri River appears to be a fairly ordinary river. Caulk the wagons and float: while you watch the wagon's cover moving from shore to shore, you never even think about going under.

You traveled west eight years ago in a Chevrolet. Your route was not the trail gouged out of the land in the early nineteenth century: you began on Route 80 in New Jersey, took 90 through the Midwest, 94 through the northern plains, 90 again in Montana, and rode that all the way to your new home, your promised land, your city of destiny: Seattle.

You have only three memories of that overland adventure: a gas station convenience store where you bought Skittles, a hotel room, and a sign warning you to watch out for rattlesnakes. You, twenty-two and wrecked by liquor and meds, needed a fresh start. In the West, the trees stayed green in the winter. You didn't know that the West would maim you worse than the East. It wasn't the overland trail that would do it, three and a half days without cholera or dysentery. Your demise came from provisions you tried not to pack into your wagon.

You've traveled three miles when you get the itch to select your rifle and stare at the flat expanse of green. A squirrel hops across the prairie. You want to kill it, but you are a patient hunter. Your boyfriend of a month, Philip, is a week into his monthlong vacation in China and you haven't heard a word from him. His motivation for going, in the ways of the whites, is to be enriched by another culture. He is an honest man. That is why he doesn't say he'll miss you.

If you had any real patience, you wouldn't have committed to the first guy you went on a Tinder date with after being dumped by another. You and Philip have nothing in common—he's a programmer, a libertarian, an optimist, a board game enthusiast, and an upper-middle-class white man who keeps saying his parents met in Mensa, which he calls a "social club"—but you're attracted to him and he's harmless. What is the right fit, anyway? People say relationships stop feeling like magic eventually, so you figure you might as well start one without any spark to lose. Anyway, you have no frame of reference for the right fit, only models of danger, disrespect, and indifference.

No deer, no bears, no meat. You shoot a jackrabbit. Firing 3 times, you shot 4 pounds of game and were able to carry all of it back to your wagon. If you continue to hunt in this area, game will be scarce.

You stop in town. A woman with a bonnet tells you about a party that came through, "several mean scoundrels" who "tore up the local saloon and right terrorized some of the people here." The white man's mask you wear inside the window has her fooled. You've torn up your share of saloons. No, that's not right—you've torn yourself up in your share of saloons.

Twenty years ago, you, your parents, and your brother huddled around a PC monitor and started your first journey after coming home from an after-church mall stroll. The world inside the window soon felt like another room in your house. Now you're alone in your apartment and it's getting dark.

Moving out to the suburbs seemed like a good idea in the winter, when you were trying not to drink. You wanted a big place and you wanted to be as alone as your heart felt. You chose a suburb where you'd seen evergreens; a road that gives way to Puget Sound, where cars cross the dotted stretch of the map only by ferry; a block with salt-water-smelling air; an apartment so large, bare-walled, and under-furnished that your mumblings to your cat echo around the living room only three people have visited in the nine months it's been yours.

Now you've lifted your forearms off the condensation-slick tavern slab that your spine curled over like a fern that would never open. There are no bars within walking distance of the new place. You spend evenings in your apartment, watching your brain do the same thing over and over, which is scan itself for the flaw that is going to kill you. While your body stays safe at home, you need to travel out of your isolation through this window.

So you've come back to the trail, where you have someone to talk to. The faces are more familiar than the teachers and clergy who instructed you in how to live, the preformed lines of dialogue a part of you in the way Bible verses never were. If they're living in your memory, are these people not real?

In New Jersey, the only Indians you knew were the two others in your house and the ones who lived in TV and helped white people find their inner noble savages. Disney's *Pocahontas* showed you Indians who were shot by the colonizers they loved; the year of its release, you first slipped through this window into the trail, where you sucked venom out of wounds, ignored any ailment that wouldn't kill you, and drove your oxen until they couldn't stand. You were always a good colonizer.

You continue.

You shoot at a deer with your shotgun and miss. When it runs across the grass, you feel as if someone has a finger in a hole in your chest, stretching the wound. You stare at the neat line of the horizon, wait for another animal apparition, and wish you could administer some laudanum. In another window, you ask, *What is laudanum?* Laudanum is drugs. That you surmised as a child fascinated by the teachings of D.A.R.E. You wanted to see visions and act like you weren't yourself. *Laudanum is an alcohol-based opium tincture* wouldn't have meant anything to you. Things have happened. You have grown. You understand laudanum.

You thought the West would free you from the version of yourself you'd gotten tangled up in. Instead you became more bound to it than ever, tethered to the toilet bowl, wed to caustic drink. You concocted laudanum from whiskey and painkillers, mixing up a patent medicine you were sure could cure all your ailments, your own version of Duffy's Elixir.

But the dry goods and grocery store was miles back. Laudanum is sold only in town. You've checked every penny-ante outpost on this trail, just to see. And anyway, no trail ailment is improved by administering laudanum; there's always a better way to heal.

You still long to yank yourself out of feeling. You get so lonesome you go to the high-end grocery store to talk to the artisan yogurt bar man who always mentions his time as a schoolteacher. Inside the window, you're always with your party. You shoot your rifle at a deer and it turns from a grazing thing into a lump. The hole in your chest closes. You have a purpose here. Firing 1 time, you shot 166 pounds of game and were able to carry all of it back to your wagon. If you continue to hunt in this area, game will become scarce.

Two years ago, you began weekly sessions with a therapist whose office was filled with crystals. The only thing you knew about astrology was your sun sign, but your therapist said you were experiencing your *Saturn return*. The planet, once every thirty years or so, returns to the spot in the zodiac it occupied when you were born. In this rite of passage, Saturn, celestial taskmaster, breaks apart and reassembles your life. Your job became intolerable when your boss snapped into tyranny, your first book came out, your long relationship with Kevin ended, you moved outside the city, you got sober.

FOUR OF CUPS, featuring a person under a tree, arms crossed, refusing the cup offered by an extended hand. After weeks of this, you understood it was time, once and for all, after fits and starts and trials and failures and dry spells flooded, to get sober.

But you still needed to buy the other supplies you'd need for your journey: a new moon webinar, a book of spells, a baggie of dried mistletoe, a tin of incense, a tiny cauldron. You recently turned an end table into an altar and learned to read the shapes left in a spent candle's wax, because you've come to believe you might be a witch like that one character on *The Magicians*, a show you and Philip watch: Julia, denied entrance to the school for magicians where her protagonist friend matriculates, becomes what they call a *hedge witch*, cast out on her own, forced to learn magic without instruction. The internet says hedge witches are real, and you haven't told anyone, but you think you might be one.

You've been hoping for a sign, something to make you feel in your gut that it's real, not just TV. One day, while you were frying tofu and kept getting bitten by the tiny drops of oil popping from the pan, you thought, *I just want one thing in my life to be a little easier. And less painful. Just one thing. Maybe I should get a FryDaddy.* Hours later, outside your office on campus, the free-book table had no books, only an unopened box holding a brand-new FryDaddy. *God is everything or he is nothing,* your sponsor likes to say. That was the moment the mystery dropped from your head to your gut. You have always been in the mystery. The choice is not to be a witch or not be a witch, not to believe in magic or to believe in reality, but to be an open door or a closed one. You are good at making choices. You continue.

You stop at Pawnee Village. A man with a porcupine quill headdress says, "Now is a good time for trading." He says if you don't want to, perhaps you're not a friend of the Pawnee. No! You need him to be your friend. As a child here, you talked to every Indian twice. They dressed like the Indians in *Dances with Wolves*, not in oversized Looney Tunes T-shirts like you, but you still knew they were your people. The white men in cotton vests and women in bonnets were not your people, everyone wringing their hands over wagon dust or pushing you to get a move on.

Tall Rain Cloud has 1 5-lb. sack of tobacco that he'll trade for 1 ox. He sees you as another white man, a taker who owes a debt. You need your oxen more than his friendship. You move on.

You meet a Pawnee woman with long hair. She looks sort of like you do under the white man mask. She says, "Why do you bother me? I don't want to trade. The things that we get from the white travelers don't make up for all that we lose."

"Tell me more," you say.

She says, "We didn't know the whooping cough, measles, or the smallpox until your people brought them to us. Our medicine cannot cure these strange diseases, and our children are dying."

"Do you have any advice?" you say.

"No. I just want you to leave us alone."

So you do.

You once believed that there were two kinds of Indians: the real ones in buckskins who used every part of the buffalo and died before 1870, and the ones like you. But then you thought about the black-and-white photo hanging in your hallway. You'd seen these two women a dozen times a day your whole life, and you knew they were your relatives. The standing woman wore a black Edwardian dress with a high neck and puffed shoulders; the seated woman's black shirt was covered in white threads you later learned (or guessed—you can't recall) were dentalia, skinny shells of scaphopods used for trade and high-status adornment. Your great-great-grandmother's dress was covered in money.

You looked sort of like the women. The women were Indians. You knew the best way to be an Indian was to look the part. But you didn't feel real yet, not as an Indian, not in any way at all.

At Mormon Island, you wonder when you'll encounter missionaries, but there's nobody but a sad-faced lady who will trade you 228 pounds of salt pork if that's what you want. You don't need any meat, and *want* has no place here: you're supposed to carry what keeps you alive. Morale is high.

This trail began as missionary work. In 1836, Methodists Marcus and Narcissa Whitman went west with other missionaries and fur traders. The Whitmans established a mission at Waiilatpu, near the Walla Walla River in present-day Washington, which was unceded Cayuse land. They intended to save Indian souls. The Cayuse didn't want to be saved. In 1843, Marcus Whitman returned east, then came west again with a thousand pioneers, making the first "Great Migration." With settlers came disease. An 1847 measles epidemic killed half the Cayuse people, including most of the children. At the mission, the Whitmans treated whites and Cayuse, but more whites survived, and the Cayuse retaliated for treachery and held the missionaries responsible. They killed the Whitmans and a dozen other whites and destroyed the mission. But the white people opened more. Some of them made Native converts pledge, "From this point on, I will be a white man."

Your gun is not for killing people—yours is a fun gun. On the hunt, you choose. The hunt isn't like the scripted trail-goer dialogue or guidebook-defined path. You aim where you like and you shoot what you please. You can do anything. A gun is a possibility machine.

Before Philip left for China, you drew him three tarot cards. He doesn't believe in anything, but when you talk about tarot and astrology he listens and doesn't tell you belief makes you stupid, so he's an improvement. THE DEVIL: "This means fucking," you said. He said nothing.

Now he's on the other side of the world, and still nothing. You tell yourself maybe he's busy or dead, maybe he doesn't have internet, maybe he's fucking. Your new psychiatrist gave you, along with your new PTSD diagnosis, language for the way your body holds its breath so hard that even at a cellular level, you feel taut: you're *triggered*. Every violation came with new filaments of memory you'd associate with the harm, all forming a long rope of disorder. You're always unconsciously seeking a sign that a man will kill you soon. Silence trips your wire.

You can't explain any of this to Philip. He's a regular at Burning Man. He has a face like a little baby's, unmarked by pain. When he hits your ass hard during sex, you can't say anything, because you know this is called *spanking*; this is not being hit, this is not the same as when your first rapist punched the wall, and you're supposed to be *good, giving, and game*, so you bury your face in the pillow and you are not triggered, you are good at fucking and you are giving yourself instructions not to cry and you are, above all, game: a doe, bending your face toward grass.

You suffer an accidental gunshot. If you die, you'll have to restart. Your options: Continue as usual; Rest here awhile; Increase rations; Clean and dress the wound; Treat with an antiseptic; Rub salt in the wound; Get advice.

Most of these treatment options seem fine; outside the window, most options are bad. Gallbladder failure: Continue as usual or get surgery. Ovarian cysts: Continue as usual; Take Advil (though your inflamed stomach can't handle it); Take Vicodin; Get a medical marijuana card. You've been so busy killing your pain that you never learned how to treat your ailments. Pain won't kill you. But this gunshot wound might. So you get advice.

A man with a dead fox hat holds his rifle like a baby and says, "I've had me some experience with gunshot wounds back in the Illinois frontier wars. Let me see what I can do to help." A man with a mustache says, "You sure it was an accident? We don't want any murdering varmints hanging about!" Yes, you're sure:

the only violent one here is the empire. The men know nothing. You're good at rubbing salt in your own wounds, good at increasing rations, good at rest, best at continuing as usual, so you know that these actions won't heal you. You treat with an antiseptic.

Your injury becomes infected. You clean and dress the wound, and you plan to stop for rest, but you meet a man with the biggest knife you've ever seen and also one of the biggest mustaches. He looks like bad company. Your condition is poor, with bleeding, discoloration, pain, and reddening. You wonder whether there's still a bullet inside you, and where. Removing it was never an option.

You continue.

You're staring at a green rectangle of hunting grounds and thinking about a question your therapist stumped you with—"What do you like about Philip?"—when a deer walks across the sky, levitating above ground. You shoot and miss, and the deer runs. You look for another sky deer but find only geese. This was not a glitch, but an apparition.

At Ayres Natural Bridge, you meet a woman in buckskins who resembles your grandma, young. She says, "Ah, more wagon people. Are you here to slaughter more buffalo like the group that passed by four days ago?"

"Tell me more," you say.

She says, "I'd never seen such waste. They killed ten times what they needed for food, and left most of the carcasses to rot. Luckily, after the coyotes had finished with them, we gathered the bones to make tools."

"Do you have any advice?" you say.

"If you must kill for food, good. But don't kill any more than that. The well-being of our people depends on the buffalo."

"So long," you say.

You're done looking around.

You understand the message, but why do people keep telling you not to kill the animals? What is there to do out here but hunt? You've always thought of the American West as a place where the land's story recently got its stakes raised by revolver blasts, esophageal corrosion, torn petticoats, snapped necks, and stripped skulls. Violence has no homeland: you pick it up like a pox and carry it. You got sicker in the West, but maybe that was less about place than about time: the longer you lived, the worse you got, following your mapped trail to death by man or by poison. A trail is both more and less fixed than a narrative. When you're writing the narrative, choices are infinite; when you're reading it, your only choice is whether to continue or not. The trail is somewhere in between: when you get to the river, you can cross or not. You assess the river and decide to ford or float. Decision-making becomes rote as you practice. This is what it's like to live without intoxication: no escape, only facing choices.

This river may prove a little tricky. You ford the river. This river may prove a little tricky. You ford the river. This river may prove a little tricky. He's been silent for a week but you don't know what it means. You ford the river. Text him or don't. The way up the hill appears fairly steep. You double-team and continue.

It is night. A long weekend for Thanksgiving. And your birthday, actually. *No thank you* to every holiday dinner invitation. No messages from Philip, even as your thirty-first comes and goes. Sealed inside a dark room, spine hardening into kyphosis in this rolling chair, eyes fixed on a luminous screen. This portal lets you travel by memory teleportation through jaunty songs, cornflower blouses, and the same text prompts appearing over and over at every hill and river. Your destination is a time when you felt wonder. With every month sober, you strip away another layer of buildup— or maybe armor. The little witch inside surfaces.

Nested inside a lonesome pause, you can take stock of what still hurts, if you're ready. You've been told to think about how you want a man to treat you, but that kind of reflection feels like indulgence in fantasy. Reality is hard enough without imagining the impossible: a tender man who loves you. Real men are snakes. Some the poison kind, some constrictors; some are harmless but slither away when you get close.

Alkali water. Morale is high.

No grass. Deep sand.

Mia Zapata has a sprained ankle. You immobilize the affected joint.

You've traveled so many miles but you still haven't seen the sun or the moon.

Injured livestock: 1 mule. Get advice: "An injured draft animal is no good to nobody. Shoot it!"

In your gut, you know that your relationship is bad, as in expired, like milk. Philip's white man face is not a mask, and he can't see it. He doesn't love you. He is not wicked, never abusive, never mean, so you know you must hold on to this for as long as you can, because if you lose him, the next man might kill you.

Fallen rocks. Try to clear the path—You were unable to clear the path. Try to find another path—You were unable to find another path. Wait for conditions to improve—

You decide to enact a plan you hatched when you found one of his pubic hairs on the bathroom floor. You folded it up into a little scrap of paper. Just in case. And now, he hasn't even emailed, so you take the logical next step in your occult development: you put the hair into a glass pillar candle, reach into your vagina, pull out fingers wet with cervical fluid, and scrape the ooze into the glass. You light the wick. You don't really believe it'll work, but you burn it to the end.

At the Grande Ronde River, you meet a cavalryman with a gun and gold buttons. He says, "Used to be you could count on Indians being here to help you cross, but not no more. Too much tension now between them an' the settlers." You hope he'll tell you more about these particular Indians, who would have been trading partners with your ancestors, but he does not.

In the space of five miles, near Deadman Pass, a wild animal bites you, Layne Staley gets a bad cold, you become snowbound, Kurt Cobain gets the grippe, you get stuck in the Blue Mountains, the trail floods, a mule is injured, and your party goes through most of its food. You don't celebrate the new year of 1856. You never see death here and yet its promise is everywhere.

You're nearing the Columbia River when: No fruit. No vegetables. Low food. Hunting turns up nothing but rabbits and rocks.

Before colonization, your Columbia River Indian ancestors brought in food according to the seasonal round, moving from fishing to picking to gathering to hunting and back through again. They preserved food to carry villages through the winter. People celebrated the arrival of first foods with ceremonies that would ensure future abundance. They did this for thousands of years; it took only a few for whites to upend the system.

Your freezer is full of salmon you won't let yourself eat because you don't deserve it. Your pantry, canned pineapple for the apocalypse you don't fear. Your belly, a birthday cake you bought yourself and served with no song, no fire, no wish.

You stop at the McDonald Ford of the John Day River. This is your traditional territory. Your ancestors should be here. You find only a white man with suspenders who says, "What are we waiting for? Let's cross!"

You cross on the ice.

You hunt.

You stop in Biggs Junction. Your guidebook doesn't tell you this is the first place on the Oregon Trail where settlers would see the Columbia River. Your guidebook doesn't say anything. You see who's around, but find only more white men in vests.

You stop at Celilo but can't see the river. You can see only white snow and white people.

Celilo. Intact, here in this window, the kind of miracle that feels like a backhand.

You stop.

The Columbia River originates in the Canadian Rockies and curves through volcanic ridges, basalt scablands, and flat basins, flowing so forcefully the white people knew they had to take its power from it. So they dammed the river to capture water for farming, stop the flooding of riverfront towns, control the water's course, and generate electricity.

Your mother was five years old when the Dalles Dam was completed. The Army Corps of Engineers flooded Celilo Falls, an important salmon fishery since the beginning of time, drowning the village with a reservoir. Your ancestors and other people once gathered at Celilo to trade, fish, play stickgame, talk, and snag.

Before white people found the river, their diseases found its people: first smallpox, then malaria, influenza, and whooping cough. Deaths gutted kinship systems and decimated whole villages. Lewis and Clark cataloged lands to claim, peoples to overtake, and riches to split: furs, logs, waterways.

For a while, some of the people tried to get along with the whites and strategically traded with them at forts to get the horses and guns they made necessary. Intervillage marriage had always been important in maintaining kinship systems; now, some of the men of the Hudson's Bay Company became marriage partners for the women. Some of the new men were just fucking the women. Sometimes by force.

By the 1850s, the Oregon Trail brought the arrival of thousands of settlers per year. Fort Dalles served as a US Army outpost along the river, and in 1857, a few miles west of Celilo Falls, settlers established The Dalles as a town at the site of a mission popular with trail-goers. Then white people found gold. Then white people wanted land. Then they took it and farmed it. Through treaties largely unclear or wholly unintelligible to the headmen signing them, the US government formalized the land theft its citizens had initiated. The people would no longer live along the river as they had since time began. They were clustered into "tribes" whites could understand, and these tribes were pushed onto small pieces of land far from the territory they moved throughout to live, fish, hunt, and gather. White people didn't like these Indians: they weren't as exciting as the peoples of the plains, and they ate fish, even when they didn't have to.

The white people never understood the river. They still don't understand the river.

Elissa. Do you?

You've spent more time at wimahl, the great water, inside this window than you have outside it. As a child, you made trips to the Columbia River every other summer. You watched salmon move through the fish ladder at the Dalles Dam, looked at fishing platforms from the bridge, and traveled by sightseeing boat. As a teenager, you tried to walk from your grandparents' house to the river, but walking from memory with no guidebook, unable to tell the scorched flats around you from the scorched flats in your recollections of drives from The Dalles, you walked deeper into Washington.

Now, a few hours' drive away, you can't ever seem to get there. You're perpetually rushing to finish some task for money or going to the doctor to see why you feel like you're dying (it was the drinking, and then it was the lack, but now, you don't know). But the real drain on your time is the men. One after another. In the last year alone: your man of four years who drank even more than you did; a man who demanded your affection until a court ordered him to stop; a man who choked without asking; a man with his ex-wife's name tattooed on his chest who yelled at you for making everything about race when you told him you were pissed that an event host introduced you and a Black writer to the audience after saying, "We have diversity"; and now, this white man Philip, whom you're trying to understand. Who listens in silence when your darker-skinned Native friends talk about being followed around stores by security guards, and who later tells you he didn't like that conversation. Whose sense of self seems dependent upon formative experiences with substances Native people discovered to be hallucinogenic. Who was raised by wealthy white genius people fifty miles from the graveyard where the bones of all your ancestors, back to Tumulth, lie, and where you will be buried when you die, maybe at the hands of a white man.

Elissa. What do you think you're going to find on this trail?

At Camp Dalles, a white man with a gun and buckskins tells you this last stretch is the roughest. You can raft down the Columbia or take Barlow Toll Road; he recommends hiring an Indian guide for the river. You consider paying $80 for someone to raft you, just so you'll see another person like you. But you decide to do it without help because your Indian senses are strong—right?—and your people have lived with these rocks forever. For a while, you do move your cursor with precision, and your wagon dodges every rock, rapid, and whirlpool. But then you capsize once. You capsize again. You capsize four times before you're yanked from the ultramarine river, the adventure tune changes to a dirge, and you see five settlers wringing their hands at an unmarked grave.

Elissa died.

Elissa drowned.
Save diary. End game.

No. You're not going to do either of those things. Your ancestors didn't do the things ancestors do for you to fall off your wagon and drown.

You load a saved game. Back at Camp Dalles, you try the river again, and every time you capsize, you wonder how white people made it as far as they did. The river feels almost as long as it did when you were a kid in the back seat of your aunt's car, waiting to reach Grandma and Grandpa's house, or at least to get to the place where your aunt would point to a stone outcropping on a hill and tell a story you've never seen written.

Your rafting ends without death. You've lost the following supplies: 2 blankets; 1 pair of boots; 1 16-oz. bottle of brandy; 1 butcher knife; 1 fishing spear; 4 25-lb. kegs of gunpowder; and various other items. At Cascades Portage, you find yourself down to no fruit, no vegetables, no beans, no bread, and 11 pounds of meat. You meet a man in a bowler and a checkered jacket who says, "Let's head for the rapids! Sure, it's dangerous, but it'll be fun!"

No. You portage.

At McCord Creek, you have to raft again. Your Indian senses are strong; you don't capsize. You reach Fort Vancouver. It appears to be an ordinary fort, but you think your spirit heard about it from your mother's spirit, who heard about it from her mother's, who heard about it from her mother's, who heard about it from her mother's, because she was forced to linger in that place, and maybe her spirit is still there a little, and maybe you can even see it through the window.

Visit the fort.

You look for your great-great-grandmother and her sisters, but they're not there. Eventually, outside the window, their father will be executed, the Klamath will take the girls as slaves, and the US Army will attack the Klamath and take the girls to Fort Vancouver. You know nothing of their life at the fort, only that soldiers collected gold for them because it was known that Tumulth had been wrongly accused of treason. In the window, you don't find any known hangmen or any Indian girls. A white man with a buckskin vest says, "It always pleases me to see more people moving out west. This will be a great and grand country some day, you know!"

"Tell me more," you say.

He says, "Why, expanding the horizons of civilization out here in the wilderness. Just thrills me to the bone to think on it!"

"Do you have any advice?" you say.

"Don't be led astray by anyone or anything promising short-cuts or quick fixes. There ain't any! Stay on the main trail and work hard. That's the only sure path!"

"So long," you say.

A man in a bow tie will sell you supplies. He has 118 5-lb. tins of biscuits. He has 91 10-lb. sacks of cornmeal. He has horses for cheap. He has pemmican, salt pork, rice, and sugar. You have 61 pounds of meat and no idea how much longer this trail is. But you won't leave a single dollar at this fort. You'll take all these settlers' money. You sell your mules, your extra clothing, and half your oxen. You sell your rifle, bullets, and gunpowder. Someone

on the internet said if you heal yourself you heal your ancestors, your whole family line. How would that work? You want to
think time is not linear and all of you are alive at once. But even
games have been training you to see your life as a quest, trail, or
narrative, time flowing like a river pushed through narrows. *Stay
on the main trail and work hard. That's the only sure path!* You're
staring into this window so hard because outside it, you're stalled
in a dark room lit by a weak flame you fed with your own cells
because they put you on this path and compelled you to follow
it: your mother has a husband, and her mother had a husband,
and her mother had two husbands, and her mother had three,
and her mother was one of a chief's wives. The ancestors are in
the beautiful wagon of your body, your eyes like a rifle, your lean
hips like a horse. A long time ago, your ancestor women married white men because no Cascade men were available, you've
heard. Your mother and grandmother didn't model that: they
built marriages from love and healthy interdependence. But
your body, somehow, seems to remember the fort. The scarcity.
The huckleberry crop dwindling as the white men stopped the
people from tending the fields. Your body carries something you
need in the thin pillow of fat around your waist, right where the
huckleberry basket would be tied. Your body holds. When you
pair with a man, even if he is not good to you, your body holds.
Philip will return and you won't ask him why he didn't write, not
even on your birthday. Months from now, at his birthday party,
you'll surprise him with a unicorn-shaped piñata filled with can-
dies you took care in selecting from WinCo bulk bins; he'll save
it to break later, at a karaoke party to which you are not invited,
and afterward, he'll tell you nobody liked the candy, so they left

it on the floor. In late winter, he'll break up with you, saying the problem is that you won't trash-talk when you two play *Dance Dance Revolution.*

But you don't know any of this yet. You only know that you have a man right now and are meant to have a man forever. You leave the fort. You continue rafting. You don't capsize.

The music changes. The orchestra sounds happy. It's January 28, 1856. Rainy. 1,864 miles traveled. You've reached Oregon City! You stake a land claim. A man behind a desk gives you acres. Save diary. End game. Are you sure you want to end your game? OK.

The game is over, but it's not *over*-over. You didn't get what you came for, which was not land: you were the Oregon City you were looking for all along. Seriously, what did you think you were going to get out of this nostalgia exercise? This game was not made for you. Not for the person you want to become, anyway, the descendant of your ancestors. The game was part of the project of whiteness: you were expected to colonize, to strive for an arrival into land theft, to see it as a great adventure, to see the Natives as helpers or hindrances or frightening shadows. When your mother was born, Native people still weren't welcome in some stores in the white towns near her river. By the time you were born, the hostility had lessened, but whiteness was still working hard to erase you, positioning its desires as the only ones that would lead to a win. This game has only two outcomes: death or settlement.

You go back to the trail again and again, hoping to meet your relatives. You try an alternate route. You try hunting to excess, filling your wagon with a thousand pounds of meat as a provocation, hoping the Indians might retaliate. You leave as late in the year as possible and stretch out your time on the trail so your arrival at the Columbia Plateau, in a time before treaty making, coincides with the arrival of the salmon runs.

And this works. In June 1851, you stop in to Fort Walla Walla and see a Native man with a Pendleton blanket in his hands and a drum and basket at his feet. Finally, after miles and miles of no Indians but those on the prairie, here is one of your people.

He says, "We are Tsinuk traders. Maybe we have something you need. We can do business."

"Tell me more," you say.

He says, "The Tsinuk live near the western ocean, but we travel far to trade, as far as the plains to the east. To trade well, one must know many tongues. I speak English, French, some Spanish, and six Indian languages—including Tsinuk, of course."

"Do you have any advice?" you say.

"Trade with us. We offer much better deals than the fort trading post here. We can do well for each other."

You realize that *Tsinuk* is *Chinook* but you've never seen it written that way, and you realize that when he says *the western ocean* he means *the mouth of the river* because that great water is the center of the universe, so you, an upstreamer from another Chinookan people, trade with this relative. He offers you 5 pounds of bacon for 1 ox, and you accept. The moment is anticlimactic: this is the middle of the apocalypse, after all, and here this man is, trying to make a deal.

But this is right. The end of the world was long: more than half a century of skin turning to sores, necks snapped by rope, blood pouring from bullet holes, vaginas trespassed by unwashed bodies. Through all that, the people had to find ways to keep living. So they say to your white man mask, "My people will gladly trade with you here and on the road ahead." A child with a basket says, "Hey, wagon-people! Look here! I have some very good salmon. Maybe you want to trade?" At the Grande Ronde River, "Let us help you cross. The river can be difficult at times, especially after heavy rains. What do you have to offer in exchange for this help?"

Friendly and cooperative, ones the whites would have liked, not like your actual relatives, whom they hanged, whom they called "siwash," who did not agree to leave the river.

You can play this game over and over for the rest of your life if you want to, and maybe you will, until your old computer finally gives up the ghost and you have no way back in. But you won't find the women you're looking for. You'll see them in photos, dressed like the ladies you imagine going to Victorian-era séances, and you'll look for your face in theirs. You'll recognize them in movies like *The Revenant*, which you'll see in the theater with Philip. You'll hold your breath during the scene in which white fur traders sidle up to drunk Native women on a cold night at the fort while men speak about pelts. You'll close your eyes when a French trapper rapes an Arikara woman against a tree. When a Pawnee man is hanged, you'll gasp. Minutes earlier, he caught snowflakes with his tongue. After the movie, when you are quiet, Philip will tell you it's just a movie, nothing to get upset about, and you should be glad they were historically accurate and used Native actors.

Let me tell you: that's not even right. In reality, there's no recorded evidence of a Pawnee wife for Hugh Glass, the settler

Leonardo DiCaprio played. You know why they gave him one, right? If not, your real quest will be to first figure that out, and then to beat that game. You don't know what's history and what's fiction in the film, but when the unnamed trapper rapes Powaqa, the made-up daughter of a chief, you'll think of Toussaint Charbonneau, a real trapper who enslaved Sacagawea as his teenage wife. Lewis and Clark arrived later that year and asked Charbonneau to join them and bring his Indian wives. Sacagawea was there at your river when Lewis and Clark pushed their expedition into it. There in your homeland when the party met a principal chief covered in sores and his wife racked with pain. Clark would later write in his journal that the chief's wife was "a Sulky Bitch." In *The Revenant*, the trapper says in French translated into English subtitles, "I need a woman with big tits" and "Bring me the girl, those five horses weren't free."

You were promised to the white men, but that doesn't mean you have to keep playing. You know you're going to restart this game until you find what you're looking for. You know why you're not done: because—unlike the theater where you'll see an anguished face that feels like your own, or the bed where you pray for protection before you sleep—here at this window, you don't even have the option to be a Native woman. Because your man is off the continent, which you haven't yet been. You're not ready to stop trying to suck the poison out of yourself. There are snakes everywhere. What do you want to do? Continue as usual? Rest here awhile? Slow down? Increase rations? Use tourniquet/suction method? Use antiseptic on the bite? Give patient lots of exercise? Get advice? None of this will cure you. Listen to your grandma: don't go where the snakes are. Listen to grandpa: wear Western boots whenever you walk outside. If you must stay on this trail, hope not to be bitten and hope not to drown. Look for the Salish child who will guide you across the river. In exchange, he wants something. Close the window and figure out what you need to give up to reach the other side of this thing that could kill you if you don't learn to choose well.

We will guide you across the river in exchange for
1 Winter coat

Is it a deal?

CENTERLESS
UNIVERSE

All my life,
since I was ten,
I've been waiting
to be in
this hell here
with you;
all I've ever
wanted, and
still do.

—Alice Notley

If a man was never to lie to me. *Never lie me.*
I swear I would never leave him.

—Louise Erdrich, "The Strange People"[9]

---

9. Do you think this is a good book? How do you know? Is it because you compared it to other books? I do want to make you uncomfortable if you're accustomed to being the ideal audience, your wants prioritized. This is how I treat so many of the people I get close to: I try to give them exactly what they want in some ways, withhold in others. Can you love a person even if you don't understand them? Or: How much do you have to understand someone in order to love them? Does one have anything to do with the other at all?

FROM THE DEPOSITION OF JENNIE Davis (Duwamish), March 28, 1927, US Court of Claims:

> QUESTION. In the old days, when you were a girl, did the Duwamish people use to use all parts of their country?
>
> ANSWER. Yes.
>
> QUESTION. Was it all covered with big timber then?
>
> ANSWER. Yes.
>
> QUESTION. Was it well stocked with fish and game and roots that they used to eat, and with berries and everything that you required?
>
> ANSWER. Yes; plenty of it.
>
> QUESTION. Did you use to go out and pick berries and dry them for your use?
>
> ANSWER. Yes.
>
> QUESTION. Do they let your people go out and get any game now or fish?
>
> ANSWER. No; they can't go out and get fish and game or they will be arrested.
>
> QUESTION. Are your people poor because they got no reservation and no lands?
>
> ANSWER. Yes.

QUESTION. Have they suffered hardships because they
     have been forced away from their own country, with
     no place to go?
ANSWER. Yes.

The spring and summer of 2016, when I was one year sober and
knew everything, Facebook and Twitter kept showing me an image of John Trudell's face with an overlay of his words: "Protect
your spirit, because you're in the place where the spirits get eaten."
I liked it. I loved it. I shared it. I didn't really think about it.

Before settler imposition, late May would have been a time for
gathering and storing blackberries, clams, and cockles; that
year, for me, it was for getting the key to the bridge tower. Two
afternoons a week, I would ascend the Fremont Bridge's northwest tower stairs with dried mango, LaCroix, and a thermos of
hot canned soup. The bridge spans the Lake Washington Ship
Canal, opening for boats, closing for cars. My perch was a room
with windows on all sides, one holding an air conditioner, one
holding a neon sign of Rapunzel. Vehicles rumbled over the
bridge: cars, trucks, buses, the Ride the Ducks land-into-water
vehicles.

Seattle's Office of Arts & Culture and the Seattle Department of Transportation selected me as the bridge's writer-in-
residence, a role that would not actually involve residing. My
task that summer, according to the call for applications, was to
occupy the bridge tower a few afternoons a week and "under-
take an in-depth exploration of the historic bridge's role and
meaning for the city of Seattle and create written materials in

response to this residency . . . The writing shall represent or illuminate some aspect of the bridge and the bridge's history, be it real or metaphorical."

I wasn't going to apply. I had nothing to say about a bridge. I felt that bridges were fine. I liked walking over the one between the university and Madison Park, but there's no narrative tension in liking. A bridge never did anything to me.

I needed the money, though—ten thousand dollars for a few months' work. My salary at my half-time job was twenty-five thousand, I was living in an expensive city, and money was running out. I realized I had something to say about a bridge.

My application letter said:

I propose to write an essay about the role of the Lake Washington Ship Canal in the transformation of the Little Crossing-Over Place into the city that is central to my work, life, and relationships. The non-Native settlement of the shores of Lake Washington drove away a'yahos, a shape-shifting serpent spirit that lived in the lake and in the sky above it. A'yahos caused landslides and was feared and avoided by the Duwamish people, and though it was known to be malevolent, it was a respected source of personal spirit power. I am interested in the role of the creation of the ship canal and the changes it brought to the lake in driving a'yahos away.

After my interview, selection, and informal orientation, I received a key tagged FREMONT BRIDGE and instructions to call the bridge operator before arriving and leaving because of an alarm on the door. On the first day, the operator asked, "Will you call me when you go anywhere and when you come back?" like my first long-term boyfriend always asked in high school.

I looked upon shimmering water, rustling trees, and pale sky. The ship canal was a straight, wide, concrete-edged street for sailboats (the Land Rovers of the sea), superyachts (the tricked-out RVs of the sea), police boats, barges, and Argosy cruises packed with tourists pointing phones at the bridge. Most boats were white; most people on most boats were white; most barges carried porta-potties and garbage; some white boats carried smaller white boats; other boats were pushed or pulled by tugboats; one tugboat was labeled BEARCAT. I knew the carving of this canal was a mark announcing white dominance over the breathing, squirming land, but my eyes deceived me: I only saw beauty I wanted to take in forever.

I began to worry about the vastness of this project that had seemed so manageable when I was spewing words into an application window: I'd promised a (limited) history of Seattle, but I was not a historian; a personal essay, but I was writing it for the government. I wasn't sure how much of my pain I wanted to make into a deliverable for them, even though they had claimed me generations ago.

The water below me seemed like the kind of place where the *dangerous beings* of old Cowlitz stories lurked, waiting for a person to approach so they could attack. I was most drawn to those stories. The dangerous beings were never explained; they were simply dangerous. Maybe there were messages about humanity and evil in their movements, or maybe there was no sense at all, no narrative motivation, just desire for rupture.

I didn't see anything in the water, but I felt something; then again, I always had.

Before Seattle, there were steep hills, bent rivers, tideflats, lakes, bogs, spirit powers, forests, people, longhouses, and prairies forming a system of fluctuation and movement of time and land. Then the bostons—the word people up and down this coast used for *white men*—turned places into property: terminals, shipyards, mills, railroad beds, dumps, cesspools, homesteads, parks, streets, wharves, trestles, bridges, canals. The boston men dredged, regraded, dumped, removed, sanitized, engineered, straightened, renamed, mined, seized, settled, procreated. Where they saw useless, unsightly, progress-impeding land and water, they imagined *real estate*: navigable waters, land to build upon.

In 1978, city engineer Roy W. Morse wrote, "It is apparent that the first settlers could not have envisioned the great city that would grow on and spill beyond their claims on the shores of Elliott Bay. Nor could they have foreseen the significant land-.scape surgery needed to mold the townsite for the future safety and economic well-being of its people." Those early city engineers, he said, "translated the problems into effective solutions." The implied *problem*: land the Duwamish people had been in relationship with for ten thousand years. *Solution* turned out to mean:

Removal: In 1855, Chief Si'ahl and subchiefs Ts'huahntl, Now-a-chais, Ha-seh-doo-an, on behalf of the Duwamish people, signed the Treaty of Point Elliott, establishing a government-to-government relationship between the United States and the signatory tribes and legally recognizing the tribes as sovereign nations. This treaty's terms include tribal cession of the land from the summit of the Cascade Range to the east, the western shore of Puget Sound to the west, Point Pully (approximately the latitude of the current location of the airport) to the south, and the Canadian border to the north. That land has become some of the most valuable in the United States. Small tracts were reserved from this ceded territory to establish four reservations, but no land was retained by the Duwamish in their territory. The treaty specified that tribes would retain their rights to fish, hunt, and gather roots and berries. I refuse to say that the tribes received these rights and reservations in exchange for anything. What they were promised had already been theirs.

In 1865, three weeks after the town of Seattle's original incorporation, Ordinance 5 was passed, decreeing that "no Indian or Indians shall be permitted to reside, or locate their residences on any street, highway, lane, or alley or any vacant lot in the town of Seattle," with exceptions for the Native people present for employment. White progress demanded the labor of these people they saw as troublesome, unsavory, and indispensable: settler construction would've been impossible without Duwamish labor at Yesler's mill, which spit out boards to build the new town. When Seattle's government was dissolved in 1867 and reincorporated in 1869, the ban on Native residents was not renewed. But settlers would keep them out by burning villages.

Assimilation: The Indian Homestead Act of 1875 gave Native people the settler-legal ability to own land if they agreed to live like white people, no longer tribal members. This willingness had to be proven by white endorsements like "We, David

Denny and Luke McRedmond, do solemnly swear that we are well acquainted with Bill Sbedzuse and know that he is an Indian formerly of the Duwamish tribe—that he was born in the United States—that he has abandoned his relations with that tribe and adopted the habits and pursuits of civilized life—that he is over the age of twenty one years."

Surveying: In 1863 and 1881, the Northern Pacific Railway identified steep hills, lapping tides, and flood-prone rivers that would pose construction problems. To reduce flooding, surveyors proposed a sea-level canal between Lake Washington and Elliott Bay. A city surveyor was appointed to plan the flattening of the land's natural contours into a uniform grade system for the streets. "Surveying" was not neutral learning; it was cataloging for demolition.

Regrading: I picture a topographic map's contour lines sliding apart as Seattle's steep grades were pushed down and its low points tugged up. In reality, millions of cubic yards of hard blue clay, sand, gravel, glacial till, and soil were removed, and in the seventeen years between regrades, a steep cliff was left to be cut down later. It's estimated that between 1910 and 1929, over one-eighth as much earth was moved in Seattle's regrades as was moved to build the Panama Canal. Some of it became fill for swamplands and tideflats; some was shaped into what was then the world's largest manufactured island; some was dumped into deep bay waters.

Straightening: The Duwamish Waterway was once a meandering river that rose to flood at high water and tides. Merchants' trips down the river's eight miles took a week, and the winter and spring flooding changed the navigational route. In *Native Seattle:*

Histories from the Crossing-Over Place, Coll Thrush writes that Reginald H. Thomson, Seattle's city engineer from 1892 to 1911, "called the Duwamish's [River's] natural curves 'ugly' and 'unsightly,' preferring a channelized and useful river to one that was messy and unpredictable." In 1913, Washington State began removing twenty million cubic yards of mud and sand to shorten and straighten the river for large oceangoing ships. The flooding ceased; the shores that had once held Duwamish villages were readied for industry. The riverbeds were full of misplaced earth. The new people called this land *reclaimed*.

Dredging: Settlers wanted to link the lakes and the sound. In 1854, at a Fourth of July celebration, Judge Thomas Mercer (one of Seattle's earliest settlers) suggested a canal be cut to make that water chain. The lakes had names, but he labeled them with his own.

In the 1860s, a white man tried to dig a channel between the lakes, but he was just a man with a pick, a shovel, and a wheelbarrow, and he failed.

In 1886, a little channel was pushed from Lake Washington and Lake Union, just enough of a waterway for the passage of logs.

In 1910 or 1911—my sources vary—the War Department and the city approved canal plans.

From 1911 to 1916, dredging happened.

In 1916, the canal was finished, the locks opened.

In June 1917, the first vehicle crossed the Fremont Bridge; on the Fourth of July, a ship canal dedication celebration was held, but by then, the water level of Lake Washington had already dropped, the Black River had dried up, and the world had been upended.

Assembling the above history felt like pulling out bones through pores. I spent most of the first month of my residency taking notes from books I hauled to the tower. In planning to write the history of myself in a place, I had tasked myself with too much. The past had its own ecology of interdependent memories and facts. I didn't know what I'd find as I searched, much less what I'd write. My contract required me to interface with the media and the public, but I was given time to settle in first. I was nervous to let them in. I thought I might never be ready to explain.

Once I began regularly walking the length of Lake Union from my apartment to the bridge to avoid traffic, I encountered a sidewalk sign below the southeast tower that summarized what I'd been piecing together and let me link it to my bridge:

> Before straightened into a channel, this site served as a seasonal home to the Duwamish people, who fished and hunted here on marshy banks and were supplanted by settlement. In photographs, as the Lake Washington Ship Canal was being built (ca. 1911), the site is revealed as a mud flat, houses and shacks on its banks, weirs controlling the flow of water, and the neighborhoods on either side straggling up the banks and hills. Snapshots of the opening of the canal, on the 4th of July, 1917, show a more orderly landscape with crowds filling the streets and canal banks. This is still a place of nature and people, commerce and leisure, a crossroads of water and steel.

Still, I was glad to have done my own work to understand the narrative of place and people regularly flattened into land acknowledgments that opened Seattle rallies and lectures, often prefacing Native erasure with *We want to begin by acknowledging that we are on Duwamish land.* The US government fails to recognize the Duwamish as a sovereign nation, making the tribe ineligible for the fishing rights they had secured in signing the Treaty of Point Elliott. In 2001, the federal government granted recognition, but within days, following a turnover in the US presidency, the decision was reversed.

The Duwamish Tribe is made up of groups that, before settler arrival, were distinct: the Inside People, Saltwater People, River People, and Lake People. The portage stretch between lakes was a meeting place for the Lake People. The Zakuse and Cheshiahud families lived on the Portage Bay (part of Lake Union) shores. The development of the Montlake Cut, the canal portion between Lake Washington and Lake Union, displaced the Lake People living there, sending them north (although they continued to visit their important places).

The lakes, rivers, streams, and overland portages formed a system unifying the people living in longhouses on or near their shores with access to food, routes, woods, and tucked-away places for the keeping of treasured, ceremonial, or spiritually dangerous objects. Along the broken water string that would become the ship canal, there were two major villages: Tucked Away Inside, near Puget Sound at Salmon Bay, had two large longhouses and a potlatch house; Little Canoe Channel, just north of Portage Bay, had at least five longhouses. More villages were in the river valley the ship canal changed. Today, the

Duwamish Longhouse stands at a major village site along the Seattle Fault.[10]

The Black River drying up was not an unintended side effect of the creation of the Lake Washington Ship Canal; river elimination was part of the design. Seattle's hills, tides, trees, mudflats, and floods had to be dealt with for land to become property. Boundaries were set between water and land because impermanence and change made for poor real estate. Nature wasn't good enough for settlers; it demanded transformation. Erastus Brainerd, employed by the chamber of commerce to lead a promotional campaign for the city, said the canal would "carry out nature's outline but uncompleted purpose."

In 1906, rivers and creeks flooded, destroying towns, farms, and bridges. Hiram M. Chittenden, Seattle district engineer for the Army Corps of Engineers and namesake of the locks later installed, called for "discipline" for the rivers. The Duwamish was straightened. The White River was diverted. The canal was dredged. Lake Washington's waters poured into the sound. The Black River disappeared. Land emerged where there had been water, and in the eyes of the settlers, it looked real.

But Duwamish villages lined the Black River. A long-haired man-shaped monster, skaitaw, once lived in a deep river hole. A person could draw power and wealth from skaitaw. I don't know what happened to the being. I imagine a dry hole filled with the

---

10. Along the lakes, rivers, and sound were more villages and significant sites than I can elegantly list in these sentences with no map. For an extensive annotated list of significant places, see "An Atlas of Indigenous Seattle" by Coll Thrush and Nile Thompson, with maps by Amir Sheikh, which appears as a kind of appendix to Thrush's *Native Seattle*.

memory of a monster, a cold spot of warped energy, the residue of power sucked from the world.

In my favorite old Cowlitz story, a girl devours everyone who loves her before turning into a shark. I've tried to tell it but only ever recall that she kills her husband's women, she kills his children, she eats her baby, she kills her husband. She goes to the ocean and there she becomes a shark, a dangerous being.

Our old stories are about things like excrement, dreams, and learning to copulate, because they're meant to teach us how to live. I asked my tribe's spiritual leader about what I was supposed to take away from the shark girl story; he said I needed to do my own work to figure out the lesson. I think the story could explain the whole universe at the bottom of my throat.

The day before I began office hours, Carl left for a few weeks on tour in the Midwest. I dropped him at the airport with two guitars and a suitcase containing a small bag of protective stones I'd given him. Alone in my perch over the water, I wondered what he was doing and how he was feeling while I read books and drank sparkling water. I texted him photos and said, *I wish you were here.*

A woman-shaped neon sign filled the window facing the Fremont neighborhood. Visible from the street below the tower, her long waves of yellow neon hair hung below the frame. This public art piece, Rodman Miller's *Rapunzel*, was installed in 1995. While I sat at my desk in the tower, the flat line-drawn figure looked in at me looking out at the world. Her neon-yellow hair hung in wavy lines on the tower's exterior, obscured from my view. I felt her watching.

Wikipedia says a tower isn't meant to be lived in: much taller than they are wide, they exist to be seen (a clock tower) or to see from (a watchtower). There are niche towers for functions like measuring atmospheric conditions or supporting bridges, but Wikipedia says skyscrapers, being habitable, are not towers. How can this be possible? What about *SimTower*, the PC game in which I spent much of my adolescence building hundred-story skyscrapers? What about the Columbia Tower, where I briefly worked for Amazon, judging a novel contest while looking out over the bay and the city buildup? I will concede that the ClockTower, my first Seattle apartment complex, is not a tower, but only because it's much wider than it is tall. Whatever. The important thing I learned from Wikipedia is that the primary purpose of a tower is not, as I would've guessed, to be so high up that nobody can reach you. It's to see them coming before they do.

Most of my attempts at research into dangerous beings in the lake led me to the sea monster seen in Lake Washington in the 1970s and '80s. Some thought it was a shark. In 1987, when it turned up dead, it showed itself to be an eleven-foot white sturgeon, vaguely sharklike in shape. Born around the turn of the century, the fish got into the lake by an unknown route: maybe through the ship canal after the opening of the locks or via the Black River before it dried up. Sturgeon may have been released into the lake after being kept in a small pool on the University of Washington campus for the 1909 world's fair. A few others have been found alive and dead in the lake and canal in recent years.

The sturgeon's direct ancestors, predating dinosaurs, evolved during the early Triassic period; not long before, a mysterious calamity—maybe asteroid collision, carbon dioxide ocean poisoning, or volcanic eruptions—had caused the "Great Dying," a mass extinction that wiped out nearly all animal life on earth. The sturgeon is still the long-bodied bottom-feeder it always was, similar enough to its ancestors that it's often called a *living fossil,* but while those ancient fish were bony, the skeleton of a sturgeon is now almost all cartilage, much like a shark's. In the Columbia River, they grow to twenty feet long and can live for a century. In an old photo that has been on the wall in my parents' hallway for as long as I can remember, my great-grandfather Morris carries a sturgeon, nearly as long as he is tall, slung over his back by rope.

Though they're bottom-feeders, they occasionally leap into the air, nose to the sky, body spinning. Their reasons for doing this are unknown, but the percussive pounding of the fall against the water's surface can reach the tactile sense organs of sturgeon deep below. The jumping may be a kind of talking, messages sent down where there is no light.

My second week, I saw my first superyacht, the two-hundred-foot *Lady Lola.* While the big boat passed under my bridge, I learned from Google about its remote-control curtains, Technogym exercise equipment, two Jet Skis, six sets of dive gear, heated pool with waterfall, eighteen-hole golf course with floating buoys that allow passengers to use the sea as though it's the green, outdoor theater, and helipad space. The closed-off upper deck has an office, hot tub, salon, and sheltered terrace. A summer charter went for $430,000 a week. The boat was for sale for $49.9 million.

I had no way of understanding such a boat. My dad's seemed huge when he was shoving it into the water from the lakeshore, but it was just a fishing boat propelled by an electric motor smaller than a toaster oven. I drove the boat down the Delaware River once, when I was about ten. I'd crossed that river countless times on our trips to Pennsylvania to visit my grandparents or the big mall. The water drew the line between home and that country of steel and coal. To be *in* the line was to be in no-place, to wedge my body into a divide.

My mom grew up near the banks of the Columbia, the largest river in the Pacific Northwest. Its drainage basin encompasses most of Washington, Oregon, and Idaho, as well as portions of several other states and part of British Columbia. At its mouth is a little point of land called Cape Disappointment: a British fur trader went looking for a massive river he'd heard about, but he found only what he thought was a bay, so he decided the river wasn't real.

For thousands of years, this river was a community core, transportation link, food source, and world center. The river didn't divide; it unified disparate villages. Over the last century, settlers have dammed it to curb flooding, ease passage, make land, and generate a staggering amount of power for the region.

From land or water, a river is slightly visible, mostly obscured. A canal wants to be a river. It wants to carry what a river carries, but without flair: tidy banks, no tricky bends. A river doesn't want to be a canal, but now that the settlers are here, a river doesn't have a choice.

My elementary school class took an educational boat ride down the Morris Canal, constructed in the 1820s and '30s to bring Pennsylvania anthracite from the Delaware River through North Jersey and to New York City. People had cut down the trees and needed something else to burn. The canal starts in

Phillipsburg, New Jersey, where I went to Catholic grade school; goes through Hackettstown, where I attended high school; continues through Sussex County, where, at the restored canal town of Waterloo Village, I went to poetry festivals as a teenager; and passes through four counties before ending in Jersey City, where my parents would take Nate and me to the science museum. From the museum's cafeteria, I took photos of the tiny-but-not-so-distant-now New York City skyline.

In 1924, after oil became favored over anthracite, the canal was abandoned. Only remnants remain. To a child who knew only rivers, the canal pieces looked like the real thing, a waterway with only a middle and no ends.

The Bridge of the Gods spans the Columbia River in my ancestral territory. It was built in 1926 at the site of a massive landslide that blocked the river about nine hundred years ago. The river broke through, creating the Cascades of the Columbia, river rapids that were an important fishing place long before they were a treacherous spot for settlers on the Oregon Trail. At the end of the nineteenth century, for easier passage, the US Army Corps of Engineers cut a canal and installed locks.

When I was a kid, my family would visit my grandparents and my mom's siblings every other summer. Grandma Kate and Grandpa Bud lived in Dallesport, Washington, a dry place upriver from the Bridge of the Gods. As a teenager, I decided I wanted to walk to the river and cross over to Oregon. I think the distance to the river from the house was about half a mile, but the distance to the bridge was three miles, and I didn't walk in the right direction anyway, instead going deeper into Washington, attempting to take photos of Mount Hood with my chunky new digital camera. I had only half accepted my mistake when I turned around and retraced my steps along the road splitting an expanse of scorched grasses. I didn't know why I wanted to go to the river. I knew that Native men fished with dip nets from platforms, but I didn't quite understand that the platform-construction techniques and fishing methods had been handed down from men who could have been my ancestors. I knew my mom had grown up in Dallesport and other towns along the river, but I didn't truly understand what it meant that her mother and grandmother and great-grandmother had grown up along the river, too, and so had everyone else in my maternal line for ten thousand years, even after our community was broken by US government violence in the 1850s and most of the people were removed to reservations. My family hung on in their homeland at the edge of the new white people's world.

One day at the bridge, through my open window, I heard the Ride the Ducks tour guide say, "I want you to take out your phones. And I want you to go to Google Maps. And I want you to search for 'Center of the Universe.'"

I did this.

"Center of the Universe Hypnotherapy," 0.3 mi away, 3 reviews.

"Fremont Center of the Universe Signpost," Historical Landmark, No reviews.

I wondered what it meant for Fremont to be the center of the universe. I saw this designation on street signs and sidewalk sandwich boards enticing potential renters to live in new apartments above the expensive grocer. According to the Fremont Chamber of Commerce's website, this neighborhood was built upon a geographically special place with a gravitational pull that brings visitors back over and over again.

The research question that brought me to the bridge was, *What happened to a'yahos, the serpent spirit that lived in and above Lake Washington?* I knew it had left. Did it go when the ship canal opened and the lake dropped so many feet?

I made a hole-ridden timeline of colonization and "progress" in Seattle, and upon rereading Thrush's *Native Seattle*, I saw the problem with my hypothesis: a Duwamish elder told ethnographer John Peabody Harrington that by the 1910s, a'yahos was "gone, not there now." The canal opened in 1916, leading to the water level drop I'd thought could be the reason a'yahos left. But a'yahos had vacated its home years before that.

What drives a spirit away? Maybe it happened when the white people first arrived to claim their pieces of wilderness. Maybe it wasn't driven away at all; maybe it just departed.

Why did it leave? The question of my heart. *Where did it go?* The boundary line of my imagination.

A month before getting the bridge keys, ending my year in the suburbs, I moved to Capitol Hill. The neighborhood had been the center of my social life since moving to Seattle nine years earlier: bars after class, karaoke after long days, readings any night of the week. After my first year in the city, I started an internship at Richard Hugo House, a literary nonprofit in a weathered Victorian on the Hill, and sometime after, I began dating Kevin, a writer who lived in the neighborhood. His apartment seemed as if it could be demolished any day, like so many of the other dusty homes that would turn to vacant lots, then frames, then gleaming structures. The leveling and rebuilding happened grotesquely fast, the little world of the Hill remade every time I returned. Kevin's building still stands, with him still inside it. Hugo House has been torn down and rebuilt under a slick stack of apartments. I moved into a prewar brick building under no threat of demolition. The neighborhood paper reported two weeks after I moved in that when the big earthquake hits, these elegant old brick buildings are most likely to collapse.

My research turned up no details about the place's significance before colonization. "We were unable to identify any traditional cultural properties on the Capitol Hill uplands," wrote Jay Miller and Astrida R. Blukis Onat in *Winds, Waterways, and Weirs: Ethnographic Study of the Central Link Light Rail Corridor.* Prepared for Sound Transit in 2004, this 262-page study brings together document review, elder testimony, and ethnographic research to present Native histories of traditional cultural properties near the proposed light-rail route, and to contextualize the project's land use within histories of movement, destruction, and change through colonization.

Under Section 106 of the National Historic Preservation Act, federal agencies must "take into account the effects of their undertakings on historic properties," and "consultation with an Indian tribe must respect tribal sovereignty and the government-to-government relationship between the Federal Government and Indian tribes." While planning the light-rail expansion through Seattle, the Federal Transit Administration, Sound Transit, and the Washington State Department of Transportation consulted with "interested

Indian tribes"—Tulalip, Duwamish, Muckleshoot, Yakama, Snoqualmie, and Suquamish—and the Washington State historic preservation officer. This is not a courtesy; this is the law. At my desk in the tower, I pored over the ethnographic study because it was a real-life example of a legal process that had been theoretical to me when I worked for the USDA in DC more than a decade before, using Microsoft Word to create best practices flowcharts for people interested in developing their lands but unclear on tribal consultation. *Winds, Waterways, and Weirs* showed me that the process could not only reduce harm and preserve sacred sites but also honor the continuance of Indigenous knowledge.

Seattle is one of the fastest-growing cities in the United States, and many sacred sites have been disturbed and harmed. Foster Island, a small island in Union Bay on the east end of the ship canal, is now part of the Washington Park Arboretum, but settler damage has already been done. The lake's big water-level drop enlarged the island, and settlers later firmed up shorelines with dredged lake soil. The floating bridge split the island in two. sčəgʷučid was once a graveyard. Nearby on the shore, clothes and food were burned, sent by the living to relatives on the other side. People placed boxed dead bodies in the trees. When the boxes fell or disintegrated, bones fell to the ground; settlers took them when they made sčəgʷučid into part of the arboretum. The land is said to be protected from development now. I say the land was turned curio, changed to suit settler tastes and rendered static. Even with their bones gone from that place, the people on the other side are still at sčəgʷučid. Among the invasive purple loosestrife and yellow flag iris, there is no place for burning.

In 2011, a decomposed human leg bone and foot were found in a plastic bag under the Ship Canal Bridge, the two-layer span carrying I-5 and its express lanes over Portage Bay. This is listed on the Wikipedia page for "Salish Sea human foot discoveries," although it seems unrelated to the rest, this one being bagged, with no mention of the sneaker that encased most of the others (at least twenty) that have washed up on shores around the Salish Sea in Washington and British Columbia since 2007. The cause is unclear, and the internet loves the mystery. People seem to want it to be the work of a serial killer, the long setup of a true crime drama unfolding in news bulletins.

The cause has mostly been settled: marine animals and churning water disarticulate the feet. The sneakers are buoyant, their solid synthetic architecture protective of the feet inside. Sea currents, unpredictable in the straits, carry the feet long distances. Two of the feet are known to belong to a woman who committed suicide by jumping from a bridge over the Fraser River, which empties into the sea. It seems likely that suicide was the cause of death for some others whose feet washed ashore. And yet the internet still wants to have fun with it: a website called Cool Interesting Stuff.com files its write-up under "Modern Mysteries"; the National Paranormal Society says "eerie mists" and ghostly cold spots have appeared where feet were found; Ripley's Believe It or Not! features a write-up with a photo of one of the feet, tibia and femur still attached, no warning. I'm reminded of shrunken heads in Ye Olde Curiosity Shop in downtown Seattle, whose "curiosities," at its opening in 1899, largely consisted of Alaska Native artifacts and art. Princess Angeline, Chief Seattle's daughter, who refused to leave her land after treaty signing and remained there for life, sold baskets there. The shop remains as a tourist destination where souvenir trinkets share space with mummified corpses propped up in glass.

From my tower, I could see the Aurora Bridge, carrying Route 99, high above the canal. People began jumping from it to die before construction was even finished. Hundreds have jumped since. A fence was added in 2011, a result of advocacy by Seattle FRIENDS (Fremont Individuals & Employees Nonprofit to Decrease Suicides), self-described as "a group of individuals who live, work and play in the Fremont neighborhood."

Play—I become tense at the mention, despite myself. This group's accomplishment undoubtedly saves lives. But "live, work and play," well-worn language in Seattle's newest self-styling, calls to mind the ways in which Seattle tries to wield quirk against sinister gloom. The concentration of oddball whimsy is highest in Fremont, home to statues of a famous clown, Vladimir Lenin (intended, apparently, as kitsch), and, under the Aurora Bridge, a colossal troll holding a Volkswagen Beetle. *De Libertas Quirkas*, "freedom to be peculiar," is the neighborhood motto; "Entering the Republic of Fremont, the center of the Universe, throw away your watch," instructs a sign. Every summer solstice, as an unsanctioned part of the annual parade, a group of cyclists remove all their clothes, paint their skin, and assemble to ride bikes through the parade route.

I avoided the neighborhood and its curiosities for a long time. I was cheerless, trying to die slowly. I did not go to the high bridge, but neither did I go on the tour of the nearby chocolate factory. While Seattle was playing, I was drowning myself, carried far down some river, lost at sea.

It was finally time for me to interface with the public, so I allowed a few reporters and their accompanying camera people to ascend the stairs. All asked me to describe the office, and I was never able to estimate the room's size, even when they told me to "just give a rough number."

Some wanted to know why my project was valuable. A white TV man sat a foot away from the window through which the bright colors of the Google logo nearly glowed behind his smile-sharpened chin. He asked whether my project was worth ten thousand dollars. I told him it was valuable to have a Native woman in this office, on this bridge, writing this story.

I didn't tell him that in the early 1800s, many of the earliest white explorers regarded Native women as bodies to use by force and coercion. In the ensuing years, many settler men married Native women in earnest, intending to be good husbands, but in the mid-1800s, Washington Territory law disenfranchised my "half-breed" ancestors by legally voiding legal marriages between Native and white people and limiting the rights of their descendants. In Seattle at that time, as part of the ongoing colonial project of portraying Native people as lesser beings with no claim to the land, writers of newspaper editorials made wildly untrue proclamations that Native women would destroy the town with drunken fires, smallpox, and depravity; in 1873, the passage of Ordinance 42 banned Native women "or other disreputable persons" from being in the city after dark, unless they were leaving. In truth, it was settlers who brought the pestilence and poison, the Duwamish women and their families who were shuttled away to suffer. That is what happened here. The land and the people know it.

The month I got my bridge keys, the Department of Justice released a report on intimate partner and sexual violence against American Indian and Alaska Native women and men: of the women, four out of five had experienced violence in their lifetimes, one in three in the past year; 56.1 percent had experienced sexual violence in their lifetimes, 14.4 percent in the past year.

Later that year, newly hired as director of the Urban Indian Health Institute in Seattle, Abigail Echo-Hawk opened a file cabinet and found a folder labeled "Sexual Violence," containing questions from a 2010 survey conducted by the UIHI and the Centers for Disease Control and Prevention, who sought to learn about sexual violence against Native women in Seattle. Previous leadership decided against making the data public, possible fuel for further stigma and stereotyping; Echo-Hawk pushed for the development of a report. The findings were released in 2018: of the women surveyed, 94 percent had been raped or coerced into sex.

While I was in my surplus chair in the tower, pinned down to permanence by the camera, I wasn't thinking about violence, only about representation and responsibility: my Coast Salish face on the news, the blessing of an opportunity to speak, the burden of getting it right. I felt I needed to hold myself accountable: a non-Duwamish visitor driving settler streets, walking settler-flattened hills, crossing the settlers' fake river by bridge. I was reliant upon the products of this violence, moving across the land by way of "improvements" that bludgeoned it into something nearly unrecognizable to the glaciers that carved it. I wanted to express that I knew I was complicit, living in someone else's homeland, protected by what strangers took to be whiteness. I saw this as my responsibility.

But where else would I live? Not my ancestral territory, where I couldn't imagine a way to make a living. Now, I wonder whether I wasn't taking on a share of settler guilt, willing to suffer for them—*for* meaning *in their place*, but also as in *for their entertainment*, because they want the suffering. Settler colonialism wants me flagellating myself, because it's a good distraction: nobody might notice the DOJ findings that, of the Native women they surveyed who were victims of sexual violence, 96 percent were harmed by non-Native perpetrators.

A settler man I once matched with on Tinder said he liked that I was Native, it was sexy. I asked him to explain. He said, "I think a psychoanalyst should answer that question but if I attempt to analyze myself, I would say that there are multiple reasons for that, such as: Native American women are gorgeous, they are protective, strong and kind mothers. Native American people are (at least seem to me) very honest and honorable, they seem very exotic which they are, and people find exotic sexy and etc . . ."

How many settler boys learned through stories that a Native woman should be expected to be a chief's daughter waiting to be promised to a warrior or saved by a white hero? How many times have I showed up doomed to fail them just by being myself because they said they liked me for who I was when they meant they liked the fantasy maiden they were prepared for me to be?

Settler colonialism wants me to call myself "white-passing," and I do, I am. The mortgage lender and the cops don't treat me as a menace; they think I'm white and so they let me live. But on dates or at work, being known to be Native makes some things change. Settlers speak as though difference is only what's visible, lying to us all while fine-tuning the structures wrapped around our lineages, constricting, trying to get us to disappear. In "The State Is a Man: Theresa Spence, Loretta Saunders and the Gender of Settler Sovereignty," Audra Simpson writes about the 2014 murder of twenty-six-year-old Inuk student Loretta Saunders, who "looked like a white girl":

> Her violent passing is teaching us that one cannot "pass"—this structure, this assemblage, those people that articulate themselves through and for it, will find you, and subject you, it can kill you . . . One's life, one's land, sovereignty, one's body, emptied out, in order for other things to pass through . . . If you are an indigenous woman your flesh is received differently, you have been subjected differently than others, your life choices have been circumscribed in certain ways, and the violence . . . will find you, and choke you, and beat you, and possibly kill you.

This, Simpson says, is what the settler state demands. They could not kill me, so they told me I wasn't Native at all. When I defied them and would not be made a white woman, they asked me, *Are you sure? Are you sure? Are you sure?* and over and over I said, *I'm sure I'm sure I'm sure.* I became so busy insisting on the fact of my existence that it was only through strain that I could summon up the words for anything else.

But in the tower, I did. I described my project to the white newsman. Say it one more time, he kept telling me, this time without the word *confluence*, too big for broadcast. *Yes,* I wanted to say, *it is too big. It is all too big.*

Later, he called to ask what neighborhood I lived in, and whether I had an apartment there. He asked whether I was ever homeless and said, "I promise this isn't a leading question." Leading to what, other than my reluctant disclosure of that personal detail and his admission that he thought I was living in the bridge to get off the streets? I asked him what gave him that idea. In Seattle, Natives have, by far, the highest rates of homelessness of any racial or ethnic group. But he didn't say that. He said someone told him this was the city's program for homeless artists. Was that it, or was it the narrative he liked so much he convinced himself it was true?

The interview was broadcast on the evening news and on the station's website, accompanied by text with three mentions of the sum. On the station's Facebook page, in comments posted under the headline "City pays writer $10,000 for summer-long project to chronicle Fremont Bridge" and a photo of me, a Native woman who wouldn't have been allowed to live in the city its founders dreamed of, or would've been sold for sex, or wouldn't have even made it to age thirty-one, people wrote:

RIDICULOUS !!!! They just squander the peoples money away and families can't even afford food for their table.
can think of better ways to spend that money
Nice waste of 10k.
And you'll vote to raise your taxes again anyway.
Theres your tax dollars for ya
Who's bright idea was this?
I can write some poems . . .
really? arent there more worthy things to do with 10000?

Wow and then Seattle wants to raise taxes! Glad I don't live there!

A year earlier, after a colleague was quoted in a news piece about her scholarship on her community's whaling tradition, a man called my office and yelled at me: "Why do you wanna kill the whales? Why do you wanna kill the whales? It's part of your culture? Well, killing Indians is part of *my* culture." He called four more times. I trembled for ten minutes and put my head between my knees, hair brushing the floor. At my request, a university cop came by, called the guy back, and told him not to contact me again. He told me, "Typically, they don't call back. This happens fairly often. An ex-boyfriend is calling a girl, we call him and tell him to stop, he stops."

One month after the phone call, in an email to an entirely different man, one I knew, I wrote, *I just need for you to stop contacting me. Don't reply to this message. Don't initiate contact if we are both in the same public place. Don't assume I have changed my mind about this unless I explicitly tell you so.* One month after that, he emailed me again, begging me for friendship, then followed me out of a campus building, saying, "I just want to know what I did to hurt you." A university cop called him and told him not to contact me again. He stopped, but he later called the cops, asking if he could mail me a gift, come to my reading, because he couldn't believe the law would deny him access to me. A court, satisfied with my articulation of fear, called it stalking. They granted my request for a protection order and forbade him from contacting me for two years.

And now—I've gone and opened a door, introduced a wrinkle of a plot point, and I will have to deal with the stalking on the page or delete it. Can I ask you to deal with it for me? In my opinion, I've given enough. I've served as a sturdy container for men's anger and need, so often overlapping. I've disclosed for the curious. Learned to wear my suffering like a mimesis of suffering, a tolerable performance, heart turned human interest story. Is it enough to know that when the protection order expired, he contacted me again? That my body and mind have to keep holding him? Simpson writes:

> Force qualified as violence moves through us, trying to empty us out, transiting through moving to the flesh that is the subsurface of "identity" as peoples possessing bodies with living histories of relatedness to territory that is constantly being violated, harmed, ignored—allowing some of us to be devalued to the point where we are denied bodily integrity, denied philosophical integrity, flattened, sometimes killed.

I am trying to write about a tower. Let me write about a tower. When I write about the windows, know I'm not saying (because I barely recognize it myself) that when I was up there, under all thought ran a current of worry about who might look through.

For a few days in mid-June, I went to a wooded island in the Salish Sea to write. The evergreens hung dark and heavy over the cabin. I walked paths cut through nettle and blackberry brambles. In the evenings, I called Carl, who had returned from tour after I drove to the woods. I told him I'd found my dream:

to have land in the woods among the salal, Oregon grape, ferns, and cedars my ancestors would have known as relatives.

As a child, I drew maps of the island I dreamed I'd own, laying out plans for all the buildings I would need to make my life. In the woods, I took up the practice again in my mind. Hemlock, fir, cedar, alder, maple, cottonwood, camas, lilies, nettles, ferns, salmon, smelt, shellfish, deer, elk. Before the world turned over, it was forest and prairie, burned to let the bulbs grow unfettered. I imagined land that didn't know the suffering settlers had inflicted. I'd build a cabin for me and one for Carl. The woods felt safe, a hiding place. We'd leave everybody.

Back in the city, Carl brought me lunch at the bridge. While we sat and ate, I asked him if he ever wanted to live with me. "Maybe," he said, and I regretted asking, so I tried to sound like I was joking and talked about the mansion I wanted. I told him I'd build in the city if I could, but I'd never be rich enough.

"What about squatters' rights," he said. If a person openly occupies and pays property taxes for an otherwise neglected property for seven years, they're eligible to claim title. Washington State came into being, after all, through settler squatting, an American tradition; white people tried to take my great-great-grandmother's land through squatting.

Carl and I watched the bridge open for a pirate ship, complete with men in eye patches. I explained that it was a *simple trunnion bascule* bridge, using a system of counterbalance and leverage; the installation of an automatic control for the bridge-opening machinery made openings quicker and reduced the bump at the meeting of the spans, the moment that wore on the machinery more than any other.

He was quiet. I worried I'd been showing off. We watched the bridge close, and after it returned to its flat line, he said, "That part seems like a metaphor. That one spot that takes the most wear."

The next day, he told me he didn't want to move in together, not so soon, but he hadn't said so because he wanted to say what I wanted to hear. I hadn't been asking about doing it right away, but he knew that's what I wanted. While I told him I appreciated his honesty, waves of an impending earthquake rippled through my core. I wished I could leave my shaking body, suddenly alert, afraid I was not safe and would be abandoned again. Sobs quaked in my gut until I fell asleep.

Seven months earlier, my bipolar diagnosis had been reversed, a PTSD diagnosis added. My therapist taught me to locate panic attacks in my body before they began and track them as they erupted. At first, the change in diagnosis brought on a mild identity crisis—bipolar disorder had been a major part of my routine and my self-conception for most of my adult life—but more troubling was the loss of my belief that, in medicating for an illness with chemical and structural causes in the brain, I had control. PTSD was the external turned internal, a constant string of triggerings, a body and mind set against the world.

A few weeks after we started dating, I told Carl about the rapes and assaults—not secret, but not easy to bring up in conversation, and he hadn't read my writing (and still hasn't, but anyway). He asked, "What are your triggers?" I said, "Silence. Not knowing what a partner is thinking. A man who's not talking can seem like he's fine, then a switch flips and he's angry.

Angry and dangerous, sometimes. I'm afraid of a man when he's not saying something. I'm afraid of not knowing what could be in there."

After I learned what was hidden in Carl's silence, which began to crowd our relationship, I realized that not knowing was not the problem: the problem was my intuition sparking like the flame of a lighter, and I feared the way it burned, the way it illuminated what I didn't want to see.

The morning after my panic attack, I went to the bridge still quaking and pulled tarot cards for a relationship spread. *How he feels about me*: THE TOWER, two people flung from the windows of a burning keep. *How I feel about him*: FOUR OF CUPS, an outstretched hand offering a cup, a person with crossed arms refusing it. *Obstacles*: THREE OF WANDS, the back of a robed man standing at a cliff's edge, looking at the mountains beyond. *Outcome*: DEATH, a black-armored skeleton riding a white horse while the sun rises or sets.

A couple of days after his admission and my panic attack, we went to an island. Weeks earlier, we had agreed it would be good to take a trip after his return, so I'd booked a couple of nights in a "tent cabin," on the beachfront of the Salish Sea; it turned out to be a translucent plastic hothouse warmed by our sweating bodies. We hiked in misery, dined in misery, fucked in misery. He said everything was fine, or said nothing. On the ferry back, I said, "You keep getting quiet, and I just need you to tell me what's wrong."

He paused. He did not look at me. He said, "Sometimes you irritate me so much, I don't know what to do."

In 1926, Mary Iley, who was Cowlitz, told the shark girl story to Thelma Adamson, a white ethnographer who edited it and included it in *Folk-Tales of the Coast Salish*:[11]

There were five Crow girls and one girl who was small in size. The small girl had no father or mother. She was a dangerous being; whenever she played with children, she fought terribly. She would tear the flesh from their faces. The Crow girls, accompanied by the small girl, went in a canoe to an island to dig small camas. The small girl alone could dig as many camas as four or five girls together. She got more than all the others. Since they got only a few, she divided with them. They visited the island four times. The fourth time, the Crow girls sang,

> I'm going to have a best-love,
> A rich man.

They did not know that the small girl was a dangerous being. She sang a song of her own, to let the pretty girls know that they could not underrate her,

> I'll have the best man of all,
> A richer man than yours.

---

11. I've edited the story, too, to clarify original text by changing two archaic terms to *camas* and *Raccoon*.

As usual, she dug a great many camas. Although small in size, she was rather oldish. By this time, a quite desirable man had taken a fancy to her. On their fifth visit to the island, the other girls said, "We'll throw her away, so that she can never get back home." "Put your basket into the canoe first and then go back after your digging stick," they said. They had already taken her stick. When she started to go back for it, they pushed off and left her there.

A rich man, who had a number of wives and many slaves, lived near the island. One of his slaves was Raccoon. She was on the island trying to dig camas but could do nothing but scratch around. She had her basket full but there was more rubbish than camas. After a while, something caught her attention. "Who can that be over there?" she thought and crooked her finger at the person. The person came over to her; it was a girl. "What are you doing?" the girl asked. "I'm trying to dig camas but I can't manage to get anything but the tops," Raccoon said. "Well, I'll give you mine," the girl said and filled Raccoon's basket.

The women were surprised when little Raccoon came home with her basket full. The fourth time, her master asked, "Did you do this yourself?" "No, a girl over there did it for me," Raccoon said. "How big is she?" he asked. "She's as big as I," Raccoon said. The man went over to see the girl. "Where did you come from?" he asked. "The Crow girls left me here. I dug with them here for several days and then one day they went off and left me." "I'll take you home with me. You can be my wife." "Do you have any wives?" the girl asked. "Lots of them," the man answered. "And do you have any property?" she asked then. "Thirty-seven slaves," the man said. Raccoon was his youngest slave. "All right," the girl said. "You'll be well-to-do when you become my wife," the man said, "I'll forbid my other wives to whip you."

The man treated all of his wives well. There was plenty of work to do, berries to pick and camas to dig. The small girl always managed to get more than any of the others because she was a fast worker. The other women loved her at first because she was such a good worker. But gradually they began to fear her, for when she became angry, she fought them terribly and nearly killed them. At times, she also fought fiercely with her husband and nearly killed him too. Finally, she became pregnant. When her baby was born, she killed it and ate it. By this time, everybody was afraid of her. At last she killed her husband and all the small children that had not already run away to escape her. "I'm going to leave you," she said one day. She went to the ocean and became a dangerous being. When a person, she was much like a shark, and it was a shark that she became. She was the best possible worker; she could work and work and dig fast. When she did any basketry work, her fingers moved with great speed.

On the last day of June, I saw the *Invader* superyacht. At 163.7 feet, the *Invader* is one of America's one hundred largest yachts, worth more than $40 million. When it passed under the bridge, I saw expressionless people in dark suits standing on its deck. I took their photo, tweeted it, and immediately worried I'd invaded their privacy. But what is a superyacht for? It wants to be witnessed taking up space, never committing to any patch of the earth.

In July, a time for drying clams and picking blackberries, I began having panic attacks every few days. "What are you thinking?" I kept asking Carl. *Nothing.* Or: *[Pause] Thinking about my schedule for the week.* Or: *[Pause] Nothing.*

When *Pokémon Go* was released, I was slow to download it, even though, as a kid, I'd tried to catch all the little monsters. I didn't care about games or anything else; I was collecting information, tracking Carl's Instagram likes. I woke up one morning after another night of useless sleep broken a dozen times by my cat's howling and my own nightmares, and, drinking my coffee, considering the interminable day ahead, I decided to install the app.

The bridge, I quickly learned, was the site of two PokéStops (GPS-designated landmarks that function as collection sites for items) and a gym (for Pokémon training). My tower was a PokéStop; the description read, "Rapunzel: The siren of the ship canal." The bridge operator's tower was the other: "Gate Keeper: Late at night on June 15th of 1917 the first vehicle crossed the Fremont Bridge."

In my tower, I attached a lure to my PokéStop. The lure's gameplay purpose was attracting Pokémon; because it was visible to all players, it began attracting people from the Google building, and I watched as they gathered near the base of my tower, staring at phones. I wondered about their inner lives a little, and whether they ever had to do night math, the calculations that kept me from sleep as I worried about how long my money would last before I had to leave Coast Salish land.

Instead of writing, I caught creatures:

Oddish, which "buries itself in soil to absorb nutrients from the ground using its entire body. The more fertile the soil, the glossier its leaves become."

Clefairy: "On every night of a full moon, groups of this Pokémon come out to play. When dawn arrives, the tired Clefairy return to their quiet mountain retreats and go to sleep nestled up against each other."

Drowzee: "If your nose becomes itchy while you are sleeping, it's a sure sign that one of these Pokémon is standing above your pillow and trying to eat your dream through your nostrils."

Eevee, with "an unstable genetic makeup that suddenly mutates due to the environment in which it lives. Radiation from various stones causes this Pokémon to evolve."

None of these was the creature I was looking for.

I spent the summer searching for more details about why a'yahos left, but I've already shared everything I found. The resolution of this essay will not, as I had hoped, be some answer about exactly which acts of dredging, excavating, regrading, chopping, filling, and otherwise "improving" would have driven the serpent spirit from the place that had always been its home. Maybe a'yahos knew what was coming and wanted to leave first. Maybe I'm assigning a'yahos the abandonment motives I know. But a'yahos was not a man.

When a hypothesis is wrong, what then?

A long time ago, animals were people. Nobody was fully animal or fully person, as we think of a person now—these delineations appeared after the Changer transformed the world and turned the Animal People into animals, people, mountains, tideflats, and rivers. Most Cowlitz traditional stories (like those of Salish Sea peoples) come to us from the belly of the change. The Changer turned some Animal People into the spirits that watch over the land.

When a'yahos lived at the lake, healers visited it to tap into its power. They did so with caution, because that power could turn a weak person wicked.

A'yahos is gone, and I don't know where it went or when it left.

Will the new people drive away all the spirits? Who will keep watch then?

A regrade moves earth like a landslide. Mining and fracking—cracking deep rocks with high-pressure fluid injections—have begun inducing earthquakes worldwide. A'yahos is easy to wonder about because it has a shape: horned, two-headed, hot-eyed. Shapeless, unimaginable malevolence is what gets me: on constant watch, I wait for it, but it never arrives because it never leaves.

It didn't take long for internet people to start talking shit about Pokémon. I began feeling self-conscious when I walked around Capitol Hill after dark, looking for invisible animals and trying to exhaust my brain. I could feel a threat in my body but couldn't locate its source. I kept my brain occupied with the to-do list of Pokémon to catch.

I hoped to find a rare water creature under the bridge in the dim, sea-dank place accessed by stairs descending from the towers. I rarely went down: opening the door to the bridge belly would sound an alarm in the operator's tower, and if I hadn't phoned already to warn them, I'd get a call asking me if I was down below, and for what purpose. Art purposes, but that didn't feel adequate, because they would not open the bridge with me underneath, and with an average of thirty-five daily openings for boat traffic, the Fremont Bridge is opened more often than any other drawbridge in the United States, and it is one of the busiest of its kind in the world. Even if I was standing in one of the under-bridge areas marked safe by their absence of yellow warning paint—the unsafe areas being the ones that shifted and went vertical when the bridge opened—the operators wanted me out of there during openings. I had no business under the bridge until I learned I could cross on foot, use my key to enter the other west-side tower, take the stairs to the underbelly, take the catwalk, enter the bridge operator's tower, and find a bathroom at bridge level. I just had to call first. The bridge supervisor gave me a hard hat, which he told me I was welcome to use for cutesy photo ops, but it was meant for fall protection.

There were no water monsters under the bridge. I would only ever spot a goddamn Pidgey, Pokémon vermin. Music blared under the bridge to discourage pigeons from gathering. Bells blared to signal openings. No rare monster would live in that water.

@josebold, July 18, 4:41 pm: You were the pokemon you were looking for all along

Within weeks of the game's release, Seattle burn center researchers reported that *Pokémon Go* kept patients distracted from pain. In July, I played Pokémon late into the night. In July, I kissed Carl while looking into eyes he'd keep open to look beyond me. In July, he asked me, "Do you talk about me with your therapist?"

This is most of what I remember about that July, a month for gathering and drying food to carry us through winter. It was the month I tried to leave my body because it knew too much about the scarcity to come. I tried to walk the panic out of me: from home to the bridge and back, from work to home, from home through unplanned loops of blocks around the Hill, to downtown, to the waterfront from which this place's transformation radiated. I walked until my feet and ankles felt broken. I wanted to crack myself and let the dread gush out of the hole.

In July, Rapunzel's neon hair, attached to the tower's exterior below her window, was cut. The light had been going out for months, and once the city determined the office responsible for the art, they took it away for repair.

I read on witch blogs that head hairs are intuitive conductors. The authors always mentioned Native American hair and said it heightened our Indian senses. Like cat whiskers. Like we were never changed from animal people. My hair is dead and it doesn't know anything. But something in my body sensed an approaching disturbance then, obscured, a kind of deep hole. Carl said everything was fine, nothing was wrong, fine, nothing wrong, fine, nothing.

I sat behind a table at the Fremont Sunday Market to answer questions about my project. A tourist asked, "Where can I find the Seattle of the grunge era?"

"It's gone," I said.

"Which neighborhood is closest though?"

"There's none. The grunge era is gone."

I didn't admit that I'd come west looking for it, too. Seattle's sense of self is built on nostalgia, but yearning for the past too loudly invites reminders that the city changed. Our dearly departed dives were knocked down to make room for badly needed housing.

On the days I chose not to walk but to instead sit in a hot bus that inched up the regrade-softened Denny Hill during rush hour, I thought, *South Lake Union is hell.* Amazon's campus had packed it with people and their cars. The arrival of tens of thousands of tech workers made for a city that grew too rapidly, leading to displacement and gentrification, but long before Amazon existed, the ship canal formed a hard boundary segregating the city: according to historian James N. Gregory, until the late 1960s, African Americans were effectively banned from being in the part of the city north of the ship canal after the end of the workday. "The ship canal was a special kind of boundary, an unmistakable dividing line between the part of Seattle where anyone might live and the part of Seattle that was off-limits to those whose skin was not white."

In 2016, north Seattle was 69 percent white, south Seattle 28 percent. Between 1924 and 1948, racial restrictive covenants in property deeds prevented Asian American, African American, and Jewish buyers from purchasing homes in many neighborhoods, especially in north Seattle (in 1948, the Supreme Court ruled this practice unconstitutional). Discriminatory lending practices persisted longer in redlined Seattle. In recent years, historically Black neighborhoods like the Central District have been overtaken by white residents in an onslaught of gentrification due to racial wealth inequality, rising property taxes, predatory lending, and white homebuyers' demand for housing.

Sitting on the bus, I thought about the malevolence and how it got here, imported from the white world settlers sought to suck this place into. They made it into what they needed, in large part, through the regrade: scraping, cutting, flattening, earthmoving.

Before colonization, Lake Union was full of salmon and suckers. After white arrival, it became home to perch, bass, and crappies. On one of my walks home along the lake's full length, passing the yacht store with PRIVILEGE MARINE lettered in white on the window, reading the metal plaque engraved with the words of Frank Fowler (Duwamish)—"In the thirties, forties, everybody had a canoe, that's where me and my uncles made a lot of canoes, people wanted them. If you didn't have a canoe down there, and the fish were running so good, you'd just about die in your heart, to see all that and no canoe"—I touched my phone, opened the *Pokémon* app, and collected half-dead-looking Magikarp that flopped and struggled against death.

At some point, I had to pivot from research to writing, but I'd given myself an assignment that seemed too big. The research could be endless. The essay's organization was loose, no arc or resolution in sight. I kept forgetting to write about the bridge. The essay was like a river, mostly obscured from my vantage point of the paragraph. Bridges make water invisible, in a way: eyes on the road ahead, we might not even see what flows under us. That, for sure, was a metaphor, and I was instructed to write something that would *represent or illuminate some aspect of the bridge and the bridge's history, be it real or metaphorical,* but I was lost in the meaning maze.

I had just a few more weeks in the tower and had produced only a sliver of what I expected of myself. In *Winds, Waterways, and Weirs*, I found reassurance in a quote from Blukis Onat:

> Most legends were not structured to have a beginning, middle, or end. Elements and characters of significance were strung together much like beads on a string. Each element would have contained a teaching and could have many facets. Elements could be assembled and reassembled depending on the circumstances . . .
>
> Neither the storyteller nor the audience necessarily knew exactly how long the legend would be or how the story would finish, nor did the story need to be finished, and often it was not. The legends could also move from the myth age, an unspecified time before the world became as it is now, to the present time, the recent remembered past, and to daily tasks that needed to be accomplished, all within the same story.

This comforted me. But maybe, beyond the essay, that comfort was part of my problem: my stressed, post-trauma brain didn't believe that the story of my body in danger was over. Concocting possible threats became a perverse routine. Carl's secretive silence was familiar, my favorite fear box. I could've told him he had to tell me what was going on or I'd end it. That never occurred to me. I loved him too much, or I loved the dream, or I loved the worry: the promise to myself *I will never let anyone hurt you again because I will see it before it happens.* I thought I could build a story to keep me alive, not a single linear narrative but a thousand tendrils of possibility, imagining the ways every pause might bloom into violence.

For work, in late July, I went to Santa Fe, a dry, high-altitude place where my face swelled and my throat ached. I called Carl every night before walking around the hotel vicinity looking for Pokémon. There had long been a spider inside me, most restless at night, and I needed to go outside to let it out. The moon shone onto the adjoining Santa Fe Outlet Mall parking lot, empty except for the unusual cluster of cars at the curb. I couldn't sleep, but also, I *wouldn't* sleep. There were too many animals to capture, monsters I'd never seen: a scowling rock with fists, a horse on fire, an ambulatory fossil with beady eyes.

People inside parked cars looked at their personal pieces of the glow. On my screen, I saw the Pokémon gym they'd pulled up to. I finished catching, walked back across faded white lines past the RVs and Silverados, and returned to the bed that was mine that night in a room that was simultaneously too hot and too cold, too close to people and too lonesome, too small and too roomy: no matter how many thoughts leaked out my ears, the room stayed empty.

When my relationship with Carl was new, he picked me up from the airport with a bouquet. When I headed back from Santa Fe, he asked if I was okay finding my way home by myself.

What are your triggers?

Audra Simpson, "The State Is a Man":

> Indian women "disappear" because they have been deemed
> killable, rapeable, expendable. Their bodies have *histori-*
> *cally* been rendered less valuable because of what they are
> taken to represent: land, reproduction, Indigenous kinship
> and governance, an alternative to heteropatriarchal and
> Victorian rules of descent. As such, they suffer dispropor-
> tionately to other women. Their lives are shorter, they are
> poorer, less educated, sicker, raped more frequently, and
> they "disappear."

Silence. Not knowing what could be in there.

Silence. Knowing.

Before colonization, Coast Salish people often depended on each
other because of their reciprocal contributions in hunting, fishing, gathering, and other work, much of it gendered masculine
and feminine. My research turned up similar descriptions of het-
eronormative marriage patterns among Cowlitz, Columbia River
Indian, and Salish Sea peoples, although queer, trans, and two-
spirit people were and are part of these communities. One book
after another talked about married men and women splitting up
work by gender: generally, women gathered and made food, wove
baskets, and did other chores; men hunted, fished, built, and took
care of heavy labor. Sometimes people chose partners, sometimes
they were arranged, depending on the community. That's what I
read, anyway. In those books, there is no love, only tasks.

After I got back to Seattle, Carl said, "I don't know if I'll ever get married. Fuck the patriarchy."

I can't imagine that after settler violence broke up the Cascade people in the 1850s, the white men who married Cascade women knew how, in that ancient system of shared responsibility, to be useful.

If there is a future, and historians to look back at us, what will they say we married for?

Carl slept while I scrambled eggs. I used his method, not mine. I made his espresso with exactly as much cream and water as I knew he preferred.

We liked to walk around my neighborhood and point out houses we'd buy if we could. After he changed, he said, "I don't know when I'll be able to afford a house. Not for years." I wanted to tell him, *That is something we can work toward together*, but I knew better.

When our ways of life were disrupted, Native women were asked to do more than ever before: to become everything we needed, everything they needed, healers for the world.

When I was in high school, my aunt took my family to see Tsagaglalal, or She Who Watches, a large petroglyph/pictograph of an eerie-eyed face looking down from a bluff on the Washington side of the Columbia River near Horsethief Lake. That place was once a Wish-ham village, Nix lui dix (the Trading Place), but in 1957, the opening of the Dalles Dam flooded it along with Celilo. Now it's a state park. Tsagaglalal has been protected by a locked gate since vandals spray-painted petroglyphs and pictographs nearby. Somebody scarred her face with bullets.

I like the way Wasco/Warm Springs/Yakama artist Lillian Pitt tells Tsagaglalal's story on her website:

There was this village on the Washington side of the Columbia Gorge. And this was long ago when people were not yet real people, and that is when we could talk to the animals.

And so Coyote—the Trickster—came down the river to the village and asked the people if they were living well. And they said: "Yes, we are, but you need to talk to our chief, Tsagaglal. She lives up in the hill."

So Coyote pranced up the hill and asked Tsagaglal if she was a good chief or one of those evildoers. She said, "No, my people live well. We have lots of salmon, venison, berries, roots, good houses. Why do you ask?" And Coyote said, "Changes are going to happen. How will you watch over your people?" And so she didn't know.

And it was at that time that Coyote changed her into a rock to watch her people forever.

Signs in the park warned of rattlesnakes. My grandparents always did, too. On the way out, we stopped at the strange ruins of a little stone house, and I took photos of the rocks against the hot blue sky. The house seemed as though it should be haunted, but I felt no ghosts, only snakes.

When I told a Native friend about the stalker, he asked, "Elissa, tell me the truth: Did you do love medicine?" I hadn't—I didn't even know anything about love medicine that I hadn't read in novels—but what had I done? In the only language I had, I called myself *cursed, punished, worthless, abusable.* I wasn't thinking about the old stories about people who know where dangerous beings live and go anyway. You're supposed to figure out the story's lesson for yourself—it's not part of the plot, but beyond it, situated in the listener. Sometimes, the old stories don't take shapes I know, don't resolve as I expect. I can't learn the intended lessons until I understand relationships between actions. Story is a system of cause and consequence that builds sense from the incomprehensible. Settler colonial stories take shapes like mountains and send us scaling the side, focused on the summit. We reach it, and everything after is the comedown.

I've gone to the mountain. There was plenty of work to do, berries to pick. I didn't think about the summit. And I've gone to the mountain that destroyed its own peak and obliterated life with lava and ash. I sat by a lake the eruption made, then left. What kind of story is that? There are shapes inside me that look like the ocean, flat and unchanging only if you look from the wrong place.

Carl's neighborhood, still, to me, is *the Seattle of the grunge era.* The houses are mostly the same, with boxy old Volvos and world-weary RVs in the driveways. Seattle is part mirage, an idea divorced from material reality. As soon as I moved to the city, I updated my Facebook profile with a quote from Dave Grohl: "All I really had was a suitcase and my drums. So I took them up to Seattle and hoped it would work." Carl seemed like hope in a body, the dream rising from a black stage, pushing through the soles of his Vans into his sliver of a form roughly the same size and shape as Kurt Cobain's, though they look nothing alike.

In the car at night, driving to a dive for dollar tacos, we moved through the mirage. When I was with him, I could pause the work of propping up my dream with money and plans. We slid along a loop of magnetic tape, unspooling toward an end point, a decision needed: stop or flip.

August was for picking salal. The bushes all over campus were full of berries nobody ever picked. I ate them even though they were probably sprayed with toxins. I thought about going to the forest to pick from unbothered bushes, but I didn't. I thought to ask Carl, but I didn't. He kept getting surly with me, and I didn't want the salal to see me upbraided.

I got an email from my ex-boyfriend Kevin:

> This is going to sound really weird, but do you remember a few years back you thought you saw yourself from the future on the bus? I think I may have seen you from the past. Once or twice a week I work from home in the afternoon and walk from Denny to my apartment around 12:00. Every time I walk up there I see a young girl with black framed glasses wearing pajama bottoms and boots sitting against the wall smoking and playing with a cell phone. Sometimes she's wearing a wool hat, even when it's hot. I swear she looks just like a younger you. She has a round face and freckles and looks like she's in her own world. I almost thought about asking if I could take a picture to send you but I couldn't think of a way to ask without sounding like a complete freak. I get the sense that she might be high.

It didn't sound weird.

That night, I cast a spell: I wrote the attributes of my ideal romance on three circles, buried them next to my $200/month parking space, and burned a candle carved with the word MARRIAGE. One of the documents I read in the tower said Cowlitz people used to dig into the ground with their hands so they could contact the other side. I didn't know whether it was true, but I had to ask the spirits to intervene, or else Carl would leave me.

The next day, he broke up with me. I was intimidating, he needed space, and it was time for him to work on himself. I could not change his mind.

I got in my car and drove all over the city, ending up in Madison Park. It was night. I waded into the dark lake. Looking across the expanse of ripples, I felt, for the first time, that I was inside the water, made of it. I wanted a'yahos, or any spirit power, to tell me why my happiness had to be destroyed, but I heard only sounds from bars where I used to get wasted.

For days, I couldn't leave my bed but I couldn't sleep, either. I couldn't eat and so I didn't walk much.

I told my therapist about a prayer I'd been saying, something another sober friend told me that summer. I liked the prayer so much I said it over and over in my head hundreds of times a day: *Show me your will in ways I cannot possibly misunderstand.*

"When you say a prayer like that so many times," my therapist said, "you could be praying for a purging." Like THE TOWER card in tarot: something is leveled. An earthquake, a fire, a cataclysm. And then a beginning, inevitably. She suggested I take a break from that prayer and try another for a while: *Heal my heart in ways I cannot possibly imagine.*

The following day, my friend Elissa Ball wrote on her "Hit the Deck Tarot" Facebook page that we might be "wrapping up major life lessons in The Underworld," work that began in fall 2012. She said some of our blocks and fears might be illusions. "Desire, sexuality, personal truth, obsession, power: These swampy waters are shifting deep inside you." We could shed old patterns "like snake skin."

I was crossing the underworld river. Not by bridge. By a canoe with a hole in the bottom.

By August, I'd been filmed by three TV crews, each of which asked to capture me unlocking the door, entering the tower, ascending the stairs, typing, and looking out windows. Some wanted me flipping through books; some wanted me walking the bridge. They filmed boats and trucks, bike people, the bridge breaking itself in half. They all got shots of Rapunzel from below. One trained the camera on the big crystal I kept on the corner of my desk, glimmering and shaking while cars rumbled over the bridge. The reporters asked what I was writing about. *Land,* I said. I didn't say, my sad heart, my forever subject I knew nobody would think was worth the money.

All summer, over and over, with lenses trained on me, I leaned out the window and arranged my hair to mirror Rapunzel's. I unlocked a door for show. I typed on demand: *I don't know what to do. I don't know what to do. I don't know what to do. Universe: show me your will in ways I cannot possibly misunderstand. Heal my heart in ways I cannot possibly imagine. I think I am going to cry and they are still here and I don't know what to do. I don't know what to do. I don't know what to do. Show me what to do. Show me what to do. Show me what to do. I was betrayed and lied to. He's still lying. I don't know what to do. I don't know what to do. I don't know what to do. I don't know what to do. Help me. Help me. Help me. Help me. Help me. I'm pretending to take notes on a book. I'm not going to cry on TV. I'm not going to cry.*

Carl killed a spirit we'd birthed in dreaming, a third body spun from expectations and hope. Alone, I had no chance: there would be no house, no stability, no rest; no sharing, no company, no comfort. I had never grieved like this, all electric feeling, no hiding place from pain—sober.

A friend said, "Grief doesn't ever go away. We just shape ourselves differently around it, around them. Around whatever is painful. And that's the way it should be, even though it hurts. It's part of us." And I thought, *That is the meanest thing you've ever said to me.*

There, of course, had been someone else. I made him tell me. The way I made him tell me was by asking.

One of my last photo shoots at the bridge came in the days after he broke up with me. I was crying too much for makeup. My eyes were dark-ringed planets. The photographer, making small talk, said she worked at an escape room: groups of people got locked in rooms where they solved puzzles and riddles together to get out. This sounded like torture, but then again, everything did: sitting in my office chair while she documented my stinging face; looking out the window and pretending to ponder something deep but really just imagining my way out of the dead dream alone. In the photos, you can see my soul left my body for a little while. Or maybe I'd buried it deep in me for safekeeping. I was no longer a person who drowned feelings in whiskey; now I drowned them in the fluid of my own wrung-out body.

Under the bridge on one of my last days, crossing the catwalk to the bathroom, I noticed a sign: "100% fall protection required beyond this point."

The writing shall represent or illuminate some aspect of the bridge and the bridge's history, be it real or metaphorical.

I'd spent so much time watching yachts I'd forgotten all about bridges. I felt as if I hadn't thought about a bridge in months. Just now, all this time later, I did what I should've done first and googled *bridges*. A bridge, it turns out, is a structure spanning an obstacle, allowing passage. The metaphor only works once the obstacle shows itself to be a river and not, say, a cliff's face. Even if I work my metaphor until it locks in—what then? What good comes from saying one thing but meaning another?

Rapunzel got her hair back in August, hot yellow like the belly of a star.

At the end of August, the Volunteer Park Conservatory had a corpse flower about to bloom, a rare thing; this was to be the twelve-year-old flower's first blossom. Since I was trying to live in the moment and develop interests beyond work and infatuation, I decided to visit the conservatory, a Victorian-style greenhouse stuffed with cacti and tropical plants; it was always closed when I passed during one of my long walks. Making an intentional trip struck me as a frivolous use of time. Without a man, why do anything but work? But I knew I was being asked to solve a divine riddle, and I'd located my next move in a self-help book: I'd embrace my freedom, start a self-discovery journey, get intimate with myself, grow my power.

I tried to recall the odor of the botanical rot that had coated me when I fell into a swamp and thought I might die two years earlier. The corpse flower, though, was said to smell like Limburger cheese, garlic, rotting fish, and sweaty human feet. I had a head cold and couldn't smell anything. "I can't stand here anymore," said one of the people crowded into the glass room.

I didn't realize until I googled later that the flower wasn't in full bloom yet; the spathe (the frilly green leaf jacket) had yet to open to show its dark red inner surface and fully expose the spadix (the yellow spike). Wikipedia said the rotting smell beckons to its pollinators, carrion beetles and flesh flies, while "the inflorescence's deep red color and texture contribute to the illusion that the spathe is a piece of meat . . . Both male and female flowers grow in the same inflorescence. The female flowers open first, then a day or two following, the male flowers open. This usually prevents the flower from self-pollinating."

The conservatory tweeted that the flower would probably open overnight. This made sense: a solar eclipse was happening that night, and if a pubescent plant was going to bloom for the first time, I figured it would want to do it on the solar eclipse that astrology Twitter was waiting for. I returned the next day before going to the bridge, but the flower hadn't opened.

On the phone a few days after our breakup, when I told him I hoped we'd be together again someday, Carl said, "We don't know what's going to happen." Maybe that was true for him, but I was going to know. I burned candles to ask spirits for protection, tracked the transiting sun and moon around the zodiac wheel to see change-bringing eclipses ahead, and asked my tarot deck the same question too many times. I wanted to see every change coming so I could harden myself into a landform.

On my last day in the tower, I stayed late to watch the sun go down. I'd never been in that office after five. *Red sky at night, sailors' delight,* my mom has always said; pink clouds lingered above the tree line beyond Salmon Bay. I felt okay. The bridge's shaking sent my hard hat to the edge of the desk and then onto the floor with a bang. I began to cry because I was going to miss that place, and I never wanted to have to miss anything. *You are human,* a friend texted the night before when I told him I couldn't stop missing Carl. *Humans miss.*

When it got dark outside, I didn't turn on a lamp. My hands were illuminated by the blue, pink, and yellow of Rapunzel's line-rendered shape, bright and constant, her arm never moving away from its protective stance across her body. Maybe she and her long hair knew more than she wanted to, more than she thought she could take.

A reporter had interviewed me earlier that day. We talked about bridge sounds: constant car traffic, boat horns and bridge operator responses, bells signaling openings. The quietest moments came when traffic stood still, the bells stopped, and the bridge's pieces soundlessly separated. How interesting, she said, that the largest movement is the quietest.

The opening: one smooth deck suddenly two; joined pieces showing they were never fastened; counterbalance obscured beneath, in the place too dangerous for free access. The bridge, for a few seconds, was no longer a path, its halves pitched as steep as a cliff's face, and as a boat passed under, stopped motorists were made to remember that the reason for a bridge is the water.

The opening: the corpse flower's blossom never did. Its progress stopped sometime around the eclipse; the flower died and began decomposition. Gardeners thought the young plant may not have stored enough energy to go through with a full blooming.

It didn't open, but did it really not bloom? Local news outlets announced it was blooming. The conservatory did, too, and I thought what I saw was the whole spectacle because I'd never known the full onslaught of that big petal peeled open, red and pungent as a rotting heart. The plant made its flower but kept it shielded. Did all that count for nothing?

In *Emerald City: An Environmental History of Seattle*, Matthew Klingle writes, "It is the singular pride of humans to place themselves at the center of the universe they did not alone create."

By the time I returned my tower keys to the bridge operator, I didn't feel I had made a complete thing. I hadn't realized I'd be attempting to tell the story of the entire known and unknown world. I am not a historian. I could use only the tools I had: texts and pain. I wanted to tell a story that would link the present and the past, but to what end? Does the collecting of details get me any closer to meaning? What is my research question? How will I know when I'm done? Have your people suffered hardships because they have been forced away from their own country, with no place to go? What can you tell us about your project and why it's important? When a spirit gets eaten, who eats it? Why do we want the universe to have a center?

Traveling along my research questions, I went off course and ended up in no-place, a hole, right where I needed to be. At the end, I finally had the words for a starting point: my belief that the settlers desecrated the land and disrupted Duwamish life, and at the same time, that the settlers could never destroy Duwamish life or the power in the land.

The Bridge of the Gods, like the Aurora Bridge, was built using cantilevers, anchored on a side and projecting horizontally into space from there; both bridges have trusses for additional support. Tension, compression—metaphor is too easy. Easier to avoid the full dive into understanding the bridge and how it works, skipping right to the meaning I want. What I understand: Tatoosh, the Thunderbird, used to live in the river, terrorizing everybody, bringing in storms, shooting lightning from his eye. And I understand this: the original Bridge of the Gods, the land formation, was made when two brothers fought over love. They threw boulders at each other and flung fire, laying waste to the land, and their shaking opened a deep hole. The woman they wanted hid in a cave. The Great Spirit had placed a bridge over the river, and with the brothers' earth-shaking, it fell, land in water.

What purpose do metaphors serve? Adding texture and vividness. Making the abstract concrete. Disrupting the familiar through proximity with the unfamiliar. And to what end? The bridge fell into the river and blocked it, but the river broke through. I'm stalled here. I can't stop the metaphors that make themselves because all my language, all my structures, are built—see?—on mechanisms that want to span the distance between one thing and another thing and join them in the mind. When something reverberates with meaning beyond itself, it can break through obstructions and make new routes. I have lost my land, my language, a thousand choices that should have been mine to make. But I have these felt connections, nearly supernatural, one thing transformed into another. Metaphor doesn't always cheapen things by turning them into devices in service of clarity or art: it can point to relationships between the spirits in everything.

A small creek once entered Salmon Bay, the stretch of the canal that was as far west as I could see from the tower. The creek was called spədak, "a kind of supernatural power," and through it, people could go to the underworld to meet their guardian spirits. By the beach of the bay, in what's now downtown, there was once a little hole in the ground that served as a portal to the creek. Baby whales and turtles passed through it to get to the lake.

When I dug into the ground with my hands and buried scraps of paper in the small hole, everything changed. I can't name the spirit I met because I don't know what it was.

A voice in my head said, *Do you trust me?*

Yes, I trust you, I thought back.

My world turned over.

ACT III.

THE MAGICIAN.

A person in white and red robes stands behind an altar, one arm raising a baton, the other pointing at the ground. On the altar lie a cup, pentacle, sword, and wand. Red roses, white lilies, and green leaves fill the top and bottom of the frame. An infinity symbol floats over the magician's head.

THE EMPRESS.

A person in a white robe patterned with red and green fruit sits on a plush pillow atop red cloth, one arm raising a scepter, the other resting on her knee. Under her seat lies a heart marked with the Venus symbol. Evergreens, a leafy tree, and a stream are behind her, gold wheat at her feet, a crown of stars on her head.

THE WORLD.

A person, nude but for the wrapping of a pale ribbon, holds batons in both hands and floats in blue-sky space, ringed by a leafy laurel. Red ribbons wrap the laurel, forming infinity symbols. In each corner, there's a disembodied head on a cloud: person, eagle, bull, lion.

IF YOUR BODY IS FEELING the arc, you know what's ahead: our narrator faces the monster in a final showdown. Act three is for crisis, climax, resolution, and dénouement, meaning *unknotting*.

Eight years ago, I began this book as a drawn line marked by plot points. I outlined a novel about a girl who turns into a shark. When I realized the girl was me, I drew a new line, but I didn't know where to put the only plot point I had: the narrator sees herself from the future. I wrote messes and disappeared them into hard drive folders. I downloaded articles about ghosts and intergenerational trauma. But I couldn't write a book, because a book is the dénouement of a problem worked through in life. I had to descend into the gloom, the underworld. Writing a book is living out the final battle, a long face-off with what my mind has resisted resolving because it feels safe in the pain.

I suppose I should tell you where I am now, and by *where*, I really mean *when*, or maybe *where* is right—the location of this narrative present. Where: I am in Ohio, in my attic. The date is October 6, 2019. I have written and arranged the book, and now I am passing through, sentence by sentence, to tighten and unify. I know what happens next because for me, that's over. For you, it's not.

While revising, I made a Google map of all the important places in these pages and saw points nearly on top of each other, ringing the Salish Sea: fictional worlds, filmed worlds, the spirit world from which a'yahos emerged, the world called "Seattle" I lived in from 2007 to 2017. I needed a better form than a story, an experiment, or a map. I needed to build a memory palace, a set of mental rooms filled with images, a route to travel through it. But the memory palace was outside me, in the land and the calendar, the seasons dragging through both.

The problem with a narrative is that it must end. I knew, in the last year of writing, that I was cursed with a blockage and would not find love until I finished this narrative. I felt myself traveling toward the final time loop's exit, or close to solving a riddle. I thought I had solved it by believing there was nothing greater than my assemblage of patterns. That wasn't right, but it worked, because even though the solution was wrong, the block was lifted, the gate opened, and I was dismissed, as though walking out of a cave.

The day I left the time loops, I was in an old fort on the Salish Sea, in barracks repurposed as state park visitor housing, sitting in a first-floor bedroom while a doe sat outside my window and watched me work.

When I finished the draft, I felt it: resolution. I could stop hexing myself with cursed names. The book ended but I continued, and the next day, my world turned over. The symbols and synchronicities had appeared when I was looking to be convinced by magic, but they made their sense and disappeared, leaving space for a real person. He came to me two days after a lunar eclipse, four weeks before Venus met the sun and plunged into the underworld. He came to me two years after he came to live in Seattle, right where the I-5 bridge spans the ship canal, just as I was about to leave without having met him yet. He came to me under meteors, atop a cliff, at the Salish Sea beach where Salish canoes had just landed and left. When he came, we walked up a path to a forest clearing filled with poems on tall slabs and a concrete vault that once held battle plans, now empty. Two concrete thrones, empty.

But I have to stop before the narrative reaches that confluence point where the symbols gather to resolve themselves. My own resolution arrived without them. I, arranger, am changed by having written these essays, and I come to you from a narrative present beyond them, but also still embedded in them. I have asked my body to suffer a little more. My disorder demands that I feel the past in my body, like a medium channeling spirit. The reliving is an illusion, because I am safe now, but still, my hair is falling out, my legs ache and tingle with the pain and pressure of displeased nerves, my mouth sprouts canker sores, and my inflamed hips weep. My body props up the stakes of this book by summoning ghosts. It is time to finish this and exorcise the last of them.

Now I am the magician. For my finale, I will try to make you feel the wonder I felt. Spectators feel the greatest delight when they don't know how an effect was achieved. What is your tolerance for ambiguity? Stay with me. For you, I will perform the final trick, the magician's unknotting of the wrist-binding rope, the dénouement.

MY HEARTBREAK
WORKBOOK

Understanding the nature of your wound is the key to your healing, for it has affected all your behavior, your decisions, and your life choices, especially in the arena of intimate relationships. It is the healing of our wounds that we seek, consciously or not, in committed relationships.

—Harville Hendrix, PhD, *Keeping the Love You Find: A Personal Guide*

THE INTERNET SAYS NOBODY WILL love me until I learn to love myself, but the internet never gives instructions. I told myself, "I love you," but I was thinking, *You're the worst*. Nothing would change my mind. What a terrible impasse. The bookstore self-help section, though, said something different: nobody will love me until I engage in sequential self-exploration exercises. Harville Hendrix's self-help book for wounded singles says there is a riddle wrapped around my heart. I have a highlighter, a composition book, and a pen. I have time. I do not have any better ideas.

The self-help book says the brain turns all that has happened to us into points. From the points, it makes patterns. The book says the collected memories are like pixels in a digital image we store of the only person we believe can close the wound.

The last few years have been like this: a cord of twined images of white boys with plastic glasses and plaid shirts and bad posture and two-thirds-full pints on outdoor bar tables. My finger presses into a flattened mouth to pull it left or right. I could build a man in my sleep. Look:

Whiskey and IPAs. Snowboarding is my life. Been single for a while now due to avoidance of drama but I'm ready to put myself back out there for the right girl. Nice guy, not a serial killer, lol. Looking for my partner in crime.

Bourbon and scotch. The kid is my niece. Just moved back to the northwest. Taking applications for a travel companion. Enjoy a healthy and active lifestyle. I have near perfect straight teeth for never having braces, and have no clue why I don't smile with my teeth.

Craft beer enthusiast. Not here for hookups. Podcasts, adventures, movies, guitars, hiking, whiskey, dogs, Star Wars, sushi, snack plates, coffee, wine, motorcycles, dancing, drinks, travel, positive vibes, minimalism, bacon, passion. Looking for a discreet lover. Must be fit and in shape. I want us to be like an old Nintendo console: blow on it hard and shove it back in the slot.

School of Hard Knocks, University of Life. 6'1" if it matters. Poly dude with a big heart. I want to beat you at pool. Caring, compassionate, level-headed, drama-free, honest, loyal, humble, passionate, easygoing, funny, adventure-seeking, and so on. Looking for a wife to start a family colony.

420 friendly. I love the outdoors. I am that serial killer you have been looking for lol jk. I enjoy meeting people and going out and trying new things. I like to be active but also enjoy staying in. "Follow your passion, be prepared to work hard and sacrifice, and above all, don't let anyone limit your dreams." Must love dogs, be low maintenance and love hiking.

Living every day like it's my last. I like beautiful smiles. I'm a good guy. Good job. Not an asshole. I love exotic women, and different cultures. What's your fantasy?

Growing old, but never up. Dream big. Work hard. Die living.

It's like a game, each match as dopamine-rich as a sunk Skee-Ball: *Congratulations! You have a new match.*

The self-help book says that when I read it, I'm like a mystery solver. The hurts I can't get out of my head are clues. People, places, dates, and times: I fill my dossier. Somewhere in the sheaf, between my troubles and attempts to fix them, I will find myself.

When I was fourteen, riding the bus home from school, a boy asked me if he could cut open my chest, pry apart my rib cage with his hands, and rip out my heart.

"Sure," I said, so he'd like me.

He looked so much like my celebrity crush that he could've been his doppelgänger. His name was Salvador, and he was one in a long line of the boys and men I called upon to save me. Not the first or the last, not the worst, not the source, just another crush.

He said he was going to wait to open my rib cage. He said it's much easier to pry apart a rib cage than you'd think. I started thinking of him as *the incubus*, something I found on the internet. At night, I kept my bedroom window open and hoped he wouldn't come in with the spring air, boy turned demon, broad shoulders as vessels for the unfurling of wings.

I stood at the door to the woodshop classroom and watched his hands. If he had opened my chest, he would have found the hole, bigger than a heart and a stomach. I thought it was an organ, maybe the *soul* I had learned about in Catholic school and imagined as a limp gray sac. The hole had always been there, and when I was little, I filled it with Cadbury Creme Eggs. In high school, I used it as a hiding place for the NyQuil I drank from the Gatorade bottle in my locker. Later, I would keep all sorts of things in the hole: whiskey, Vicodin, cheese, a butterfly knife, Nintendo games, teeth, boxed wine, antipsychotics, condoms. Salvador was expelled for knocking over a soda machine and threatening to kill us all.

The self-help book says we face a paradox: relationships inflame the wound, but it's only through relationships that we'll heal it. It is not the relationship that fixes us, but the reclamation process we enact through it. We are carrying the picture of the person who can take us through the final movement in our failing search for wholeness. We keep falling for them. But as long as we face them with imperfect courage, "we are in a waking sleep, fated to repeat the same mistakes over and over."

Tinder's founders liked the idea of the spark that starts the fire. My phone is a portal to an otherworld of strangers stretched out next to zoo tigers or scaling mountains I'll never visit. The book says I'm looking for someone whose fingers fit into my wounds. The author thinks this is a good thing, a way to heal. But I won't know which wound opener I need by the species of fish he shows the camera. We have to meet.

The author tries to coax me toward the site of my original wounding, but I won't go. A scene repeats in an infinite memory loop: In a bar with sticker-caked walls, a man sits down. He looks just like his pictures. I know he can see the hole. I try to fill it with whatever he wants to see. I can see his teeth when he speaks. He drinks whiskey. I drink soda. I look at his hands and imagine them inside my chest. I swear he's looking at me like he's going to be the one who saves me.

The self-help book says our reality is a fabrication of our own making, formed from our thoughts and actions. And yet—the book says thinking alone is no fix. Changing our beliefs isn't as easy as wanting them changed. We'll only let go when we can no longer stand the pain.

The day after Carl broke up with me, I saw a psychic in a blinds-down building between the Cash America Pawn and the discount gas station. She brought her brow toward mine and froze me. "You were a man in a past life, and you were a womanizer. That is why you are being punished. That is why they use you."

I nodded.

"You are five years behind where you should be in love," she said. "Did you know that?"

I nodded.

"You are empty inside," she said. "Did you know that?"

I nodded.

At a meditation-based sobriety meeting, a woman talks about the hole. I didn't know she could see it, but it turns out she has one too. She tells me she saw the hole once she stopped drinking. The only thing that can fill the hole, she says, is God. I don't even know what that means. When I think of God, I think of Catholic grade school and the laminated cards of Jesus opening his robe to show his cloth-draped chest burning with a heart on fire, ringed with a thorn rope, staked down the middle with a cross.

I imagine the hole like a yellow plastic ring full of irides-
cent bubble solution catching light. I try to keep God in the hole
but God is a bag of sand, and the hole gets empty before it can
get half full. I fill the hole with crystals, candle wax, handwrit-
ten affirmations, auspiciously shaped stones, tarot cards, spent
matches, shells, photos of ancestors, herbs, astrological charts,
shiny pennies, essential oils. I wedge a cauldron into the hole.

The woman at the meeting says, "We all have a hole inside
us, and we're supposed to show it to others."

Mary, like her son, showed her heart, radiating light, encir-
cled by roses, lanced with a knife.

Every night, I draw the same tarot card, THREE OF SWORDS:
a trio of blades through a red heart.

I touch my hands to my skull and ribs. I try to find the hole so I
can show it to anyone who will look, but my hands grow hotter and
hotter against my skin as they search. The current rips down my
spine and I feel it: not a hole but a channel, a tube filling with light.
In my mind, I line up all the holes I've ever reached into, holes cut
into everyone I've ever tried to love, and I just look at them.

The self-help book asks itself what happens to the parts of ourselves we deny. The book answers right away: this self disappears
underground. We recognize it in the partners we try to love. It
looks like a fight.

To make a paper fortune-teller, you have to cut a piece of loose-
leaf into a square, fold, fold, fold, fold, fold, fold, fold, fold, fold,
fold, fold, unfold, fold, unfold, put your fingers inside, push out,

write your desires and fears all over it. That is how I love. I give a softboy the pen and tell him to write about his hole and how he thinks he can fill it. A paper fortune-teller gets old fast. You have to move on, play MASH, divine whom you're going to marry and how cool your house will be and how many babies you'll have. You have to keep playing until you get your perfect life.

Some people don't identify abandonment as their deepest fear. I don't understand. When I sit down at a small bar table and take in a date, before he even speaks, I can tell how deeply he could wound me—when he stays, when he leaves. This, the book says, is chemistry: knowing he'll disappear and I'll cling because pulling away would let his fishhooks tear my flesh. To survive, I fold myself into the small thing he couldn't object to. I am the infant relying on her *Kindchenschema*, baby-cuteness, to evoke an adult's caretaking impulse. I curl my spine forward around my heart, steering conversations away from my accomplishments, asking, "But how about you, how are things going for you?"

The thing a softboy does must be survival, too: as soon as I find his hole and insert all of me, he stops speaking, starts drinking, never leaves his phone faceup on the coffee table while my mouth latches onto his mouth and my eyes try to read his mind but his eyes shift to the side before his lids close me out.

Can I really say his way of tending the fear is worse? Is hurting the one you love a worse offense than gouging out your own soul so you can stuff your brittle husk full of whatever you think he wants to feel when he delves inside you?

In my notebook-made-workbook, jumbled memories refuse to connect like dots. The self-help book says the remembering of childhood hurts will get us to ourselves, but I get to a mess of ill-fitting labels. Childhood didn't wound me and my parents didn't fail: they made a house where I could hide out. The site of my wounding can't be reached because it disappeared under the dammed river's water clot long before I was born into the nightmare. I took it in before a breath. The self-help book says we seek relationships that recreate the theft of our joy. If I never find what was lost, what then?

The self-help book knows we don't like the work of healing. We'd prefer an easier way. The book promises us that its worksheets are less painful than other people are. There is a self that just wants to find its way back to us. It fears death and wants to live. "Tell me where to go and I will," I hear it asking me, but from where?

I calcify into my mattress's divot. I believe the pain really will kill me. The hole offers to hold the pain. This, it tells me, is what it lives for.

I keep pulling the DEATH card, a skeleton on a white horse, armor-clad like a conquistador, stepping over fallen and swooning bodies, headed for sunrise. DEATH: sudden change, the old self's death, transformation, loss, failure, debacle, disaster, ruin, end, beginning.

The only way out is through the land of the dead, opposite land; the author says I must break patterns. So I take up my fencing weapon, open my third eye, cast releasing spells, summon friends with my mind while walking around the city, dress like the Virgin Mary in vintage robes, speak with the dead, pray over candles, get a second opinion from a psychic who tells me, "He is weak, Elissa, and you are strong with the power in your blood." I heal myself with my own hands. I have no other choice. I was gaping in that bed. I could fill the hole only with work and energy.

And even full, the hole remains, but now, with him dislodged, I can see it isn't a void—it's a portal through which things can enter to make me strong.

The self-help book says, "You will know you are almost to the gates of paradise when you feel like you are falling into the pits of hell." The structure of your entire self shifts and falls to pieces. Love turns to chaos. The paradise ahead goes dark, and you can try to push on toward it, but its gates are locked. The book has a promise: in this wreck, your lost self can find you.

I'm told to list the qualities of my ideal partner. No. First, I have something I need to say. Fuckboys, you are not special. This is worse for me than it is for you, because I'm the one stuck in a GIF in which I sit at a bar and smile while you tell me about this one time you were drinking with your buddies and this one thing happened. I want you—I want to listen to your collarbones and lick the skin over your ribs and slide my fingers along your iliac crests—but I don't need you the way the women of my great-great-grandmother's generation needed the men who slid in and out of their lives after the whites hustled the Cascade people onto reservations, hanged their leaders, and upended the ways of living that had been shaped over ten thousand years. One hundred and fifty years ago, the women in my maternal line learned to complete themselves because white men had broken the world in which men and women fed each other what they needed to become whole.

Softboys of Tinder, hear me: I have my own car my own cash my own large exotic zoo animals with which to recline. I cook my own meals catch my own fish write my own inspirational quotes. I am the substance I use to intoxicate myself, moving my bones for the mirror, over and over making and unmaking a cup of my collarbone and trapezius. I come from women whose dresses drip with the dentalium shells that were pulled from deep water and used like cash. I come from high-status women with cradleboard-flattened heads. From women with their own canoes, their own land in the place where they'd lived for ten thousand years.

Men of my history, hear me: When you talk down to me, fuck around on me, disappear from me, lie to me, *that's an interesting perspective but actually* me, you disrespect a woman made of women knotted in a long string stretching back before massacre. The egg that would become my mother was in my grandmother's ovary when her mother severed the cord. The first of us came from eggs the Thunderbird laid near the mouth of the river. I have my own blade my own wings my own lanced heart that might never heal but will never need your salve. I do not want you badly enough to let you grip the rim of the hole, climb in, and leave it full of emojis and cum. The hole is perfect and you cannot touch it. I delete the app.

THE SPIRIT
CABINET

"The stars turn. And a time presents itself. Hawk, watch carefully."

—The Log Lady, *Twin Peaks: The Return*

"Are you watching closely?"

—Alfred Borden, *The Prestige*

CARL JUNG NEVER WROTE, AS the internet says he did, "Until you make the unconscious conscious, it will direct your life and you will call it fate." Carl Jung did write, "The real mystery does not act mysteriously or secretively; it speaks a secret language, it suggests itself by a variety of images which all indicate its true nature." *Synchronicity* is Jung's term for "a falling together in time, a kind of simultaneity," "a psychically conditioned relativity of space and time." He wrote, "in relation to the psyche space and time are, so to speak, 'elastic' and can apparently be reduced almost to vanishing point, as though they were dependent on psychic conditions and did not exist in themselves but were only 'postulated' by the conscious mind."

I've observed that when Carl is near—not Jung, I mean, my Carl, or rather, the other Carl, the one that I used to think was mine—I feel time folding like a piece of paper creased into one of the fortune-tellers I learned to make in grade school. I've always known time to be sloppy, sludgy, full of holes. A sleep doctor diagnosed me with a circadian rhythm disorder and said, "Your clock is off," as though clocks were even real.

Do I want Carl because of what he is, or because of what I think I see flitting in my visual periphery when I look at him? What is the difference between love and a puzzle?

Carl and I met and broke up in 2016. We reconnected in 2017. Now it is July 2018 and something is happening with my blooms of intuition and things falling together in time. In a 1935 lecture, Jung called intuition "a sort of divination, a sort of miraculous faculty," and said:

> I say that intuition is a sort of perception which does not go exactly by the senses, but it goes via the unconscious, and at that I leave it and say "I don't know how it works." I do not know what is happening when a man knows something he definitely should not know. I do not know how he has come by it, but he has it all right and he can act on it. For instance, anticipatory dreams, telepathic phenomena, and all that kind of thing are intuitions. I have seen plenty of them, and I am convinced that they do exist.

I've begun noticing dates. The time loops are tightening, trying to show me something, and I'm doing my best to obey. Like the astrologer Marc Edmund Jones and the clairvoyant Elsie Wheeler, collecting visions to serve as Sabian Symbols associated with each zodiac degree, I'm using a stack of index cards, but on mine, I'm marking dates and events as I recall and experience them, then arranging the cards the way I think they want me to. I cannot stop putting this puzzle together. The universe keeps dropping clues. I want you to see what I see: the mystery, glimpsed briefly when the veil shifts between Carl's eyes and mine.

This essay will be the place where I keep the synchronicities safe, a display case for my collection. Is *essay* the right word? Is it an essay if it doesn't stand alone? Related: Do I exist if I can't be independent, can't follow my north node to my destiny? Hypothesis: meaning sits at the confluence where pieces overlap.

The way in, unfortunately for us—me, who has to explain it, and you, who may not want to hear about it anymore—is *Twin Peaks*, which, if you don't know, is a television show about mysteries, murder, and Washington State. Created by David Lynch and Mark Frost, the series premiered in 1990 and was canceled after its second season; a film, *Twin Peaks: Fire Walk with Me* followed soon after. FBI agent Dale Cooper has been sent to the small town of Twin Peaks to solve the murder of teen beauty Laura Palmer. Cooper arrives to find the town full of whimsy and evil. It is a show about the unexplained, the mystical, and the cycles of violence and neglect to which women find themselves tethered.

The killer dumped Laura's corpse by a body of water. In the show, the water's body has no name; in real life, it's the Salish Sea. The opening scene—Laura's body found wrapped in plastic, abandoned—was filmed on the Port Madison Indian Reservation of the Suquamish Tribe. Three miles up the shore, I've walked the beach at the Old Man House site, where a thousands-of-years-old village was displaced when the US War Department wanted the land. A white Indian agent burned the longhouse to the ground. It's also a place where, according to Suquamish stories cited by Ruth Ludwin et al., a waterway known as Agate Passage was created by "an underwater battle between a water serpent (not specifically identified as *a'yahos*) and a mythic bird, resulting in ground shaking, churning of the waters, and widening of the channel."

All around the Salish Sea, there are places like this, where my maps overlap. I know one place where the time loops keep getting stopped up: the portal place where Carl likely still lives.

Close to his house, an unremarkable block is home to, among other things, two karaoke bars, a diner called the North Star, the music school where he used to work, and a bar with a back room. I will tell you about these places when the time is right.

In 2017, a new season of *Twin Peaks*, called *The Return*, came to Showtime with most of the original cast, about twenty-five years after the original series was canceled and left unfinished. Carl returned to my life the same month. Things became strange.

The Return plays with time: timelines are chopped, shuffled, and overlapped. Moments are drawn out too long for TV: a bar-keep sweeps the floor forever, the villain squeezes a man's face. I become aware that I am watching time, the fourth dimension, the space between the third dimension the New Agers say we inhabit in only a limited way and the fifth dimension they say we'll reach when our vibrations get high enough. I become aware, too, that I feel that tracking the order in which things happen, and how they happen in relationship to one another, is key to my understanding of the show.

Of the show, of my life. This is what happened when I decided that either everything was meaningful or nothing was. That I could either destroy myself or live inside a riddle. The internet says Jung said, "In all chaos there is a cosmos, in all disorder a secret order." I think I've figured it out.

Twin Peaks   MIKE, a spirit dwelling in the Black Lodge, asks Cooper, "Is it future or is it past?"

1-12-18   Carl texts me a video of Phil Collins performing "In the Air Tonight." Phil Collins skulks around the stage, moist under blue lights. He sings that he can feel it coming in the air tonight. I tell Carl I'm coming to visit next month. The conversation is over.

At the heart of the *Twin Peaks* cosmology lie the Black Lodge and the White Lodge. The Black Lodge's physical manifestation is the iconic red room: instead of walls and doors, endless red curtains form rooms and corridors. On the dizzying black-and-white-chevron floors sit armchairs, fluted floor lamps, Venus statues, and a Saturn-shaped lamp on an end table. It's also known as *the waiting room.* **Twin Peaks**

Deputy Hawk of the Twin Peaks Sheriff's Office describes the White Lodge as the residence of the spirits that keep the world in order, while the Black Lodge is a place through which all spirits pass for the purification preceding perfection, requiring an encounter with the "shadow self."

Late in season two, Cooper goes into the Black Lodge after Annie, the woman he loves a little bit, who has been kidnapped. "An opening to a gateway," he says before slipping through a red curtain that appears in a grove of trees.

Love opens the door to the White Lodge. Fear opens the door to the Black Lodge. If a soul does not approach with perfect courage, the Black Lodge will obliterate it.

They call this place the Black Lodge. Maybe it's because we're all in black Vans, black jeans, black shrouds, black **1-13-17** leather jackets with silver spikes. My friend Theresa and I wear identical black boots, black leggings, and shapeless black jersey dresses. I always need a twin. In the Black Lodge, the bathroom has no door, so I use the one at the adjoining bar.

Maybe they call this place the Black Lodge because we are in Seattle, where we can touch the real world that hosted David Lynch's fictional one. In a performing hall six-tenths of a mile from the Black Lodge, the Roadhouse interior scenes were filmed.

Out on the sidewalk, we shiver far beneath the hot, roaring freeway. Carl's roommate Michael comes out from the bar next door. He's been drumming.

He and I were on this block together last year, two doors down, where Carl was playing a show. From the beginning of my relationship with Carl, Michael was a nice mystery: he never seemed to be at the house, there were almost no traces of him online, and even Carl seemed to know almost nothing about him. I only ever saw him at shows. Not long before Carl broke up with me, on a bar patio, I held his hand while I watched Michael's arms, and later, Carl said, "Sometimes, I feel like when I'm holding your hand, you're not holding it back." I can only hold so many things at a time, and that's true for Carl, too, but he thought it was okay when he was the one dreaming about someone else's body.

Tonight, no Carl, only Michael. We talk. I learn nothing but his sun sign, Leo. Later, when I see him walking away with a drum in his arms, I know I'll never see him again. If a person doesn't leave themselves all over the internet, how real can they be?

Men refuse to be permanent for me, so I need to buy   1-22-18
a house, and it has to be a hundred years old, a ma-
ture being who knows how to stick around. I choose a
neighborhood full of old houses and have dinner at one
of its taverns. While I'm eating, a woman approaches.
"Hiiiiii!" she says. She looks just like me, down to the
glasses, but she's about twenty years older. "Hi," I say.
She sets her notebook on the bar and walks away. I feel
like I'm supposed to open it, but instead, I pay and leave.

The conjunction of Jupiter and Saturn, known as the   1-27-18
great conjunction, happens every twenty years. It's seen as
an omen. The Star of Bethlehem may have been a great
conjunction. Conjunctions are said to kill sitting presi-
dents. Transiting Jupiter also makes conjunctions to Saturn in a natal chart every twenty years. Today, in my own
chart, that conjunction is exact. What is it going to kill?

We know fear opens the door of the Black Lodge. We   *Twin Peaks*
learn from a puzzle-as-petroglyph marked on the Owl
Cave that during the conjunction of Jupiter and Saturn,
a portal opens up in Glastonbury Grove, red curtains appear, and people can step through into the waiting room.

In the airport, I beg the universe and the internet for   2-14-18
signs. I'm going home to Ohio after seeing Carl in Seattle
during a work trip. His band, whose songs and aesthetic
are *Twin Peaks*–derived, played a show where I met the
girlfriend he doesn't want to talk about. Tomorrow, an

eclipse will come. Something will arrive or something will leave. On Twitter, I see a page from the book *Dead Horse* by Niina Pollari: "Without you / The killing night comes down / Like a horse from heaven"; I want to be the something that leaves. I sit on the airport floor, propped up dead among the living and their bags of things. "If you say you love me / I will open my mouth and you can live in it." On the terminal wall, a mural-flat magician and his assistant make a body disappear.

2-21-18   Tonight in Ohio, I'm alone at a charming theater to see a magician. Nate Staniforth begins his show standing at the edge of the stage, scanning the crowd, and when he makes eye contact with me, I know I'm going to be part of the act.

"A moment will come where you just don't know what to think about anything anymore," he says. He pulls threaded needles from his mouth, lights a dollar bill on fire and brings it back to form, and says illusions work on us because we're misremembering the last four minutes. He says, "There's a world of difference between being fooled by something and being genuinely amazed."

He's given us index cards. For the finale, he asks us to write down a name—someone we really care about. CARL, I write. The magician instructs us to fold the cards, collects them in a grocery bag, and selects an assistant from the crowd. She draws a card, or does he? I forget to watch closely. He asks some of us to stand, and then one by one, directs people to sit until I am standing alone, hot, organs pulsing, my nervy limbs quivering, and the magician approaches.

Close your eyes, he says. His soft voice in the darkness sounds like it's coming from inside my own head. *Imagine the person. Imagine them sitting beside you. Imagine what they're wearing.* I'm imagining Carl dressed identically to me, in black jeans and a flannel.

Imagine the person standing up, the magician says. *Imagine them walking down the aisle toward me, and saying . . .*

My name is Carl.

I open my eyes and scream.

The magician is right in front of me, smiling, really looking at me. It's been a while since anybody looked into my eyes the way I try to see into everybody else's. He hands me my card. CARL, it says.

Alone in my car after the show, I feel the magic pent up in my bones and tissues. There is no one I can explain this to. The magic can be fake and it can be real. It can. Otherwise I cannot live in this world.

"No apparitions, no incantations, no thunder. That settled it. This was witchcraft. And not only that, but of a new kind—a kind never dreamed of before. It was a prodigious power, an illustrious power; he resolved to discover its secret."

Mark Twain,
The Mysterious Stranger

Eliza, a grad student I advise, sits across my desk with a list of questions. She asks about independent study.

3-22-18

She asks about class. She pauses, looks into my eyes, and asks, "Did you buy a house?" This is a question on her list. She dreamed of a house full of doors that I wouldn't allow anyone to open. "Not yet, but I'm closing soon," I say. In one week, I will turn the key in the lock of the front door of the house I own, step across the threshold, and lock the door behind me. I will finally feel safe.

Amanda Linette Meder, "Doorways to the Other Side: Am I a Portal? Is My House a Portal?"

"A portal is a doorway, a gateway from one place to another place. It's a location where energy, matter, people and Spirits can transfer between one side and another side. It's a crack in the wall or a place with a large funnel of energy coming in."

4-21-18

When Jupiter conjuncts Saturn, two more conjunctions will follow: Jupiter (the faster-moving planet) spends about half the year retrograde, during which time it backtracks through the zodiac before turning direct and retracing its steps. This means that it will pass over Saturn three times. My second conjunction happens today.

4-25-16

Last night, my Tinder date asked me, "Do you like my white cock?" after he told me the ways he was planning to hold me down and fuck me. I'm planning to delete Tinder after I go on one last date, with this curly-haired, bespectacled hipster who looks like the typical softboy who matches with me three times and never wants to meet up. But this one does. His name is Carl. His bio is empty. His job is *Guitarist at Earth*. He likes the photo of me dressed up as the Log Lady, with a thick sweater, red-framed glasses, cradling a fireplace log.

We meet at Montana Bar, a dark, scrawled-over place. Then we go to the food place around the corner. Then another bar. I'm sober but I feel drunk, losing track of time, as if I've been shot down a pneumatic tube from eight to midnight. As if I've met someone I loved in another lifetime, and my mind says *safe* when it means *familiar*.

Cooper goes through a portal that takes him across a time wrinkle. He finds Laura in the woods, moving between her anguished goodbye to her beloved and the meeting that will kill her. He can disrupt the timeline now.

Twin Peaks: The Return

"Who are you?" Laura asks the special agent. "Right. I've seen you in a dream. In a dream. Where are we going?"

Cooper says, "We're going home."

He takes her by the hand and leads her through the woods. We hear an electrical sound, and just like that, in front of our eyes, she disappears.

Carl is visiting family in West Virginia. Before traveling east, he asked if he could come up to see my house. He thinks the drive will take an hour; it takes three and a half. I'm almost surprised to see him at my door in this city that's mine and not his, where I've never smoked a cigarette or gotten drunk. "I'm in love with

4-25-18

your house," he keeps saying. We go out for ice cream, and I Instagram a photo of us in our black beanies and dark plaid flannels. We go to the thirty-two-room bookstore, where I point out the love languages book. "Remember when your therapist had us do that?" I ask. "And it didn't help? So my therapist said we should try enneagrams?" He remembers; he reminds me that enneagrams are a concept from Gurdjieff, the mystic whose work he studied in a group that has always sounded cult-adjacent to me. We go to a bar where he tells me he was born a swindler, raised a liar, and can't stop cheating on women. This seems to be why he's here: he's cheated on his girlfriend and he wants me to make him feel better. I'm not in the mood.

I assign him to the guest bedroom. He plays on his phone with the door open and the light on while I wipe off my makeup. My loins have decided he's dead to them. I close my door.

4-26-16   We don't have to go home, but we can't stay here, in this thick block of a bar booth, so we walk to my apartment building and I show him the old Otis elevator. I draw the dingy golden cage closed and we ascend, kissing in the corner of the old box.

In my bed at dawn, Carl asks, "Where have you been? Where were you?"

4-26-18   He's learned a new scrambled-egg cooking technique, so I let him make them for us both. I don't think the new method is any good. When he leaves and I lock the door behind him, the house sighs. We are alone again.

I shower while thinking, *If I never see him again, that would be okay. I got my closure.* When I towel off, my arm knocks my labradorite necklace from the vanity to the floor. I bought it after Carl broke up with me, at the suggestion of a psychic who told me to protect my heart. I've worn it nearly every day since. The fall splits the stone in two. I take this to signify an ending, but I put it in my jewelry cabinet, not ready to discard it.

4-29-18

New at each other, we are together every untied minute. Tonight, he opens the door and stands before me as a dim shape against lamplit white walls. The image of his V-necked clavicles is seared into me like the small vision hole burned into the retina of someone who stares into the solar eclipse. "Wow," he whispers, standing still in the doorway. "You weren't here. And now you're here."

LATE APRIL OR EARLY MAY 2016

I look into his eyes, which are my eyes copied into a different skull. When one of us was made, the maker started with the eyes, accidentally made duplicate pairs, and built two different humans around the eyeballs.

He's right. There, alone, then here, poised at the threshold between lawn and living room.

In his bed, I like my hands on his compact rib cage. By his smell—a little musky, inching toward ripe—I know he's flesh, not ghost. When I tell him about my PTSD, he asks, "What are your triggers?"

My psychiatrist said ten years without a diagnosis and proper treatment let my triggers spread like toxic mold. A partner vacillating between warmth and coolness can set me off. He holds me and thanks me for telling him. Because I am a fool, I have faith he'll use what I've told him to love me better.

5-10-18   I found a *snake* in my *house*. It's thinner than a finger, and I dare myself to pick it up by its tail, but I'm not a snake handler. When I approach, it slithers away; when I touch it with a gloved hand, it sticks out its tiny tongue and I scream. I catch it in a glass and carry it outside. We are both upset. It watches me pull weeds for a while. I will make a personality for the snake if I want to. Nobody can stop me. The snake and I love each other but we are afraid. I take my eyes off him for a minute and he's gone.

5-15-16   For a week, I've been in the desert, worried Carl will find someone else while I'm gone. I can hardly think about anything but his heart emojis and compact bones. He meets me at the airport with a bouquet of daisies. He must love me. I am keeping track, tallying gestures. In my apartment, I find a stove burner I never use turned on to high. Here I'm trying to be in heaven, and some ghost wants to make it a hell.

5-17-17   I owe Carl an apology, because even though he has treated me like a reluctantly received houseplant, I tried to hurt him deep in his heart and need to resolve my guilt before I move. Two months ago, he texted me out of nowhere, telling me I was on his mind, asking how I was doing. I told him I was moving and I reminded him of all the rotten things he'd done to me. He said he was sorry, but I kept going. I didn't want his accountability; I wanted his pain. The apology I emailed him was for myself, so I would think I was a good person, or maybe I wanted something else, because now we are meeting at a taco place on Capitol Hill. We are far apart inside the house-sized booth. He presses his hands into the lacquered tabletop and stares at his fingers. He has some words under his tongue. I don't love him anymore.

He texts to ask whether I'm coming home. I am, but I don't care to tell him so. Doesn't he know this is over? 5-18-18

I watch Carl onstage, working his guitar like a scalpel to my heart. After, at the bar, we admire a painting of a ship on black velvet and he says we should have our portrait painted on black velvet for our wedding invitations. When we fall asleep hours later, his thigh between mine, his amps stacked around my bed in my tiny studio, he says, "This is the best day of my whole life." I have what I needed those nights when, as a preteen trying to reach out of the haunted forest, I listened to Delilah reading love song dedications on the radio, hoping for a message that I would be loved. This is what I thought it would feel like: a breakage reversed. 5-20-16

Nate Staniforth,
Here Is Real Magic

"Like a writer of fiction, a magician does everything possible to make an illusion feel real in the moment."

5-20-18   People caution me against love spells because I am powerful. I could make a mess. But they don't understand how lonely I am. I must be hexed: every flirtation fails. I could curse every married person who says I should be happy to be single, but instead, I go to a magic megastore and buy dried roots advertised as sex spell ingredients. I buy two person-shaped candles. I put the roots in my bra and the candles on my mantel. I anoint them with oil, scratch TRUE LOVE into the base of one and ELISSA into the base of the other, and I set them on fire.

5-21-16   We sit on the same side of a booth at the pizza place, staring into each other's eyes for five minutes. Carl's eyes are like tunnels, his skull less like a brain cabinet and more like a portal. My eyes reach in and it's like the first time I ever saw the Milky Way out on a mountain, unpolluted by light. Being seen makes my body electric. It has been a year since I began learning to feel. Everything is pins and needles, my spirit waking up.

5-21-17   To mark the hundredth year since the ship canal's grand opening, Coast Salish canoe families have gathered to paddle from Lake Washington to Puget Sound. I've shown up at the lake to visit them, and the Cowlitz Canoe Family invites me to accompany them in the support boat. I haven't been on a boat in these waters since Henry and I would travel from Lake Washington to Lake Union, and these memories assert themselves more than my research, more than my images of the water from above. But we keep going beyond where Henry would turn around, passing under the Fremont Bridge, where I see my tower from the water I stared into last summer. We stop in the locks, then charge through bay waters to meet the canoes at Golden Gardens. They're mostly empty when we approach. "How can you leave your land?" my friend asked when I told him I'm moving to Ohio. I ask myself this over and over. The answer is in the images: in my brain there will always be a row of canoes against sand and evergreens, a portal to the place and the self I had to leave.

At the end of the original series, Cooper meets his doppelgänger in the Black Lodge. According to Franck Boulègue, this is "his own Shadow, at the heart of his personal unconscious. This 'double' is an independent 'twin', a menacing inner alterity endangering the stability of his personal identity . . . Unable to defeat his inner demons, Cooper ends up being swallowed up by the Black Lodge that releases his mirror image, i.e. himself, but possessed by some of the negative aspects of the collective unconscious . . . The conscious, positive aspects of his personality are kept a prisoner of the Lodges."

Franck Boulègue, Twin Peaks: Unwrapping the Plastic

"I saw you," says a woman at a recovery meeting. "I saw you driving your car." This morning, she says, at the end

5-23-16

of Carl's block. But I wasn't there. She's sure, though. It was me, she's certain. "It must've been my doppelgänger," I say.

5-23-17   On the way to a reading in Eastern Washington, over the pass, I think about stopping at Twede's, the filming location for the Double R Diner in *Twin Peaks*. I haven't been back since I went with Henry during my golden birthday trip. I could stop at Snoqualmie Falls, shown in *Twin Peaks* in establishing shots for the lodge; I used to visit when my nighttime panic attacks needed to be broken by the sound of falling river water. Today, I have someplace to be. I do make a bathroom stop at Snoqualmie Pass, where my body is small next to the bright white peaks.

    At the college, I read an essay about how I've got a hole inside of me, a hole that's really a portal. All these people watch me, but I only pretend to look back, instead seeing through them. A mismatch of attention, a cut current. Someone shows me I've been reading to a carved sculpture, *Man Who Married an Eagle* by John Hoover, a triptych with hinged doors opening and shutting over a figure that looks like a portal. The piece is based on a story I don't know, the design reminiscent of Northwest Coast transformation masks that open in ceremony. The figure has two faces, one embedded in the body of the other. Which is the man and which is the wife?

5-23-18   Both love spell candles are burning strangely, hollowing themselves out, with the faces standing up like masks, then peeling forward and flopping toward their chests. I'm supposed to burn the candles over seven days, but in minutes, the ELISSA candle burns down far and its red wax spills onto the mantel. The figure's face and chest lie supine in the puddle. I decide the TRUE LOVE candle should be burned down tonight, too. It takes hours; along the way to the bottom, this candle's face and torso, in a move that defies all sense, leap across the puddle to land parallel to the other torso, as though they're lying in bed, talking. When the flames die, I try to read the wax. I see a mess.

Not yet, the wax says. Whoever he is, he's not ready.

"I only want to be with you," I say, meaning, *I don't want you to be with anyone else*, so it's good that Carl says, "That's what I want too." **5-27-16**

He's inside me when I tell him I love him. He can hardly say it fast enough—"I love you too, I love you so much."

Later, our sides pressed together, I ask, "What if they could stitch us together by our rib cages? I would do it. I would be sewn into you." This is not the same as saying *I love you*. It's more accurate.

Carl is going on tour for weeks in the Midwest. I take him and his guitars to the airport. When I pull up at the curb and stop the car, I look at him and know that on the other side of this, everything is going to be different. **5-30-16**

6-4-16   A few weeks ago, I tore a pretty medicine cabinet out of the wall in a building I'd once worked in that was about to be demolished. I've always liked the medicine cabinet; now it's propped up on my microwave, attached to the wall with enough heavy-duty Command Strips that it's not going to move. Except, tonight, it does: while I'm standing at the kitchen window, wondering what Carl is doing and whether he's going to text me tonight, the cabinet practically jumps off the wall toward me, all my witchcraft supplies inside spilling all over the black and white tile of the kitchen floor. I tweet, *The emoji I really need is a serious ghost that is not making a funny face.* Then I tweet, *The emoji I need is not a cat that is crying or laughing but is just existing the way we all do: in intermittent pain.* And *I want an emoji that is not a pile of shit with a smile on it, but a pile of everyone who has ever rejected me with its face covered in loss.* And *The emoji I need is not a bumblebee taking flight but a baby bumblebee eating the corpse of a male bumblebee killed by copulation.* And Carl, still, is silent.

6-4-17   In order to be happy, people say, I'm supposed to like being alone with myself. People also say one shouldn't look to one's partner to fulfill all needs. I wish I could be entirely absent from myself for a while. I get close by walking for hours. Today, I walk alone through grim, drizzly Reykjavík to the edge of the ocean, where I will dine alone. I eat my sous vide arctic char and sea beans while I read a book that was probably meant as décor. I learn about shark meat, a traditional Icelandic food with origins in starvation times. The raw meat is too toxic to eat, but when it's fermented, dried, and rotted, the decay detoxifies the flesh. Fishermen could once sell the meat of sharks caught while fishing for other species, but now, they must toss the dead sharks back into the sea.

Across the ocean, my parents are at the supermarket fish counter, where they see a species they haven't known the store to carry: arctic char. We eat it together in time, apart in space, but I don't know that yet. I walk back thinking about dead sharks in the water, caught by somebody who wanted something else.

What is he doing? I tweet, *I need an emoji that is not a*   **6-5-16** *starry sky but a diorama of my anxiety nightmares.* Carl doesn't text. I tweet:

The emoji I need is not a chipmunk holding an acorn but a chipmunk holding the beating heart of its enemy.

The emoji I need is not an arrow over the word SOON but instead an arrow over the words NEVER SOON ENOUGH.

The emoji I need is not the sun peeking out from behind a cloud but the sun peeking out from behind my overwhelming fear of scarcity.

The emoji I need is not a smiling frog but a representation of the years of therapy that gave that frog the tools it uses for anxiety.

The emoji I need is not a dove holding an olive branch but a dove holding one page on which I've written all my secrets.

The emoji I need is a pretty good likeness of my dread, which looks basically like a set of extracted wisdom teeth.

The emoji I need is not a smiling moon but a moon that is always afraid of asking a stupid question.

The emoji I need is not a disembodied dragon head but a beheaded dragon body so I can find out whether its efficacy is in the brain or heart.

6-8-17   On the way to Carl's show, which I should not go to, I'm stopped by a man on the redbrick sidewalk in front of the community college. He wants to show me a magic trick. "You look familiar," I say. "Do I know you?" He doesn't want to talk about it. He wants to show me this card trick. I'm game. It's a good trick, so when he asks for money, I give him some. "Don't you love surprises?" he says.

After the show, Carl and I go to the diner across the street and eat tater tots. The fireplace flames are reflected in his glasses, just like the shot of a shady character in a *Twin Peaks* episode I watched the other day. "You're the devil," I tell him. He says that he is. I don't want to look into his eyes, but I can see through the flames.

I excuse myself to the red-walled, black-and-white-chevron-floored bathroom, where I take a minute to think. Don't I love surprises? What is it I love, who is it I love?

The Ohio air is so humid I feel like a fish in a tank. 6-9-18 The whole room might fill with my tears. I hardly sleep anymore, and once afternoon settles onto my skin, I can't get off the couch. "Something is missing and you have to find it," the Log Lady told Deputy Hawk on the phone. That is the condition I am in. I don't even know where to begin to look.

I sometimes imagine getting in my car and driving far away, and today, I really do it, grabbing only my wallet and water and asking my phone to take me two hours south to Serpent Mound. If I don't feel wonder at the sight of a thousands-of-years-old earthwork shaped like a snake eating the sun—maybe an egg— then I must be dead inside. Standing on a platform above the built earth, the curves' shaping said to be an unsolvable mystery, I feel nothing.

"Days and days went by now, and no Satan. It was dull without him." — *Twain, The Mysterious Stranger*

Late at night, the first vehicle crossed the Fremont 6-15-1917 Bridge: an owl car, the night's last trolley run.

My back hurts and I can't dream. I'm in a forest cottage 6-16-16 on a Salish Sea island, where I am to do nothing but write. Carl and his guitars are still in the Midwest. The quieter he gets on the phone, the louder the pond frogs bellow. I walk paths for hours, legs lashed by nettles, then come back to the desk where I write about things

I'd forgotten: years ago, Henry's fingernails digging into my cheeks, bursting pores, his thumb wiping away blood. His palm over my mouth in the night. There's something I know happened over and over but I can only picture it as though I'm hung from his ceiling, watching him flip me over and tell me to just relax and let him fuck me in that hole that doesn't want him.

I rarely thought about him until my sponsor, in a move I didn't know went against all program wisdom, urged me to make amends to him for my drunken fight-instigating and my emotional affair with my best friend, Kevin. I didn't think I should contact Henry; she didn't think I could stay sober if I didn't. So I met him at a restaurant by the lake, right where a'yahos once lived.

He was late. His face was lopsided, swollen with infection around one eye, but his expression was unobscured: that smug smile when he's got me pinched between two fingernails, he's got my collarbone pinned under his oxen thighs. I apologized for psychic infidelity, picking fights, and getting drunk. He told me he was sorry he was mean to my cat. He used to pick her up by the scruff and throw her. He'd pour cold water on her head when she hid behind the toilet.

Our history was lodged between my vertebrae, stiffening my back, when we sat by the lake and he told me he thought we should stay for dinner. After a conversation that felt as if I were pulling words from deep, small pockets between my bones, I sat in my car by the lake and texted a sober friend, *I shouldn't have seen him. This was the wrong thing to do.*

She wrote back, *You're right where you need to be.*

I was in the underworld. My corpse hung on a meat hook. I've spent the last two and a half months rotting.

"We do not like to look at the shadow-side of our-selves; therefore there are many people in our civilized society who have lost their shadow altogether, they have got rid of it. They are only two-dimensional; they have lost the third dimension, and with it they have usually lost the body. The body is a most doubtful friend because it produces things we do not like; there are too many things about the body which cannot be mentioned. The body is very often the personification of this shadow of the ego. Sometimes it forms the skel-eton in the cupboard, and everybody naturally wants to get rid of such a thing."

C. G. Jung,
Tavistock Lecture I

At the end of the tour, Carl stops at his parents' house, where he gets his birth certificate so he can send me his birth time and I can finally look at his natal chart and see how it fits with mine. The aspect lines drawn between planets look like stitches between rib cages. I already knew he was a Gemini, but now I know everything, or at least the appealing things I let myself see in his chart. His north node conjuncts my ascendant exactly, which the internet says means it was our destiny to meet. Actu-ally, what it says is, "Was it your destiny to meet?"

6-17-16

I email him a detailed explanation of the ways in which we are fated to be together forever. He doesn't reply.

My spine aches as though its cord snapped like cheap elastic string holding plastic beads. It's the kind of pain that sounds an alarm.

6-18-16   On the way home from the woods, I cross the threshold into Carl's living room, where he'd once stood like a portal rimmed by soft white light. Now, he's limp and shifty-eyed when I wrap my arms around him.

6-18-18   I'm sitting in stopped freeway traffic when a coyote bolts down the shoulder. A dog that looks like a coyote. Drivers have parked their cars, left doors open, and are sprinting after this animal that has been running so fast against traffic that I don't think he'll ever be caught.

It is 11:00 AM, one hundred degrees. I'm thinking about my memory of what sex feels like. I'm like the plants I put in the shitty backyard topsoil, limp and thirsty, wanting nutrients. Before I saw the coyote-dog running, I was thinking about my upcoming trip to Seattle and the possibility of texting Carl *would you be down for a mercy fuck* or *maybe I'm considering asking you if you'd be down for a mercy fuck but this doesn't mean I've decided yet that I want it*, and then all of a sudden I was braking and an animal appeared.

I'm going to the doctor because I can't eat or sleep. There, the nurse is patient with my slow blood she drains into six vials. The doctor prescribes a pill and asks me if I'm getting any exercise. I tell her I've been cutting my lawn out of the ground with a knife.

Back at home, I lie on the couch and listen to birds chirping in the chimney. Right behind the mantel where I burned the love spell candles, I hear flapping wings and a single note over and over. The internet says these are newborn chimney swifts, and though they are hungry and demanding to be fed, they're right where they're supposed to be, and I am lucky to have them.

He'll appear when I'm least expecting it, the internet says. I'm supposed to stop looking. I think the birds might beat the bricks from the wall with their unhappy wings. Don't they know they're supposed to be independent, not wanting or needing anything from anybody?

Back from the woods, I find the stove element on high again. A bag of chocolate chips in the cupboard has melted. *Who are you?* I wonder. *What do you want me to know?* I ask.

6-19-16

Meder writes that not only places can be portals: people can, too. Certain events can open the soul, making a hole where a portal to other worlds can take shape within the person. I picture the heart as a cabinet with doors opening to a corridor.

Meder, "Doorways to the Other Side: Am I a Portal? Is My House a Portal?"

MIKE appears to Agent Cooper in a dream and says, "Through the darkness of future past, the magician longs to see. One chants out between two worlds, *Fire walk with me.*"

Twin Peaks

I'm flying to Seattle, and I've decided not to see Carl. There is no point in trying to find the magic again. This morning, I could barely heave myself off the

6-20-18

couch, lethargic from the humidity at the muggy confluence of two rivers.

Now I am high above the land, reading Staniforth's
book, *Here Is Real Magic*, which I bought after his show.
I'm not sure whether magic is real. I haven't cast spells in
ages, and haven't felt any wonder that could pull me from
doldrums. I suspect I was tricking myself into believing
in the mystery, because fantasy makes reality tolerable.

Staniforth writes, "Magic tricks are just a way to remember something you already know, or maybe knew
and then forgot somewhere along the way. Take them
for what they are and they're nothing. You can't look at
them. You have to look through them, like a telescope."

6-21-16   Carl and I look out the bridge tower window at passing
boats. Something isn't right. I have said the wrong thing,
wanting to be closer. He was just saying he hates living
in his house, a place full of intolerable memories, and I
said, "Do you ever want to live with me?" I didn't mean
it—I meant it like sleep means a dream. What I meant
was that I want us to live inside each other. We watch the
boats and I watch my dream float down the canal, like a
body making its passage into hell.

6-21-18   My back hurts and I can't dream. I'm in a forest cabin
near a river, where I am to do nothing but write. I sleep
on a pallet. I can't write because the past is dead and
useless. How do I write a story after I've killed it? I've
been asked a thousand times, *What are you working*

on? And I have said, *A book about how my heart was broken and how I became a powerful witch.* Did I? Where's my power now? I can hardly eat enough to stay upright.

This is not the place in the woods where my back told me secrets two years ago, but it, too, has moss-coated cedars, Jurassic ferns, brambles, paths, water, a cabin with a loft. Two years ago, Venus was in the underworld and I believed I was in love. Now I don't know where Venus is or if it matters. I'm susceptible to illusions and prone to spinning meaning from co-incidence. I don't remember the last time I felt any-thing more mystical than the cooling of the sweat on my shoulders in the Ohio afternoon, listening to doves cry like executioners.

I am staring out the window at a hill covered in evergreens, unsure whether I will cry or not cry, hav-ing spent the whole morning wondering what the point of all this remembering might be. I know that two years ago, there was only one way out of my bed: magic. Maybe it doesn't matter if it's real, if I'm gull-ible and naïve, only that it lets me live.

LOG LADY: There are clues everywhere, all around us. But the puzzle maker is clever. The clues, although surrounding us, are somehow mistaken for something else. And the something else, the wrong interpretation of the clues we call our world. Our world is a magical smoke screen.

Twin Peaks,
Log Lady intros

6-22-18   Down the hill from my cabin, there's a small building with a tiny library, a few shelving units of seemingly haphazardly collected books. There's no cell service out here, and no Wi-Fi outside this room. I stand in the corner and play Twitter. When I look up, I see the shelves in front of me are packed with rows of books of the teachings of Gurdjieff, Carl's favorite philosopher-mystic.

You have forgotten something, the books whisper.

Let me keep forgetting.

Twin Peaks: The Return   LOG LADY: Hawk, electricity is humming. You hear it in the mountains and rivers. You see it dance among the seas and stars and glowing around the moon. But in these days, the glow is dying. What will be in the darkness that remains? . . . Now the circle is almost complete. Watch and listen to the dream of time and space. It all comes out now, flowing like a river. That which is and is not.

6-24-16   The venue would give Carl a plus-one only for a spouse, so he said I was his wife. He meets me outside and tells me he's given us an anniversary, just in case. While I watch him onstage, I don't know whether he even sees me in the dark. *Wife wife wife wife wife.* I hold it like he holds the strings against the neck of his bass.

Twin Peaks   Benjamin Horne, owner of Twin Peaks's Great Northern Hotel, accompanied by his brother Jerry, travels north by boat upriver to One Eyed Jack's, a casino and brothel just across the border, which Ben owns and frequents. Inside, floor-length red curtains cover walls, and in low light, women and girls stand with arms on cocked hips, playing cards tucked into thigh-highs and ribboned around waists.

I'm just across the northern border in Vancouver, British Columbia, at an event focused on decolonizing sex. Most of the performers and attendees are Indigenous. In the foyer, people with fairy wings offer condoms from boxes. I have no need—nobody wants me and I want nobody—but I take a condom with an image of a playing card Jack and the words *One Eyed Jack*.

6-24-17

After the show, at a twenty-four-hour restaurant, we plan our departure for the islands in the morning. We're eating eggs and realizing neither of us has made a reservation for the ferry, so we have to leave in an hour to take the only one available for days.

6-25-16

I made a flourless chocolate cake for Carl's birthday, so we bring it on deck and eat a little for breakfast. He likes me right now. I've reserved us a "tent-cabin" that is mostly a tent. It's barely dawn when we arrive, and we can't check in, so we walk onto the dock, where the Pacific air feels like a body brush. I kiss him and he kisses back. We need to sleep, but the tent-cabin won't be ready for hours, so we drive down the shore to a park, turn off the car, and force our bodies to fit horizontally on the back seat. Hours later, I wake up hot and panicked. After this everything changes. He wakes up with a sun-cooked heart, something boiled out of him.

6-25-17 *It's late but I'm wondering how you are doing*, Carl texts. It is not late, not for a person with a free condom. I am doing fine. I tell him about the One Eyed Jack condom. He says it's interesting that a condom would be labeled with the name of a fictional brothel. *Yes yes yes*, I want to tell him, *but don't you see it's a synchronicity? Don't you see the way the narratives are intersecting?* Apparently not. His texts are stilted, as though he is choosing his words carefully. Why text at midnight if not to reach across the thin hours, grab the person's hand, and plunge its fingers into your open heart? I stop responding.

6-25-18 Out of the woods and back into Seattle, I lie in my aunt's guest bedroom and swipe through Tinder. There is Carl's grim, hollowed-out face. I want to make sure he knows I'm in town and chose not to see him. I want him to think I'm as indifferent to him now as he has been to me for two years. So I text him to tell him I've seen his profile and I think it's shit.

Twin Peaks: The Return Agent Cooper is in the lodge and he can't come out. Twenty-five years have passed since he was doubled in there, but his evil twin is gone now, out in the world. The Arm, a lodge spirit, hisses, "Do you remember your doppelgänger? He. Must. Come. Back. In. Before. You. Can. Go. Out."

It's sweltering inside the tent-cabin. This was a mistake.   6-26-16
Since we're on vacation in the islands, we try fucking,
but every thrust feels like a cut. Carl is annoyed, even
when I separate myself to sit in my car and play with
my charging phone and he comes out just to see what
I'm doing wrong so he can resent me. Today's sin: in
my sleep-deprived confusion, I've turned the engine
on, though I could've charged with the key turned only
partway. Jesus fucking Christ. He doesn't tell me right
away, just gets fed up and quiet; I won't know until we're
on the ferry home, when he'll finally tell me he's not
pleased with himself for getting mad at my stupidity.

Today I don't know what's wrong, as usual. Today he
drives my car so fast around dark cedar-lined road bends
I think he's trying to kill us. Today we take the road up
the mountain, and we do not stop at Mountain Lake,
though I ask to; we do not stop at Twin Lakes; we drive
to the mountaintop and walk to the stone watchtower,
where a little girl looks down at me from a high window and screams, "It's the witch!" And here I thought
I was Rapunzel. We climb. From the top, I look at the
evergreen-coated islands sitting like mossy rocks in the
blue sea. In the story, the knight takes Rapunzel away
from the tower. In real life, we step down the narrow
stairs, one in front of the other, and I go back to watching
him for clues and watching myself for mistakes.

Tonight I fuck a man who asks me what I want and what   6-26-17
I don't want. He tells me about his primary partner and

the terms of their relationship. He would be happy to show me the results of his most recent STI tests. He asks about my boundaries and I tell him. I ask him not to stay afterward. What is wrong with me? Carl was the last man to sleep in this bed. Why do we say *ghosting* when we talk about people who disappear from us? Still he haunts me, a phantom in the bed half I will not sleep in.

Gurdjieff, via brainyquote.com   "A man will renounce any pleasures you like but he will not give up his suffering."

6-27-18   Carl won't come out and say it, but he is desperate to meet. He says we could meet if I want to. He had some time open up midday. But I have plans. No worries, he says. A few minutes later, he says he's free all morning, actually. Fine. I do want to meet up. We get coffee and it's the same as ever: he's sad and I'm frustrated. He says he's working on himself, making positive changes. I remind him that two years ago today, we were coming back from the island and he was mad at me. He says, "I don't really remember that time."

By the time I have to go, I've upset him by saying he was careless with my heart and keeps coming back, like a scavenger picking meat off a carcass. He'll be fine. But now I have touched him, just to hug him, a hand light against his shoulders, so I won't be.

Twin Peaks: The Return   In the basement of the Great Northern Hotel, Cooper approaches a door. He has a key. This comes after everything: his return to Twin Peaks from the Black Lodge, the killing of the doppelgänger, the destruction of the evil spirit BOB, the reunion with Diane (Cooper's assistant known in the original series as a receiver of voice notes but never as an embodied character until *The Return*). She accompanies him, along with FBI Deputy Director Gordon Cole. At the door, Cooper pauses.

COOPER: Now listen. I'm going through this door. Don't try to follow me. Either of you.

COLE: Be thinking of you, Coop.

Cooper opens the door and pauses on the threshold, looking back.

COOPER: See you at the curtain call.

In the darkness, MIKE appears and speaks his incantation:

> Through the darkness of future past, the magician longs to see. One chants out between two worlds, *Fire walk with me*.

Just after midnight, I'm leaving the Baranof, a karaoke bar in Carl's neighborhood. I feel him nearby. *It is happening again*, I think. I want, suddenly, to see him. I text him:

6-28-18

ELISSA: Are you at your house?

ELISSA: I'm in the neighborhood

CARL: I'm at North Star

ELISSA: Can I come or are you on a date or something

CARL: Come over here!

At the bar, the scene is familiar: just like the last time I was here, six months ago, his School of Rock friends are gathering to send off someone who quit. Everything feels different from twelve hours ago: an electric current runs between our knees. "This is auspicious," he says: the fact that we are back on this block, in this room, with these people. "It is happening again," I say. "Do you want to go make out?"

The moon goes full. Goes strawberry. In his living room, I marvel at how his house hasn't changed. "It's not the same," he keeps saying, but I insist. The seahorse print I got him for his birthday two years ago still hangs over his bed. The bed and desk haven't moved. And he's here, and I'm here, unbuckling his belt with my left hand, pushing down the zipper with my middle finger, performing ritual movements. Sex with him has always hurt me; our shapes fit poorly. Two years ago, we fucked so much the doctor put me on *vaginal rest* for two weeks so the tearing would heal. I lasted one day. Let me be clear: I wanted him inside me every day, despite the pain, because I needed him to wedge himself into the space and open my heart. I've never wanted anything like I've wanted the pain he makes in me.

It is sunrise. I have been looking for a way out of the three dimensions my body can offer. Watching for synchronicities, I see the fourth dimension wrinkling; signs of the fifth are tucked into the creases. That is why I am here in his bed. I am here to be broken again so the universe can get in.

Cooper steps out of the Black Lodge. Diane stands before him. *Twin Peaks: The Return*

DIANE: Is it you? Is it really you?

COOPER: Yes. It's really me, Diane. Is it really you?

DIANE: Yeah.

She searches his face with her eyes. She has to figure it out for herself. Because they are about to go somewhere.

I want to do it again, I text, and he replies with a crystal 6-29-18
ball emoji, which usually means he can't be bothered to spend words on me. He said he would show up at my reading, but now I don't expect it. So I'm surprised when I see him. Rita Bullwinkel, whom I had never met, reads her story "Concerned Humans." It begins, "Karl was a snake who coiled himself into the shape of a pear and bit the children who tried to eat him."

I wonder whether Carl is mad that he got called out like that—not by Rita, who doesn't know about him, but by the universe, giving me another sign. But Carl isn't mad. He's so pleased he buys the book. After the reading, everyone goes out to karaoke. He and I stare into each other too deeply and for too long, just like we used to. It's time to go. At his house, we sit on his couch and do not fuck, a secret relief. The energy is sour, the cord tangled. He says he feels as though he has moved into a different room from wherever he was before. I'm in the same room as always, reaching hands through heavy curtains, looking for the door.

6-30-18   In the airport, I beg the universe and the internet for signs or, even better, release from this. On the terminal wall, the magician and his assistant are still making a body disappear. *I disappear*, I tweet with a photo. But really, I'm the spectator, trying to understand what I just saw.

Twin Peaks   THE ARM, TO DALE COOPER, IN THE BLACK LODGE: When you see me again, it won't be me . . . This is the waiting room.

7-3-18   Today, a woman hand-feeds a shark; it pulls her into the water. Four fishermen looking for mako off the New Jersey coast accidentally hook a great white. I sit in a patio furniture display at Lowe's and tweet photos of me and the furniture. *I would go on a date here*, I write.

I don't want to go back to my real, empty house. I've texted Carl the schedule for my brief trip back to Seattle for a wedding. Just days ago, on his couch, he told me he was happy he'd get to see me again so soon; now, he says he's busy when I'm free. I send back five texts trying to offer slivers of time when I might be free, but he doesn't reply. I'm crying on a piece of patio furniture, hiding my face behind plants, invisible to shoppers.

Ninety-nine years ago on this day, the city celebrated the opening of the ship canal. At my bridge tower office, I retch when trying to swallow my lunch, because my gut tells me Carl doesn't love me. I ask to come over, and he says he wouldn't mind. After letting me in, he resumes his Craigslist search for RVs he cannot afford and should not buy but might if he gets stressed enough. For what seems like the first time, he asks what I'm writing about, which is spirits. He wants to know, "Are we spirits or do we have spirits inside us?" I sense he has a correct answer in mind. 7-4-16

Satan says, "Usually when I go I merely vanish; but now I will dissolve myself and let you see me do it." Twain,
*The Mysterious
Stranger*

I show up for our date dressed in my caftan that makes me look like the Virgin Mary. Carl texts me to ask whether I'd be mad if he doesn't show. He needs some self-care. I say what I'm supposed to say. I stay for the show. Later, he texts, *You are on my mind.* 7-12-16

7-12-17   In five days, I won't live in Seattle. Tonight, I'm singing karaoke at the Baranof one last time before moving. My voice soaks the walls; I look down from the stage at the blank slips on tables, the mossy pool table, the regulars crouched over the bar. I'm not ready to go. But my friend Hanna and I have sung until our throats hurt, and anyway, it's nearly midnight, so we call it a night.

When I approach my car, I see Carl's Volvo parked right behind it. Auspicious, I think. I wasn't going to see him again, but maybe the universe has a different idea. I text him, *I'm in your neighborhood and I think I'm by your car is that weird.*

Twin Peaks: The Return   Everyone is in the sheriff's station. Diane was stuck in a body that wasn't hers, but she's back to herself. Cooper asks her, "Do you remember everything?"

"Yes," she says, then sees the clock going back over the same second over and over.

7-13-16   There is no reason for dread, but I feel it. I rise from my bed-sweat oval and touch his face. He always seems dead in the morning. I grind espresso. I cook eggs the way he taught me, because he seems to need to be able to teach me something. Twitter says the new Pokémon phone game is good for anxiety, so I begin to play. Pokémon appear against the backdrop of my world. There is a ghost in the kitchen. There is a dead body in my bed.

I'm not sure how long I should wait for his reply, since it's midnight and I'm standing on the sidewalk next to my car, but a few minutes after I text, he replies. The car isn't his. His is in the grocery store lot across the street, where he's buying ice cream. He walks over and confirms that this Volvo is identical to his. "Auspicious," I say. "Should we get a drink?" Instead of North Star, our old spot across the street, I suggest the bar down the block I've been going to infrequently for ten years, where candles drip onto heavy wood tables.

He drinks whiskey; I drink soda. Heading to the bathroom, I see what I've never noticed: in the small back room, the floor is decorated with black and white tiles arranged in zigzags and the wall is curtained with red velvet. A tiny statue of Venus hangs caged in the corner; a couch sits between opposing bathroom doors.

"You need to see this," I tell Carl.

He confirms that he recognizes this as a reproduction of the Black Lodge, but he doesn't seem to get why it matters. I can't explain it. It just feels extra-dimensional. I demand we photograph each other sitting on the couches. In the photos, his grin looks wicked, as if he's got a bad lodge spirit inside him.

We stay until closing. We plan to meet later.

In the evening, at a bar two blocks from my apartment, I touch my thigh to his. He says he's going to miss me; I'm surprised. I say he should come over, but most of my furniture is gone, so it'll be a "Norwegian Wood" situation. I see him shutter himself, so I don't push it.

321

But he does walk me home. He does come in. He gets into my bed for sleep. I tell him I'm worried I'll touch him in my sleep. He says he would welcome it.

I remember sex with him as the feeling of true union, our bodies made whole by the tight fit. No. As soon as he's inside me, I recognize it: the pain I can't take for long, but want more of, because it gets me close to him.

I'm in the Black Lodge again. I don't know how I'll get out.

7-13-18   A few days ago, I finally watched *The Prestige*, which my friend Hanif had recommended. The film opens with a man in voice-over asking, "Are you watching closely?" No, I was watching Twitter. On the plane to Seattle, I rewatch it. This film is about magicians who hate each other: one wrongs the other, then they have scores to settle. Much of the plot centers upon Borden the magician's illusion The Transported Man, in which he enters one man-sized cabinet and exits another. The magician Angier wants to copy it. The timeline is deliberately obscured, folded. There's a vexing subplot about Nikola Tesla and the "real magic" of his wireless electricity.

Borden has an affair; he loves his wife some days but not others. The magician's wife says, "I want you to be honest with me. No tricks. No lies. And no secrets. Do you . . . do you love me?" He replies, "Not today, no." She hangs herself.

Three times, we hear this magician ask, "Are you watching closely?"

Yes.

Soon after landing, I watch Carl's tiny music-school students play Nirvana songs to an audience of parents who probably bought *Nevermind* tapes from Sam Goody. Yesterday, an eclipse; today, he is busy working, but he comes to the bar, touches my back, and smiles. Once the show begins, I try to watch his nervous body on the stage without seeing his fear. It's me he's afraid of; it always has been. He knows I face the unrelenting terrors in my mind without escape. He knows I see the way his terrors wrap around him, and he knows I think he's weak.

Later, we walk the beach. We eat tacos at Cactus. We go to the West Seattle Summer Fest and, on the way to the main stage, stop into the back room of the Maharaja, where the drink specials aren't fucking around and all the hostile TVs show athletes' limbs moving fast. We run into my friend Emily outside. They both tell me to meditate, to be more in my body, but I remind them that's the one place I haven't been able to get out of. And then Carl and I go north, because I want something to happen.

I make morning eggs and espresso. "I'm sorry I'm so weird," he says before he leaves. "Goodbye forever." 7-14-17

    Minutes later, he calls because his car was towed. I drive him to impound and we stand in the parking lot, the ship canal behind us, the I-5 bridge looming overhead. He says it's a fitting goodbye, and I don't ask why.

About nine hours later, Emily and I go to the West
Seattle Summer Fest and, on the way to the main stage,
stop into the back room of the Maharaja, where the
drink specials aren't fucking around and all the hostile
TVs show athletes' limbs moving fast. I won't know for
a year that Carl was in this room before I arrived, and
maybe it's the scar of his absence on the air that makes
me feel like I need to get out of here. When we return to
my car, I notice it's parked in front of the music school
he works at now. "Auspicious," I tell Emily. *Goodbye forever*, I tell Carl.

7-14-18   We are tired. We get this over with. I can't tell him he's
tearing me open from the inside, because it's not like
he likes this either.

*Twin Peaks:
The Return*   Diane doesn't accompany Cooper as he walks through
the door in the basement of the Great Northern and
passes through the Black Lodge, but she rejoins him in
the grove outside. "Is it really you?" they ask each other.
They kiss, then they drive, quiet. They must drive exactly
430 miles. They kiss again, because it will be different.

They drive until they reach a motel. While Cooper
checks in, Diane sees herself—not from the future or
the past, but herself as she is now—standing outside, a
doubled body. Cooper seems like two men in one body,
hero and doppelgänger-villain collapsed. He's not exactly
the man we got to know over so many screen hours, but
is quiet now, not chipper, hardened, thinking things. He

tells Diane where to go and what to do. When they fuck, it's rote. When she's on top, she covers his face with her hands. She looks at the ceiling. He looks at her, but his face doesn't register that seeing her means anything.

After work, I watch Carl's tiny music-school students play slightly aged indie rock songs to an audience of parents who may well still be listening to the White Stripes in their headphones at their Amazon jobs. Once the show begins, I try to watch his nervous body on the stage without seeing his fear. It's me he's afraid of; it's as if his stitches are starting to come out, and I'm seeing the batting inside. I want to say I love him just the way he is, but really, I will love him better when he's perfect.

7-15-16

We head south to another show at the bar next to the Black Lodge. Carl is on drums. His rhythm's not quite right, but I don't say so. His friends Eric and Michael stop by, drunk. I like Michael because he has a drummer's arms and because he is not my boyfriend; he's not so tucked inside himself like Carl, the coiled garden snake. I catch a few Pokémon. I look at Michael. Later, in the Volvo, before dropping me off at my apartment, Carl pulls me to him and kisses me like he's finally roused. He kisses like one of us is going to be executed in the morning. I kiss like I've figured out how to suck the venom out of him.

Diane has not seen Cooper in some time. Now his evil doppelgänger sits before her; she doesn't know about

Twin Peaks: The Return

325

the doubling, only that something's off. His voice is overly deep and mechanical. "Who *are* you?" she asks her former boss. Once a lover of pie and sender of jaunty missives, he now looks like an aged Glenn Danzig. He says, "I don't know what you mean, Diane."

"Look at me," she says. He's not looking away, though. He's looking at her. What she wants is something else.

7-15-18 I show up at karaoke still in a bridesmaid's dress. Carl agreed to sing "Stop Draggin' My Heart Around" with me, but he's a no-show. When I text, he tells me he's nearby at a festival, and I should come. I want to cry and flip every table, but instead, I sing the duet with my friend Willie, who had promised to be my singing partner if Carl ghosted. I feel as though I'm vomiting up a fifth of whiskey on the stage. *Stop draggin' my Stop draggin' my Stop draggin' my*—I'm singing at Willie, and he's singing back, looking back. My friends would never drag my heart.

Carl has sent me out into the hexed night alone to find him.

He forgets to check his phone to tell me how to enter, but once I do, he won't look at anything but the screen. "You're being careless with me again," I tell him. "My heart can't take this." He tells me all the reasons he can't do this, oiled over with self-care jargon. I yell, "I don't love anybody else!" and realize I need to make it explode out of me only because it's a lie. I don't even like him.

My lie doesn't work, anyway, because he just doesn't care. I want to get food. He wants to stay. I want to fight. He wants to find my friend he likes. I let him win.

Cooper wakes up in the hotel to find Diane gone. She's left a note: *Richard, when you read this I'll be gone. Please don't try to find me, I don't recognize you any-more. Whatever it was we had together was over. Linda.*

Twin Peaks: The Return

We're headed to a diner decorated with airplanes. A car speeds past, going faster than any car I've seen in real life. I panic. "They're just street racing," Carl says. He directs me while I grip the wheel. He offers to drive, saying, "I used to race all the time." He seems annoyed by my fear. Like I'm a fool for believing that death, my only certainty, is real.

7-16-18

At the diner, he takes a photo of something aus-picious having to do with a circle. I'm tired of signs. Model airplanes hang from the ceiling, war memora-bilia on the walls, but with the red vinyl booths, glass tabletops, and omelet-and-hash menu, it's just a diner. I can't get excited. The Duwamish River is maybe five hundred feet away, but I don't know that. It's the middle of the night. I'm in a mint-green bridesmaid's gown.

I tell him I hate the gown and all other bridesmaid dresses, meant to make a body a decoration. Anyone in gowns built for weddings has to choose which body part they want people to stare at. I would rather disap-pear. I did not dance. I felt so uneasy with my naked shoulders getting clammy while guests watched me walk the aisle. Just looking at other women's bare cleavage made me nervous and I had to work not to stare. I tell him all this and ask, "Am I making sense?" What I mean is, *Do you see me?* The other night, I told him how much I have begun to hate my fatless ass and thick waist. He gave me the *Be more in your body* talk I should've known was coming. What I wanted then was to be told I'm beautiful; what I want now is to be told that I don't have to be. I want to be excused from this visible, unhappy body, and to still be desired.

"No," he says, shoulders tense in his busted fake-leather jacket, "because I'm not uncomfortable with women's bodies."

I tell him that's not it and he knows it.

He stares at my chest. He knows my body well: what I hate, what I tolerate. He knows what he's saying when he says, "Well, that's just not where I'm looking. I'm not into breasts anymore. I used to be. Now I'm drawn to . . ." He pauses and looks me in the eye. "Large butts."

The grosgrain feels so tight around my ribs that I want to cut off my dress, drop my skin, have nothing to show but bones. I excuse myself, get my change of clothes from the car, and take the dress off in a bathroom stall. I don't look down at my worthless hips, my pointless breasts, my unabashed belly.

I want to believe there are two of him: the one who loved me, and this one with the dead face. I can hate the one who is mean to me.

"We can't leave it at this," I tell him when we say good night. He agrees to meet at North Star ten hours later.

He shows up as the Carl who hates me. I trace the constellations printed on the diner table while he texts.

I tell him that if we are going to be friends, he needs to stop being careless with me, needs to stop ghosting whenever he meets some woman he wants. He talks about the things he needs to do right now; he thinks being careless with me is self-care. I look up from the tabletop star maps and finally look *at* him, not *into* him, and I see a poor conjuror struggling to keep up the illusion that he is worth the price of admission. I see a person so *in his body* that he can't get out, sapping his own flesh of vitality: wrinkles setting in, hair full of white. He's both the man struggling in the water and the man holding him down.

"The older you are, the more layers you've built. Magic shatters those barriers . . . Magic allows people to recapture their childlike wonder and strip away their defenses. Magic makes people vulnerable. That's when they're the most beautiful, because they're no longer hiding and no longer afraid."

David Blaine,
Mysterious Stranger

"Satan was accustomed to say that our race lived a life of continuous and uninterrupted self-deception. It duped itself from cradle to grave with shams and delusions which it mistook for realities, and this made its entire life a sham."

Twain,
The Mysterious Stranger

I'm in the airport again, begging the universe for signs or, even better, release from this. On the terminal wall, the magician and his assistant are still making a body

7-16-18

disappear. *Disappearing into the middle of the land again,* I tweet with a photo of the empty box and the assistant reaching his hand toward the magician.

7-17-18 "I hear you like magic," a high school student tells me after approaching the bookstore table where I am signing.

"I do like magic," I say.

"Can I ask you a question?" she says.

"Of course you can."

"Why are you looking for magic, and why aren't some people?"

Staniforth, *Here Is Real Magic* "The cultural resentment toward magic comes from the sadness found in the space between the universal human longing to believe in magic and the overwhelming evidence all around us that there is no such thing. It's not that a modern audience doesn't want magic. It's that they want it so badly but have already decided it's not out there, and dislike being told that maybe they were looking in the wrong place."

Blaine, *Mysterious Stranger* "All of these effects should astound any audience, but this next one may cause them to think you're Satan himself."

John Granrose, "The Archetype of the Magician" "Now it might be the case that the practitioners of witchcraft have been mostly women and the practitioners of magic for entertainment have been mostly men. Given the common negative associations to 'witchcraft,' this assumption might be unfair to women so let us leave the question open. Still, this controversy points to the tension between what might be called the two 'contexts' for magic: the changing of the world through allegedly magical power and the entertaining of people for the sake of pleasure. In actual cases, of course, it is not always easy to discern which is intended. Shamans and ceremonial magicians can be entertaining. And conjurors do sometimes rise to the level of performing 'real' magic."

"There is an Eastern tale which speaks about a very rich magician who had a great many sheep. But at the same time this magician was very mean. He did not want to hire shepherds, nor did he want to erect a fence about the pasture where his sheep were grazing. The sheep consequently often wandered into the forest, fell into ravines, and so on, and above all they ran away, for they knew that the magician wanted their flesh and skins and this they did not like.

"At last the magician found a remedy. He hypnotized his sheep and suggested to them first of all that they were immortal and that no harm was being done to them when they were skinned, that, on the contrary, it would be very good for them and even pleasant; secondly he suggested that the magician was a good master who loved his flock so much that he was ready to do anything in the world for them; and in the third place he suggested to them that if anything at all were going to happen to them it was not going to happen just then, at any rate not that day, and therefore they

Gurdjieff,
quoted by P. I.
Ouspensky, *In
Search of the
Miraculous*

had no need to think about it. Further the magician suggested to his sheep that they were not sheep at all; to some of them he suggested that they were lions, to others that they were eagles, to others that they were men, and to others that they were magicians.

"And after this all his cares and worries about the sheep came to an end. They never ran away again but quietly awaited the time when the magician would require their flesh and skins."

7-23-17   The movers took my things from the tiny studio apartment where Carl and I fell in love, where he ended it, where I learned to watch the gestures of malingering ghosts. I drove east for five days, a reverse Oregon Trail through deserts and forests and plains, through the atmospheric Black Hills and scorched Badlands, through the gift shop of the Montana Vortex, where I couldn't wait around for the tour so I never got to feel the "genuine quantum or gravitational anomaly that may re-define the laws of physics and nature . . . When visitors pass through the 'Portal' they can see and feel the power of the vortex and they enter a reality where some physical rules like gravity and perspective are decidedly skewed."

Still, I changed; I became more alone than ever, looking for a post office in what I quickly realized was an actual ghost town, holding my piss for hours while I sped past miles of growing grain. *I do miss you already*, Carl replied a day after I texted him a rest-stop photo of my face. When I woke before dawn in a motel room with a red door and a black-and-white floor, I swore I felt his body move against mine. I left his spirit in that bed.

After days of sweat and LaCroix, I arrive in Ohio, the place I believe will make me real because it will offer me permanence, what he never would. The sign at the state line says, "Find it here."

Carl texted me yesterday to ask how I'm doing. I told him and asked the same, and he didn't reply until today. I was going to tell him off, but I am feeling kind of nice because I just had a near-death experience: anaphylaxis from an allergy shot. Now I'm shot through with EpiPen adrenaline, resting with nurses, when he texts that he's figuring out his life. I tell him about the anaphylaxis. He asks if I'm okay. He says, *Stay safe*, and I want to throw the phone. 7-25-18

What I want to tell Carl is that, reclining in this chair, I have proved it to myself: I am being in my body. When my body reacted, I felt only wonder that it could do all this on its own when it had been told it was so stupid: blood rerouted from the limbs and head, waves of uterine cramps, itching soles of feet. I have never been anywhere but here. Carl knows I'm smart inside, and I don't think he likes it.

In the reclining chair behind a curtain, I'm googling anaphylaxis. *Empty ventricle syndrome*, I learn, can happen when people in anaphylaxis suddenly go from reclining to upright. I don't know what it means, but I know it is deadly. Dying not from a broken heart, but from a drained one. I will not die that way today.

The Prestige   BORDEN THE MAGICIAN, TO A LITTLE BOY: Are you watching closely? Never show anyone. They'll beg you and they'll flatter you for the secret, but as soon as you give it up, you'll be nothing to them. You understand? Nothing. The secret impresses no one. The trick you use it for is everything.

8-2-16   Last night my building was on fire. Firefighters rushed in through the garage door under my window. I packed my cat in her carrier and tried to remember whether I valued a single thing. I texted Carl to tell him the whole place might burn to the ground. He was busy looking for his passport so he could book a trip to Argentina with the musicians he had just toured with. As I walked away from everything I owned into the hallway, a fireman passed by and told me the fire was out and I could stay. I texted Carl to tell him I was safe. He told me he found his passport.

Does he love me anymore? Not today, anyway. I'm behind my building doing a love spell, cutting three circles from construction paper, writing my desires for a relationship on them, and burying them in the plot of an almost-garden next to my parking space. Then I carve MARRIAGE, 3 YEARS onto a candle, anoint it, pray with it, and burn it to the end. Sometimes he and I have what I want: love, respect, passion, kindness, safety, joy, honesty, fidelity.

But I've been watching closely while the void eats him. On the couch, I've been asking him to tell me what he's thinking, but he'll just say *things* or *nothing* or *I don't remember* while he drinks hard cider and we watch Bob Ross showing us, stroke by stroke, how to make a bunch of dots and lines into the illusion of a world. When we're apart, Carl texts me emojis instead of words, long nonsensical strings, single crystal balls in response to my questions.

My magic person is gone, and this one remains: Carl never looking in my eyes, Carl drunk, Carl looking out the window while hand-feeding his dick to my vagina. Carl's mail on the coffee table, a postcard in Spanish, which he doesn't know I can read a little. Carl gone to buy another used car, another guitar, another amp. Carl asleep.

"I see myself acting like my father with you," he told me the other day while I watched him eat the dinner I'd cooked him. "I don't like it."

The building was on fire. I was on my couch. He was looking for his passport. And now the soil in my hands is hot and Carl is lying to me.

I am in my little house, alone except for the internet,   8-2-17 which I know will explain everything to me if I google hard enough. There is nothing else for me, craven beast in a strange land, sweating into the couch in a dim and ancient brick room with its small windows covered. I take every *Have You Found Your Twin Flame?* quiz, read every list of twin flame signs. Some of them fit, like that we keep leaving each other and feel pulled back; that we learn important life lessons from our relationship; that we were immediately attracted to each other and had a strong sense of recognition of each other; that we are very sensitive to each other's energy.

The internet says you're supposed to *just know in your heart*, but also says it's possible to meet a person who feels like a twin flame, pulled into life with a bundle of synchronicities and magic and feelings of fate, until the lights go out. I find long lists of *counterfeit twin flame* characteristics: constant doubt that the bond is real, emotional unavailability, infidelity, codependence, dishonesty.

With nobody to love and no answers anywhere, I resume watching *Twin Peaks: The Return*. I seek out mystic symbols in every shot. I will find something there.

8-2-18   I'm in New Jersey, and at my request, Dad and I are going to the Franklin Mineral Museum, a place I loved as a child because visitors can pick rocks from a huge outdoor pile, hold them under a special lamp, watch them glow neon, and keep them. Inside the museum, there's a zinc mine replica where I start feeling low on oxygen. There's not even any ore dust in the air, but I have to escape before I faint. Dad and I pick out rocks and look at the rows of bright split stones in display cases. The fossils from Dad's hometown of St. Clair surprise us, because it's not exactly nearby.

We go home by way of Dark Moon Road, which I told Dad I'd like to see after reading about it in *Weird NJ*.

The book says a man known as the White Pilgrim was buried here. Born in Ohio, he came east dressed in white and riding a white horse to protect himself from evil as he preached about the wickedness he saw. Smallpox killed him in 1835. He was buried not in the good Christian cemetery, but in the Dark Moon Burying Ground, and so now, upset about it, he haunts the road, an all-white figure of horse and saddle and man. None of this is apparent as Dad drives me down the road. I see only wilds and clearings.

LOG LADY: We don't know what will happen, or when. *Twin Peaks* But there are owls in the roadhouse.

COOPER: The roadhouse. Something is happening, isn't it, Margaret?

In the afternoon, an email from Kevin. He remembers 8-3-16 that years ago, when we were together, I saw myself from the future a few times; lately, he's been seeing me from the past, sitting in an alley, smoking, wearing pajama pants and a wool hat and boots even though it's hot. The girl he describes reminds me of the version of myself he knew years ago, smoking in Madison Park alleys and hoping Henry wouldn't find out, getting wasted stumble-distance from home. It didn't occur to me that I might have left that sloughed-off self somewhere. How can a living person have so many ghosts?

In the evening, a visit from Carl. He recoils from my kisses and presses himself into the couch when I climb onto his lap. He turns his head to the side and says he can't be with me anymore. He needs to work on himself, by himself. He finds the idea of me intimidating. The breakup was his therapist's idea, for his self-care. But I love him, I tell him. Can we take a break and start again later? "We don't know what's going to happen," he says, so I let him leave. I drive down to Lake Washington, wade into the dark water reflecting bright beams, and tell the serpent spirit that if it's there, I will sacrifice myself to it tonight. Nothing takes me.

The Prestige Spoiler alert, sorry: in the end, Borden the magician is revealed to be a pair of identical twins switching roles as magician and ingénieur (stage engineer, builder of illusions). Of course he was: a man can't disappear from one cabinet and appear in another.

Except the magician Angier can. Over and over, he doubles himself onstage. In the end: a pile of top hats, rows of water-filled boxes a magician is meant to escape. The last lines are spoken to us in a voice-over from Angier's ingénieur, the same words that opened the film. He told us what we were about to see, and now he tells us what we have seen, a magic trick. "Now you're looking for the secret. But you won't find it because of course, you're not really looking. You don't really want to work it out. You want to be fooled."

I had to watch the film twice to understand what
I'd seen.

Instead of sleeping, I scroll through Facebook, where
some woman who looks like me is telling Carl she loves
him, and he's liking her tweet, and a feeling hits me that
scares me so much I fill a bottle of trazodone pills with
used cat litter and throw it in the dumpster, just in case,
because even though I'm sure my heart will never be
safe, I'm living out a promise to keep it running. In the
morning, I sob through my massage, and I feel the radi-
ant warmth of Reiki-charged hands oozing through me
like hot glue. Afterward, I drive. I drive up Aurora to the
psychic whose shuttered shop I pass on my way to my
Monday recovery meeting. The door is locked; from the
parking lot, I call to make an appointment for five minutes into the future, and when the clock turns over to
the hour mark, a man opens the door and invites me in.

8-4-16

The psychic herself is in a dark room with heavy,
shut curtains. "Where did you come here from?" she
asks as soon as I sit down. "Someone worked with
your energy. Your aura has been changed. What work
did you have done?"

"I came from a massage," I say. "I had Reiki."

"That's not going to fix you," she says. She can see
I'm sick, and it's because of men. They use me because
I was a womanizer in a past life, and now, my karma is
coming to me. "You are empty inside," she says. "Did
you know that?"

I nod.

She says that I don't know whether I'm a man or a woman, and my man energy pushes men away, making my relationships short; that I look twenty, not thirty-one, but I have the soul of a ninety-one-year-old; that I was a healer in a past life; that something traumatic closed my third eye; that I sleep poorly; that I bottle up my emotions; that I need to pay her a thousand dollars to fix everything. Crystals, smoke, prayers, water, she doesn't know what it will take, but it should cost about a thousand dollars. When I tell her I don't have that, after we argue, she sells me a tall red candle to attract a man.

Hours later, my therapist sees me for an emergency session. She tells me to throw out the candle, because that energy is wicked. She says I'm not empty. And to-gether we are going to cut this cord Carl and I spun between our souls.

Twin Peaks: The Return   Cooper comes out of a coma. MIKE appears.

MIKE: You are awake.

COOPER: One hundred percent.

8-8-16   I show up at my therapist's office having googled. All weekend, I watched *Lemonade*, drank Ensure, and read about this thing called the *twin flame relation-ship*. My therapist is not only a master of deep trauma work, she's also a professional astrologer, so I'm eager to ask what she knows about this. Twin flames, according to the internet, result when a soul is split in two. The halves arrive at their incarnations tasked with becoming whole alone, reuniting, and raising the vibrations of the universe. Once they meet in a particular incarnation, they recognize their own soul. But the powerful energetic connection starts a purge, and as layers of rot are stripped from the soul, it spasms in pain. One twin runs, the other chases. The point is to push the souls to purification so they can reach their higher calling; if they do the work, they'll ascend and reach reunion. *Twin flame separation*, as the internet calls it, feels evil: the soul glimpsed itself, began to glue itself to the other half, was torn away, and hangs bleeding alone.

In the middle of the night, my body felt his body against another body as I smelled his dank sweat.

I tell my therapist I've figured it out. She sort of smiles. "I do know that some people are into the twin flame thing," she says. "I don't know. All those times you stared into each other's eyes for minutes at a time—you deliberately created a bond that won't be easy to sever." She doesn't want to talk about twin flames. She doesn't want me to have a solution. She wants me to say I'm scared.

Later, on the phone, I don't ask Carl the question I want to ask, but I ask a better one: "Why did you really break up with me?"

"I told you why."

"Why did things change when you went on tour?"

"If you're asking if I cheated on you, I didn't, but you're very insightful, and yes, there was something."

Just feelings, he says. I've seen the Facebook photos: his arm around a woman with a face that looks like mine before the last ten years of fear. He'd prefer to talk about why I'm upset. "You need to be more in your body," he says. "You need to meditate."

"It's not safe in there," I say.

"That's the only place it's safe, actually. Are your thoughts safe?"

"My body—it hasn't been safe in there for a long time."

"It doesn't seem like your thoughts are safe."

"Nothing is safe in here."

He says this is the saddest conversation he's ever had. I want to believe it. I kind of want him to suffer. I'm tired of being the feeler while he gets to be the performer.

8-8-18   Via text:

CARL: Thinking of you these days

CARL: When is the Oregon teaching gig?

ELISSA: Hey, hope you're doing well, Rachel just mentioned you guys playing music, that's great. It's in February

ELISSA: I have been thinking of you too actually, had been thinking for the past few days of letting you know that I'm thinking differently about the things we talked about when we last talked in person, I feel like you don't need to feel any pressure or responsibility to me, don't worry about it and no hard feelings. I'm moving on from the desires I had and you don't need to keep me in the loop about the ways you're moving on too. If you get involved with somebody and disconnect from me, it's ok. I think you're right, our energies just don't work, and that's fine.

Delivered

I feel the cord cut, his freedom granted. Will he give me mine?

I wake up to a text from my friend Nick, who dreamed we found a portal but I was too afraid to enter it. He says it looked like a liquid mirror. This is significant. We're between eclipses now, on the threshold, in the portal, about to be transformed. I have been dreaming, too. At night. All day. My memory of the past two months is filled with holes and I worry I may have been sleeping, traveling through the land of the dead in the sweaty afternoon, thick with dread and desire. I burned off the make-believe when I stepped out into the sun. Carl is gone.

8-9-18

FBI Deputy Director Gordon Cole (played by David Lynch) learns that there are two Coopers: the real one and the doppelgänger. He recounts a dream he had in which he sat at a café with the actress Monica Bellucci (played by Monica Bellucci), and she said, "We

Twin Peaks:
The Return

are like the dreamer who dreams, and then lives inside a dream." He says he told her he understood, and she replied, "But. Who is the dreamer?"

Jung, "The Meaning of Psychology for Modern Man"

"The dream is a little hidden door in the innermost and most secret recesses of the soul, opening into that cosmic night which was psyche long before there was any ego-consciousness, and which will remain psyche no matter how far our ego-consciousness extends."

Gurdjieff, source unknown, except it's from the internet

"In order to awaken, first of all one must realize that one is in a state of sleep. And in order to realize that one is indeed in a state of sleep, one must recognize and fully understand the nature of the forces which operate to keep one in the state of sleep, or hypnosis. It is absurd to think that this can be done by seeking information from the very source which induces the hypnosis."

Twin Peaks, Log Lady intros

LOG LADY: All that we see in this world is based on someone's ideas. Some ideas are destructive, some are constructive. Some ideas can arrive in the form of a dream. I can say it again: some ideas arrive in the form of a dream.

8-13-17

I dream I'm in the Black Lodge. A good spirit tells me, *Your house is the key.* When I wake up, I know the spirit meant *my* house, one in the future, not the little house I'm renting. I've been planning to live here a long time. Something is happening.

Late at night, I drive into the Ohio countryside to watch the Perseids. I've never seen a meteor shower. I walk to a lake so dark it could be Lake Washington or Mountain Lake or any lake. The owls sing to one another. A meteor shoots across the sky so quickly I barely see it. I think I can love it.

8-13-18

As soon as I pay real money for the twin flame mastery course e-book, I want to delete not only the pdf but also myself. Even if twin flames are real, Carl is not mine. It's supposed to feel like coming home. The vibrations are supposed to match, and while I don't know what that means, I know his and mine don't. Still. Something must explain this intensity. This feeling I've had all my life that I'm missing somebody.

8-17-16

I walk without purpose in my sweltering neighborhood, trying to remember the difference between *lonesome* and *lonely*. One is worse than the other. I am feeling the worse one. I don't know how much longer I can wait for the feeling to pass. A church sign reads, "A ship in the harbor is safe but that's not what ships are."

8-18-18

COOPER: Harry, my dream is a code waiting to be broken. Break the code, solve the crime.

Twin Peaks

LOG LADY: Something is missing and you have to find it. . . . The way you will find it has something to do with your heritage.

Twin Peaks:
The Return

8-21-17   I have a last-minute plane ticket to Nashville and notes in my phone about the eclipse and exactly when it will happen. I'll fly there and back in the same day; my professor job begins tomorrow. That's the extent of the plan.

I find a public park by the river. The sky is clear all day until the sun begins to disappear behind the moon. Clouds accumulate. I watch through my special glasses. In the state of Tennessee, nobody loves me. I see Baily's beads, the celestial necklace, and then the sun and moon slip behind a veil of cloud. While night insects begin to scream, the city lights switch on automatically, and I cry while I run to the river and watch for the eclipse to become visible.

Totality ends and the clouds clear.

I'm sobbing so hard you'd think somebody hurt me. It's just that I thought I'd been getting good with impermanence, but then the sun went precisely behind the moon for a minute, and the world was so different I couldn't pay attention to all of it at once, couldn't take it in, couldn't take a picture of the feeling, couldn't pause it and rewind, couldn't restart. And now it's over. If I want to see it again soon, I have to go to Argentina. In a few years, it will happen again, and my new city in Ohio is in the path of totality. I have no choice but to wait.

The driver who takes me to the airport asks what brought me here. I tell her I'm writing about the eclipse, but not science writing—I was born within three days of an eclipse, so they have astrological significance for me, and I had a gut feeling that I needed to see it and write about it.

She is quiet for a bit, then says, "You know how they say the moon occults the sun?"

"Yes," I say.

"So that means the moon conceals the sun."

"Yes," I say.

"What I believe is that that's what the occult is. Astrology. The occult conceals the Word of God."

"Oh," I say.

The *Seattle Times* reports today that an Urban Indian Health Institute survey found that nearly every Native woman respondent had been raped at least once in her life. Nearly half had attempted suicide. A third binge-drank daily or weekly after being raped. The news gets retweeted all day. In the afternoon, I get headshots taken in the park, twinning with my reflection in the pond, alive in front of the lilacs that can't be funerary because they're still in the ground, and, somehow, I'm not.   8-23-18

I'm at the movies with Nick to see *Wind River*, set in Indian Country. Every movie about Natives is a reunion tape: there's the guy who always plays the cop, the woman who never smiles, the auntie. This harsh place— I was near there. I recognize the shrubs on the grassy hills. Just a month ago, I paused in those grasslands, legs dangling out of the car at a gas station while I fumbled with hot water and instant coffee and masticated   8-26-17 another dry bar of nutrition because the only restaurant around displayed a BIKERS WELCOME banner. I looked at the shrubs then, improbable as the backdrop of an early Nintendo game. Later, stopped by roadwork, I locked all my doors against the white men who used their hands to signal whether I could move.

In the theater, I watch a white man and a white woman develop romantic feelings across the corpse of a Native girl. When I'm found killed, I'll look like that. I'm supposed to identify with the white woman with the gun in her hand. All she wants is to help these sorry people. She and the white man wonder why they came to this godforsaken land at all.

Once we reach the climax, I've bitten patches of skin off my lips. By now, you'd think I'd know better than to wonder why I'm crying. I don't like the story I keep hearing: all these white men fracking the frontier, no wives, only work, so some of them rape.

If the oil business is the problem, why did I get raped in the city? The movie kills off a villain. At the end, text on the screen tells us that in real life, Native women are missing. Wind River Reservation is real, but justice is the climax of a white fantasy. Before colonizers fracked, they raped.

8-28-17   In the afternoon, looking through my mom's cousin Chuck's book for research, I turn to the photo of Virginia Miller with her canoe in the river. *Wind River*, reads the caption.

At night, I watch *Fire Walk with Me*, the *Twin Peaks* movie. The body of a dead girl is found in a body of water. The detective says it's Wind River.

My aunties bring me to the mountain where we've picked huckleberries for ten thousand years. Indian Heaven Wilderness is a protected area inside a national forest. I don't pay attention to how we get there, but on a map, it looks like the Wind River Highway goes north into the forest from the Columbia River near where Wind River meets it, near the Bridge of the Gods and Cascade Locks. On the map, I might see the roads but not the Milky Way. If I'm on the land, the galaxy is above me; if I'm looking at the map, it's behind me, or even inside me. **8-31-13**

The little house makes me uneasy. Two weeks ago it shut me out and cut and blistered me when I tried to enter. Now, while I wash dishes, a glass bowl explodes in the drying rack. It is happening again: someone trying to get my attention, telling me I've missed something. **8-31-17**

I wake up in a California hotel room, adding the digits of today's date in my head. Eight plus three is eleven, lucky, then it's followed by an eleven, lucky, and eights on both ends, infinity. This has to be auspicious. The numbers keep adding themselves, the brain keeps chattering, until a thought breaks through: *Carl knew he was hurting you and he did it anyway.* **8-31-18**

In *Twin Peaks: The Return*, Cooper is shown to still be held in the Black Lodge, twenty-five years after entering. The lodge spirit MIKE asks him once again, in backward-speak, "Is it future or is it past?" Another lodge spirit, the evolution of the Arm, asks Cooper in a halting rasp,

Do
You
Remember
Your
Doppelgänger

Yes, Cooper remembers.

He
Must
Come
Back
In
Before
You
Can
Go
Out

I write about Carl all morning, then, just to get away and see the ocean before my evening reading, I drive to Malibu with eyes flicking back and forth from road to clock so I can collect more special numbers to go with 11:11, the time on the clock when

I turned the key in the ignition. I want to get out of
my head, maybe by letting the ocean have my body.
I recall the scene in which Cooper's doppelgänger,
looking mean in a snakeskin-print shirt, drives fast
through a canyon like this one (filmed near here, actually). He says, "I'm supposed to get pulled back in to
what they call the Black Lodge. But I'm not going back
there. I've got a plan for that one."

I don't understand the plan. I don't have one of my
own. When I get to the ocean and walk in, I ask for a
spirit to rise up into my legs and clean me, heal me,
protect me, but all the spirits are dead, including the
one that used to live in my body. I keep trying to remember Cooper's doppelgänger's plan, as though the
show were a manual, not a story.

CUTTER, THE INGÉNIEUR, IN VOICE-OVER: *The Prestige*
Every magic trick consists of three parts, or acts. The
first part is called "the pledge." The magician shows
you something ordinary. A deck of cards, a bird—or a
man. He shows you this object. Perhaps he asks you to
inspect it, to see that it is indeed real, unaltered, normal. But of course, it probably isn't.

The second act is called "the turn." The magician
takes the ordinary something and makes it do something extraordinary. Now, you're looking for the secret,
but you won't find it, because, of course, you're not really looking. You don't really want to know. You want
to be . . . fooled.

But you wouldn't clap yet, because making something disappear isn't enough. You have to bring it back. That's why every magic trick has a third act. The hardest part. The part we call . . . "the prestige."

9-1-18   I fly from LA to another city to meet this guy Billy from Twitter. I know his history: fights, concussions, addiction, intractable depression, cheating, and loss. I choose to instead watch the signs I can call synchronicities: auspicious birthday matches, a coincidence tattooed on his body, his dog and my cat sharing a name. One day, while I was checking Twitter to see if his birthday was listed so I could look into his natal chart, he texted me to ask, *What's your birthday?*

All summer I've been seeing 1111 and retching at the sight of food. When I'm alone and have nobody to talk to, I talk to Billy. I've been imagining his world from photos he texts me and I've been sending him mine in return. I've been collecting photos of his face, so much like Henry's. One night I dreamed Henry had the evil sucked out of him. Now here I am, following signs.

When I drive my rental car into the town nearest his where I could find a cheap motel room, I feel a jolt under my tires, which I don't immediately realize is an earthquake, the first I've ever felt. I see the number 444 everywhere, which seems like a sign; I decide it means *love and luck* even though the internet says it also means *death and destruction*. I have lived long enough to know I really might die this time, meeting this stranger in an unfamiliar town, staying in a Travelodge whose street address is 444, which could mean anything.

This town is so dry, full of desert plants—it is, after all, a dry place—and it feels like the set of a movie. I'm not thinking about it, but Billy has told me, so part of me knows: a famous killer murdered people in this town. I wait in the motel bed for my dénouement. I could be the horror movie's final girl, the one who survives to the end.

In the seconds after the ending of the final episode of *Twin Peaks: The Return*, my lungs hold breath as though pausing my vital processes can eke another minute out of the show. The ending is upsetting, a refusal to close, but I think it has a message for me. As I exhale, the curtain rod in my bedroom falls off the wall and crashes to the floor.

9-3-17

I keep waking in a motel room. Billy is sleeping. After he arrived, we talked and watched *Shark Tank*. Now I watch him. My twin, as we keep saying. His pants are on the floor. His knife and keys are on the table. The parking lot lamp yellows his face. I say a silent prayer, not for my spirit guardians to show me their will, but to keep me safe and to let my heart be happy.

9-3-18

While Emily and I walk to the park, I tell her about how the other night, during one of my long walks, I had a strong feeling that I was going to run into Carl's friend Eric, and then I did. Between eclipses, with

9-4-16

Mercury retrograde, the veil is thin, the portal is open, and people return from the past. We're talking about this when Carl, grinning in his Volvo, drives through the intersection ahead of us. I'd say it was a mirage my mind made from pain, but Emily sees him too.

9-4-18   Back in therapy for the first time in more than a year, I tell my story all over again. When the therapist asks me whether I see, hear, or feel things that aren't really there, I don't want to answer. She presses, so I tell her, "Sometimes, when I'm going to sleep, I feel somebody's fingers in my hair." She writes it down. I am trying to tell her everything, starting with being raped in the middle of the night, but we run out of time. "You've experienced an incredible amount of trauma," she says. She doesn't know whether she can help me.

What if the problem is not the residual trauma from past men, but the fresh harm from those I keep in my life after they hurt me? I block Carl's number and his Instagram, an experiment.

9-9-17   A love spell candle burns to its end while I google Carl because I miss him and he didn't text me back. At the moment the flame turns to a column of smoke, I find a page about Karl Germain, a dead magician from Ohio. The same name, first and last, differing slightly in spelling but not in sound. In the black-and-white photos, the same slightness, the same loose curls of dark hair, the same hands trained to conjure things into existence and make them disappear.

I am tired of writing this and I want to exit. My thoughts are tangled. Ohio is a real place, while this book is the dreamer, written in dreams. Jung wrote, "The *imaginatio*, or the act of imagining, is thus a physical activity that can be fitted into the cycle of material changes, that brings these about and is brought about by them in its turn. In this way the alchemist related himself not only to the unconscious but directly to the very substance which he hoped to transform through the power of imagination."

The point of all these words was to change me— that is always my point with words, to get out from under something. It's not working.

9-11-18;
Jung, *Psychology and Alchemy*

I just want Carl to return my necklace. I bought the crystals two years ago when I was sad: one for protection, one for psychic ability, one for creativity. Since he won't respond to my texts about mailing it to me, I finally say he can do whatever he wants with it, can throw it in the trash even, and I'll mail his tapes back.

After I ship them, I walk aimlessly. On the redbrick sidewalk in front of the community college, a man stops me and holds out his arm. Dozens of necklaces are hanging from it, each with a crystal. He tells me I could buy some, so I choose an amethyst for healing and a rose quartz for my heart. We don't talk while he makes change until he says, "My name is Carl."

9-13-16

"Oh," I say. "My name is Elissa."

He looks at me as though he's thinking, *Why would you tell me that?* then says, "Don't forget you met me."

On the way home, I stop at the magic store and buy a black candle for a spell to banish Carl from inside me. It burns down into two lumps, shaped like my great-grandmother and her mother in the photo taped to the wall above my altar, a ratty printout of the photo in my parents' hallway. What do my grandmothers know about me? What do they want me to know about them?

9-14-18   Billy texts, *saw this on instagram and thought of you,* along with a screenshot:

Ask me a question about Tarot!

How do I know who my twin flame is?

That's not a Tarot Question! But I am sure a tarot reading may help you in determining if your partner is meant for you. When you meet your twin flame you will know because it is as if the stars have aligned, magic is in the air, and the chemistry on a molecular level between the two of you will be undeniable. It isn't lust, it isn't obsession, it isn't infatuation with one another. It's a deeper knowing. The soul is returning home.

I'm surprised to hear he thinks of me when he's on Instagram. I secretly watch his likes and follows. Hundreds and hundreds of tattooed, thick-hipped white women in thongs. I could never tell him. I'm supposed to be cool with this, not jealous like a child. My hair is falling out. I sleep only for an hour here and there. He's not telling me something, so I fear him. But the universe seems to be saying this is where I need to be, so I stay.

I'm in an office park across the lake to see a psychic named Todd. He knows all kinds of things: some he could look up, sure, but also some he couldn't, like that my grandpa could speak a bit of a blend of Eastern European languages common in the coal region. That's not exactly what Todd says—he says he's hearing a jumble of languages. He says I will find love in the springtime. He tells me to protect myself, because psychic attacks are coming. He wants me to be precise with my spells, because I am powerful and I am going to bring myself something I don't want.

9-21-16

I've been at Billy's house for three miserable days, mostly lying fully dressed in his bed. I'm his girlfriend now. He told me he saw someone make a heart eyes emoji and wanted to fight him, then asked if we could be exclusive. Everything was fine over texting; now I'm in his house and things are not fine. He had told me two dogs lived with him, but when I arrived and asked where they were, he said they actually live with his mother. What do I

9-21-18

really know about him? The Travelodge room, nobody's house, was another dimension, detached from reality.

We got naked, like we'd planned. Right away, he lost interest, dressed, and left the room. I've begun seeing images of scorpions everywhere: encased in resin on his mantel, in pendants in my Instagram feed. The internet says they live underground. The Egyptian scorpion deity Serket guards the dead, practices magic, and guards thresholds. Scorpion venom is wounding to prey, healing to the scorpion.

We fuck just once. It feels like nothing.

I feel more when I lie on the edge of the bed and press my body against the wall, desperate to reach for his neck, but he doesn't want us to touch. Paracelsus said, "The scorpion cures the scorpion." I would rather be a spider and climb out of here on silk spun from my body.

9-23-18   Transiting Jupiter conjuncts my natal Saturn for the third and final time this year. Billy drives me to the airport. He seems vexed at everything I say, so I look out the window and try to think of something better to talk about, but I can't say anything that doesn't make him mean. From the plane, I text to ask him whether he likes me anymore, and he says maybe he's not the one for me, if I'm going to keep needing all this reassurance. Is that what I need? I need to be touched, I know that much; I'm skin-starving after a week spent lying under the covers, watching him heart photo after photo of filtered phantasms I'll never resemble.

"Are you breaking up with me?" I ask, and because I can't see his face, I don't know what he's not telling me when he says, "No."

Hanif told me he was writing about *The Prestige*, and one of his poems is available online from *PoetryNow* today:

9-24-18; Hanif Abdurraqib, "It's Not Like Nikola Tesla Knew All of Those People Were Going to Die"

Few things are more dangerous than a man

who is capable of dividing himself into several
    men,
each of them with a unique river of desire

on their tongues.

Billy doesn't love me today, and didn't yesterday or the day before or, really, since the moment I stepped into his house and became real. He loves the future that never comes. We don't text or speak all day.

"Scorpion stings lead to paralysis and Serket's name describes this, as it means '(she who) tightens the throat,' however, Serket's name also can be read as meaning '(she who) causes the throat to breathe', and so, as well as being seen as stinging the unrighteous, Serket was seen as one who could cure scorpion stings and the effects of other venoms such as snakebite."

Wikipedia

9-25-18   I haven't heard from Billy and I'm afraid to text him. I have a body-shaking, breath-constricting panic attack while I drive to get my allergy shot. I realize I haven't taken the allergy pill that's supposed to prevent me from going into anaphylaxis again. No matter, I think. I'll let the universe decide whether I should be put out of my misery. If my throat closes, I will walk to my car and I will die.

The universe decides I have to stay, and so I stay.

10-3-17   Emily texts me that our friend who referred us to Todd the psychic now believes him to be a fake. She has no details and I don't need any. I was wrong about the world; there is nothing magic in it.

My mom texts me, too. Last week, our Fitbits recorded the same number of steps: 55,091.

10-5-18   Venus goes retrograde at 11 degrees Scorpio. Relationships will be reviewed, bonds tested; anything fragile will break. The Sabian Symbol for this degree is "A drowning man is being rescued."

10-12-17   Carl is coming through Ohio on tour. In June, he told me to come; in September, I texted him to ask whether he still wanted that, and a week later, he said, *sure*. So I'm in Cleveland, walking. His show is tomorrow. I want this visit to be our end.

I walk past a building painted with garish blocks of color, black and white stripes, and moon phases. It seems to be an art space, not yet open to the public. On the glass door, there's a Shel Silverstein poem:

> If you are a dreamer come in
> If you are a dreamer a wisher a liar
> A hoper a pray-er a magic-bean-buyer
> If you're a pretender come sit by my fire
> For we have some flax golden tales to spin
> Come in! Come in!

The door is locked.

It's been one week since I texted Billy a nude he never responded to. Tonight, on the phone call he agrees to every few days, he is depressed—I can't blame him, I can't get upset, I can't make a big deal—and he talks about moving to Ohio. While we talk, I watch via the Instagram Following tab as he likes a year's worth of a stranger's selfies. The internet says men cope like this. I shouldn't interfere. When we hang up, I open Twitter, where he's been having a conversation with some woman for the last half hour. The internet asks whether I love him or want to possess him. Let him look, the articles say. I fear something beyond loss. If I tell him I don't like this, what will he do?

10-12-18

Cleveland Public Library's special collections department includes a book about the magician Karl Germain. I spend hours with it, enchanted by the photos: the

10-13-17

magician as a teenager, holding a rabbit by its ears; the magician now a man, holding a card over a blindfolded lady's head; the magician watching a dim gray skeleton reach for the hand of a clock; the magician reaching for a translucent ghost lady in a white gown and veil. Describing trick after trick, biographer Stuart Cramer writes of a handkerchief color-change, "Here is real magic."

The magician's Great Vanishing Horse Illusion, a show finale, involved a white horse, a plain black stage, and black velvet curtains. A large cloth was thrown over the horse, and then the magician, with the aid of another, would remove it to show that the horse had vanished.

The spirit séance was a staple of the magician's show, and his most important tool was the spirit cabinet. The magician places a chair, bell, tambourine, and musical instrument in this big, man-height cabinet. The items become animated, knocking around inside the cabinet before escaping it. The magician goes into a trance. A vapor of a human figure emerges from the cabinet to touch the magician, then beckons for him to follow her inside. He does. He comes out. "Slowly I recover, snapping my fingers and opening my eyes, gaze at the audience, and then into the cabinet," he wrote. The illusion ends. The audience is left, according to the magician, depressed.

The magician said, "Conjuring is the only absolutely honest profession—a conjuror promises to deceive and does."

The band arrives later. Carl comes to the house I'm staying in, but he'd rather sit on the cold patio furniture in the yard stinking of rotting fruit than come inside. I tell him coming inside doesn't have to mean anything; we'll sit in the living room. He agrees, and when we sit on separate ends of the hard couch, I think about what a mistake I've made. It's still a mistake when we're sitting close together in the sunken middle of the green-room love seat and he tells me, "I've sort of been seeing someone." I tell him I know, I felt it, he can't hide anything from me. He says she takes so long to text him back that he wonders how she feels about him.

"I wonder what that feels like," I say.

He says, "Some relationships—when you see the person, you get right to the truth of things."

Carl is a kind of mentalist, building illusions that bend my thoughts. He knows what I want is a dissolution of the barrier between minds. But I don't believe in real magic anymore. I know it's all tricks.

He says things are hard. He hasn't been happy. He asks, "Did you ever cast a spell on me?"

If I like to watch his discomfort, does it mean I don't love him?

Onstage, he always gives the other musicians focused attention he rarely shows to anything offstage. I watch him closely. Every so often, he looks out at me, and I wonder whether maybe he is happy to see me.

Partway through the show, a couple of guys want to dance with me. I tell them no. They ask again, and then they're not asking, grabbing my arm and pulling. I yank my arm back and tell them no again, and they move away. When the show ends and the crowd begins to shift toward the doors, the men break against the flow and move toward me. I bolt across the room, down the stairs, and into the green room, where I hide while the band packs up. I tell

Carl what happened and he sits with me. When they're ready to go to their hotel, I expect Carl to leave with them, but he wants to stay with me.

We lie in my bed and I stroke his face. "I'm sorry I'm being weird," he says, and I realize he's trying to tell me that he doesn't want to touch, so I pull my hand back. He sleeps. I don't. I'm watching him and trying to figure out whether I love him. I need to know. He hurts my heart, but he would never hurt my body, which I can't take for granted. *I'm safe, I'm safe, I'm safe*, I remind myself all night while he sleeps.

10-14-17   They're going north and I'm going south. First, I'm going to the cemetery where the magician is buried. We've hugged goodbye. While I'm standing over the magician's buried body, Carl calls. He wants to know where I am, and I tell him I'm at a cemetery. "Is it . . . good?" he asks.

"I'm visiting the graves of a magician and his sister."

"Do you study this magician?"

"Sort of."

He asks if there's a jacket in my back seat. They're too far away to turn back, so he wants me to mail it to his house. I don't even have to think about it: I know, as soon as I hold the battered vinyl, that I'm going to push a few of my long hairs deep into the lining's gashes.

10-14-18   I send Billy a photo of myself standing sideways and flexing my glutes. I don't have a butt, but this is the best I can do. I tell him to please say something nice. *Dude your legs look hella good* is the reply. I tell him he can't treat me like this. He doesn't answer. Twitter says he's liked a tweet from @sosadtoday: *i liked you better when you were imaginary*.

I dream about Billy in a doorway, lit from behind like a prayer card Jesus. He dreams he's watching me walk through a door and look at him. Soon after we wake up in separate places, he sends me an article: "A scientific mission into the secret ocean lair of California's great white sharks has provided tantalizing clues into a vexing mystery—why the fearsome predators spend winter and spring in what has long appeared to be an empty void in the deep sea."
10-22-18

I get on a plane, and just like that, six hours later, I'm driving in the dark to his mom's house on a big parcel of scorched land, where we'll be staying for the week so we have more space. When I arrive, he hugs me, then kisses me on the cheek as an afterthought. I don't touch my hand to his heavy, unwashed hair, and I don't feel the bristles of his unshaven spots of face. He has filled the fridge with all the things he knows I like. It must have taken everything he had, I tell myself, and that is why he will have barely anything left for me when we sit on the couch and watch people on TV making dream houses.

While Billy goes to work, I spend the days alone with horses and a dog, uncomfortable in a reality I spent the
10-24-18

summer imagining, building the world in my mind image by image: dogs lazing on the covered porch, horses wandering up and down the pasture, dry yard landscaped without grass. Now, I sit on the porch, trying to write about magic, and the hot quiet feels eerie, like I'm in the opening scene of a Western, waiting at the ranch for the narrative menace to show up and take off its hat. He'd said the horses were his family's, but they belong to the neighbors, and he's calling them different names than he gave when he sent me their pictures this summer. Why would anybody lie about a horse?

In the texted photos, I couldn't hear the sounds of swarming hummingbirds in the pink bushes. I couldn't see beyond the fence, where the horses' tails swing in tandem and then don't. I couldn't feel the air turning from cool to scorching and back so fast it feels like a man. I tweet, *This morning I watched a long line of big vultures walk down a hill toward me, each one clambering over a metal gate. Happy Scorpio season.* I listen for the sounds of Billy coming back, even though it won't happen for hours. I am like a pet. Just wanting his touch. When Billy returns, he rubs the dog all over his ancient body, and the dog looks at me like he knows how much I want this love, but Billy doesn't have enough for me and the dogs and the Instagram women he will heart all night.

10-26-18   I wake up before him and walk outside. Across the field, a jackrabbit stands in the scorched gold grass, looking like an omen. When he wakes up, I tell him, but a jackrabbit is nothing to him.

Weeks ago, he asked if we could go to a corn maze, one of the world's largest. But once we're there, I can't see why he wanted to. He's sweaty and surly, not talking much. He's mad at someone and wants to fight him. He probably won't. Looking into the menacing rows of tall, secret-keeping corn, I can hardly tell a path from a wall. I let him walk ahead and make all the choices. I watch his long brown hair against his hard back, which I hope I will touch again someday. I can see nothing but high walls of corn, clear sky, and the vexed sun. The ground is hard-packed, useless dust. I feel like I'm in a movie, because how else could I be so far from my house, everything I recognize, anyone who loves me?

He kisses me goodbye lightly in the dark and says he'll see me in a month. I fly home crying. When I get home, I text that I've landed. He calls me to break up with me. He says he's a liar, a thief, and a cheat. "Did you cheat on me?" I ask, and he says, "No." I say I didn't think he did, but I'm lying. He says he needs time alone. He says he doesn't know what's going to happen—he won't rule out that we could be together again.

He wanted fantasy, maybe, his life turned into the autofiction he loves, the details changed a little for the sake of the story. But I write nonfiction. I want it real. And I want, to my constant detriment, to work other

10-27-18

people like I work an essay, conjuring up meaning where there was none.

11-5-18   Twitter says it's cuffing season. My yard is full of dead leaves. The air outside feels startled, like it didn't know the hot wetness was going to leave it, and it smells like other people's fires. Billy has never been in my house, but I think of him everywhere: at the kitchen counter, where I was standing when we first texted; at the bathroom mirror, where I took a photo meant to be a thirst trap for him; on the couch, where I sat and looked at our astrological synastry; in the bedroom, where I stood before the tall mirror and tried to bend my body into the shape I thought he wanted. But I have felt his spirit begin to vacate.

My mind still reaches for the signs I collected. Those uncanny synchronicities seemed to be telling me he was my perfect love. But maybe they were just pulling me into the suffering that would make me change.

11-6-18   C. G. JUNG FOUNDATION @cgjungny

"There are no fixed symbolic meanings . . . Every symbol has more than one meaning."
—Carl Gustav Jung
12:05 PM–6 Nov 2018

11-7-18   Months ago, I bought a ticket to Fleetwood Mac's Columbus show. It seemed like a moment that could close the circle: at the end of the documentary *Destiny Rules*, Stevie and Lindsey hold hands as they step onto a stage that, it turns out, was in Columbus, Ohio. Now Lindsey has been kicked out of the band, at Stevie's insistence, and she will perform with friends and associates who haven't, as far as I know, choked her. I have built up the event for months: maybe my book will end here as I am transformed by the conflation of the real world and the video worlds in which Stevie and Lindsey stare into each other onstage during "Silver Springs."

My seat is close, but not close enough that Stevie looks like anything but a distant, high-definition video image, moving below a massive screen that shows her close-up face and cloth-draped form. They've done this so many times. The moves are rote. Without surprise, the act doesn't feel real.

SEATTLE CRAIGSLIST > SEATTLE > PERSONALS >   11-11-12
MISSED CONNECTIONS

You were me from the future, on the bus, wearing a medical mask - w4w - 27 (Madison Park)

I was on the 11 bus to Madison Park. You were disembarking from the back door, wearing a beige wool cape and a medical mask. You had your hair pulled back and carried a book under your arm. I had long brown hair and the same glasses as you, the ones that Buddy Holly wore

a thousand years ago and hipsters wear now.
I was hung over. You looked just like me, but
older, and I know that you were me, from the
future, by how freaked out you looked to see
me. Please contact. I have some questions.

· Location: Madison Park
· it's NOT ok to contact this poster with services
  or other commercial interests

11-12-12   xxxxxxx@gmail.com via craigslist.org
Mon, Nov 12, 2012, 11:28 PM

I hope she responds to you, or you run into
each other again.
I would take the same bus, at the same
time, on the same day for a while.
Or again next month on the same day and
time.

11-13-10   I wake up in the middle of the night with Henry's fingers pinching my nose, his palm over my mouth, and
his eyes like twin occulted suns staring down at my
smothered face. He releases me, and I go to the guest
room to sleep, but I can't. So I leave. I don't remember
the next week. The next four years.

11-14-18   The *Seattle Times* reports today, "Urban Indian Health
Institute identified 506 cases in cities across the country

of missing or murdered Native American women and girls. Seattle had the most cases." On Twitter, Native women say if they go missing, they want their loved ones to assume they've been murdered, because they wouldn't disappear on their own. I don't know whether I would. There's nothing I do on my own. The men are with me forever.

I'm so bored I could die, like a lady once said on *Sex and the City* before falling to her death, so I reinstall Tinder. I match with a magician who wants to meet at a bar called Jack's, where the walls are covered in mirrored beer signs adorned with horses or women. The magician smells like he's stamped out cigarettes on the back of his tongue. He shows me a card trick and keeps finding ways to bring up Transcendental Meditation. I agree to go to his house to "watch TV" because I'm so bored I could die. I want another trick. I want to feel wonder, but I feel nothing: not a desire butterfly uncocooning, not the creep of terror spreading in my gut, just the non-feeling of a calcified soul that can't sense. He turns the heat up high and tells me I can take off my coat, but I'm chilled to the bone. Every time he gets up and returns to the couch, he sits closer to my pressed-together legs. What can we talk about? I need to keep him talking so he won't put his mouth on mine in the silence. I talk about the *Twin Peaks* art on his wall, and the *Twin Peaks* books on his shelf, and he explains the show to me. He walks away

11-16-18

to pour another drink when I tell him I'm trying to play with time like David Lynch did in *The Return*, and to play with echoed imagery like he did in the first two seasons, except I'm doing it in a book, and I know I'll never really be allowed to because I'm not a man.

The magician wants to talk about Fleetwood Mac and how they're nothing without Lindsey, who, he agrees, is "an asshole" (I said "an abuser"), but "you've gotta separate the artist from the art." He has Lindsey's albums on vinyl. He has a charred sage bundle in an ashtray. He has a bedroom decorated like the Black Lodge, he tells me, and when he lights a stick of palo santo and waves it between me and the TV playing *Beavis and Butt-Head*, I tell him I'm tired and I'm going home. He doesn't protest. He, or someone else hiding behind a caller ID block, prank calls me later, making the slapping skin-on-skin sounds of hard sex. The magician texts ten minutes later, *Hope you had fun.*

11-19-18 *Tweet, source now unknown, image saved to iPhone photos:*

> Q: What do David Lynch & your ex have in common?

> A: Neither of them owe you closure.

12:34 PM   ME: hey
12:40 PM   HENRY: hey
12:41 PM   ME: how are you doing?
           HENRY: so so
           ME: did you get to go snowboarding
           this weekend?
12:42 PM   HENRY: on satruday
           ME: cool
           ME: is something wrong?
12:43 PM   HENRY: not really
           ME: ah
12:44 PM   ME: i kind of feel like that too
12:45 PM   ME: do you want to hang out later?
           HENRY: no
           ME: oh . . .
           ME: i hope i didn't do anything . . .
12:46 PM   HENRY: ok
12:47 PM   ME: did i? i don't want to be a pest
           about it but i'd like to know if i upset
           you
12:48 PM   HENRY: yes, I am upset with you
           ME: why?
12:49 PM   HENRY: we were supposed to hang
           out, you don't show up, and then
           don't call me for a week
12:50 PM   ME: what? when were we supposed
           to hang out? the last time i talked to

you, you said you were busy doing homework and were behind on it, so i figured i'd leave you alone till you were free

HENRY: last Sunday

12:51 PM   ME: i feel like i'm losing my mind . . . what was happening last sunday?

12:52 PM   ME: i saw you last sunday, i slept over saturday night

12:56 PM   HENRY: then you left

HENRY: and said you were coming back later

12:58 PM   ME: i don't remember saying that at all . . . but i barely remember leaving . . . i remember being embarassed for snoring so loud and going to sleep in the other room . . . i'm really sorry, i just don't even remember saying that i'd be back later

12:59 PM   HENRY: ok

1:02 PM   ME: and like i said, i didn't call you because you said you were behind on homework, and then fri/sat i was at hugo house and then a gala. again, i'm really sorry, i didn't mean to ditch you on sunday, i wish you'd have called to see when i was coming over. i hope you'll forgive me because i really absolutely did not mean to ditch you and then space for a week. all week i wanted to see you. so that's all, i'm sorry.

1:04 PM   HENRY: whatever

HENRY: that is just the tip of the iceberg anyways

1:05 PM   ME: why? what's the rest?

1:08 PM   HENRY: basically you've become exteremly self
absorbed and hypocrictal over the last 3 months
ME: i know
HENRY: and not all the pleasent to deal with
ME: i know
ME: what am i hypocritcal about?
HENRY: eating and exercising
1:09 PM   ME: i just ask you about it because when you're
paleo and going to crossfit i look up to you
ME: if that's what you mean
1:10 PM   ME: i'm not being judgmental at all, i'm just
curious
HENRY: no
HENRY: i mean
HENRY: all you say is you want to eat good food
HENRY: then all you do is eat cupcakes
HENRY: and then complain about it
1:11 PM   ME: i've been primal for 3 days . . . it's not much
but i'm trying to take it one day at a time
HENRY: cool
1:14 PM   ME: while you were in NY i had the worst
mood episode ive had in a long time. and it
was convenient timing because i didn't want
you to have to see it. but i'm still not completely
right and i'm having a really hard time getting
healthy while i'm still depressed. i know it's
not good for you to be around me when i'm
depressed. but i'm working on getting better.
actually doing stuff to try to get stable again. i

can't just crawl into a hole for months while i do it. i'm sure i'm not fun to be around and i'm really sorry for that. and i appreciate that you put up with me.

1:16 PM HENRY: ok

1:21 PM ME: i think i'd be a lot easier to deal with if i weren't trying to pretend i'm totally ok all the time, but i feel like that's what i have to do

1:22 PM HENRY: i guess

1:23 PM HENRY: you can't keep getting a free pass beacuse you are in a bad mood
HENRY: doesn't work that way
ME: i know

1:24 PM ME: but i feel like things might be better if i felt like i didn't have to attempt to hide it from you

1:25 PM ME: i feel completely alone in trying to get better and it's not working

1:26 PM HENRY: so you want to break up?
ME: not at all

1:27 PM ME: i would really like to feel better about telling you when i am not doing well. since i'm bad at hiding it anyway.
HENRY: that is pretty much what you just said
ME: no it's not

1:28 PM ME: what i mean is my attempts to get better aren't working
ME: i want to be with you and i want to be better to you and i want to get my moods straight for the long term

376

1:29 PM   ME: if we could find a way for me to talk to you about my moods when they're not good, without making me an extra burden to you, that would help me a lot

HENRY: when have I ever said you cannot talk to me about it?

HENRY: I am confused now

ME: you havent

ME: ok

1:30 PM   ME: my reasoning is often that i'm not feeling well, but i don't want to bother you about it, so i try to pretend that everything's fine, and then i end up being way more difficult to be around than if i'd just been honest

1:31 PM   ME: i know that what you have a hard time with is the moods themselves, not me talking about them, but i guess when i'm feeling bad i convince myself i should try to hide it altogether

1:33 PM   HENRY: sounds like I am bringing you down then

ME: you aren't

ME: i'm down as it is

HENRY: I don't see how not

1:34 PM   ME: it's not you though, i know it's in my head, i just think i might have an easier time getting out of this if i could just get over my fear of talking to you about it. you aren't bringing me down because without you there'd be no one

1:36 PM   HENRY: ok

1:40 PM   ME: i'm sorry that we keep having this conversation. i'll let you go now, i don't have anything else to say right now. i hope i can see you soon.

1:41 PM   HENRY: ok

11-24-18   RICHARD SIKEN BOT @sikenpoems

We have been very brave, we have wanted to
    know
the worst, wanted the curtain to be lifted from
    our eyes.
This dream going on with all of us in it.
5:17 AM–24 Nov 2018

11-25-18   I am thirty-four years old today and I am still alive and Jupiter, auspiciously, conjuncts my natal sun, which means I should have the best year of my life. My friends come to dinner with me at a place called the Northstar, which has nothing to do with the North Star I used to go to in Seattle. After dinner, at karaoke at Ace of Cups, I sing "Total Eclipse of the Heart" on a stage newly masquerading as the Black Lodge, with black and white chevron paint and a red curtain. During my song, everyone watches closely. We sing together. I inhale their delight and exhale my old dread. In the news today, a man who survived a shark attack to his head and neck says he's more grateful than ever: "It reminds me that God's in control. That you can't

plan for something like this. It's given me a new perspective on how I want to live my life."

Carl wants to meet for coffee. He looks like a corpse, his   11-27-16
hair and skin graying. Even ghosts have memories; he
does not. He's like the body the ghost no longer needs.
I do not miss him, finally. He says if there's anything I
need to say to him, I should say it. "You destroyed my
heart," I say. "And then I became a powerful witch."

KENYON REVIEW @kenyonreview   11-28-18

> "If the doors of perception were cleansed every-
> thing would appear to man as it is, infinite."
>
> Happy birthday to Romantic icon William
> Blake! #literarybirthdays
>   5:30 AM–28 Nov 2018

I keep my memories like figurines shut in a cabinet.   12-3-18
New additions: horses chattering, hummingbirds
fighting, a dog watching for his person while I listened
to passing cars, unable to recognize the one I wanted
coming in. In the parking lot of Billy's work building,
I saw an emerald-green frog flattened and bloodied.
Down the house's long driveway, checking the mail one
night when I knew he didn't want me around, we saw
a spider too large not to be auspicious. Of what, I don't
know, because a spider has more than one meaning.

Maybe the images are more like cards in an oracle deck. What is going to happen? In the news today, a boy bitten by a usually harmless nurse shark is recovering, and he says, "I think I will swim with sharks again."

Staniforth,
Here Is Real
Magic
"I can lead an audience down the hall to the doorway and open it for them, but the final step from 'trick' to 'magic' comes from them . . . You don't want them searching externally for a solution—you want them to believe in their bones that there isn't a solution, that it was magic they saw, and you want this conviction to resonate inside, deeper and deeper, so in the end the vanishing coin was nothing but a vessel for this inward experience of wonder, which was the real goal when you asked to borrow a quarter in the first place."

Karl Germain,
quoted by Stuart
Cramer, Germain
the Wizard and
His Legerdemain
"A scheme of deception may be used in simplicity as a puzzling trick, or may be elaborated by patter and circumstances into a fine magical effect, or so veiled in an atmosphere of the pseudo-supernatural as to become a veritable miracle."

12-15-17
Carl told me it would be good to see me while I'm in Seattle. Whatever. A few days ago, we met up at the bar with the Black Lodge back room, and when I told him about my plans to take a look at the house in Everett that was the filming location for Laura's house in *Fire Walk with Me* and *Twin Peaks: The Return*, he asked to come.

Now that he's in my huge rental SUV, he's not comfortable with the number of live and studio versions of "Still Loving You" by Scorpions on my playlist, but I frankly do not care. I feel that if I can't stop loving him, I can at least make him feel uncomfortable for as long as he keeps doing the same to me.

It's one of those indifferent Seattle nights—the air can't be bothered to smell like anything, the summer honey sun is so long gone it may be a misremembering, and even mist doesn't feel like coming through. But as soon as we turn off the main road and head uphill toward Possession Sound, climbing closer to Laura's house, torrential rains pour down. We park and run to the sidewalk in front of the house. There's a Christmas tree lit in the front room, lights on upstairs. Something doesn't feel right: I thought it would feel different, like something clicking, this house from inside the TV suddenly in my real world, but I feel nothing. Maybe I'm inside the TV now. We take photos with the house behind us and a photo of the house alone. On my phone, the photo looks like the establishing shots. I don't like what I am coming to understand: sometimes, it's not the real but the imagined that unlocks answers that save us.

Carl sees a hand move a curtain in an upstairs window. I run back to the car; he walks.

As soon as we return to the main road, the rain stops.

Back in Seattle, we go to karaoke at the Baranof. He sings a pretty good "In the Air Tonight" and I don't tell him so, but I'm delighted, because now I get to end my book with an ending that circles back to the beginning, and I don't need anything else to happen to me. I sing "Total Eclipse of the Heart" to him. He takes out his phone and stares down into it.

Across the street at the North Star, his School of Rock friends are gathering to send off someone who quit. We sit in a booth in the corner, and it's as though our thighs are magnetized, two poles the same, repelling each other. His friend asks him to sing backup on her "Total Eclipse of the Heart." He doesn't know the words.

Twin Peaks: The Return — In the final scene, Cooper has brought Laura—or someone who looks like Laura, but says she is not Laura—up to Twin Peaks from Odessa, Texas, where she's working as a waitress and has a man's dead body in her living room.

The last two episodes aren't easy. Answers don't come clearly or neatly; the viewer has to work to piece them together, but there's no key. Cooper once said something about breaking codes to find solutions. According to forum users at welcometotwinpeaks.com, the symbol of Odessa is a jackrabbit. In an earlier episode, Jack Rabbit's Palace is introduced as an entry point to the White Lodge, just as Glastonbury Grove allows entry to the Black Lodge. It's a place where a vortex can spin in the sky, opening a portal.

A lot has happened off-screen; Reddit has guessed that Laura has been hidden in some other timeline. Cooper, by traveling through the secret door in the hotel basement, and then by having a rote fuck with Diane in the motel, has unlocked something and can now find Laura.

Cooper looks for her at the diner, then finds her at her house. She doesn't know herself to be Laura, and she doesn't know Cooper, but, like I said, there's a body, and, interested in distancing herself from it, she agrees to go with Cooper on some journey.

The long-but-not-long drive seems to bend time and transport the characters into a reality that is ours, not theirs. The whimsy is gone. They get gas not at the familiar Big Ed's Gas Farm, but at a Valero.

When they arrive at Laura's old house, they park and cautiously approach. Her eyes are open wide. She's watching, taking it all in. Cooper knocks on the door and a woman answers—not Laura's mother, but a woman who says her name is Alice Tremond. She's played by Mary Reber, the woman who, in reality, owns the house and lives there.

Laura's mother isn't there. The woman closes the door. Slowly, Cooper and Laura turn back to the street and walk away. Watching his back, we don't need to see his face to know he's figuring out his next move, but once they reach the street, the camera moves, they turn, and we can see Cooper thinking—trying, maybe, to retrace his steps, track the shifting of time. They both look at the upstairs windows. He looks down and takes a few steps, running through something in his head. "What year is this?" he says. There's something going on in Laura's mind, but she doesn't say anything, blinking hard to shut and open her wide eyes.

Laura! Her mother's distant voice comes from inside the house, or somewhere. Laura's eyes are already open wide when she screams. The house's lights shut off.

12-15-18   Ace of Cups is still decorated like the Black Lodge, but now there are Christmas decorations, too, and when I arrive, the band onstage is playing a song from *Rudolph the Red-Nosed Reindeer*:

> There's always tomorrow
> For dreams to come true
> Tomorrow is not far . . . a . . . way.

I worry about seeing the magician prank caller, because he told me he spends a lot of time here. But my smiling friends feel like a house around me. For a second, I think I do see the magician, but it's just someone who looks like him. My glasses are off, my contact lenses are in, and my hair is tied up high in a ponytail as I try to become unrecognizable. In the bathroom mirror, I see it: the promise that I can make a new self inside this long-remembering body that flinches as it stores twitching fear. I am all new cells since Henry smothered me. I am twice new since I was first raped. In the mirror, I haven't even aged, as though not a minute has passed.

12-20-18   ILYA KAMINSKY @ilya_poet

> "You might as well answer the door, my child,
> the truth is furiously knocking."—Lucille Clifton
> 12:26 PM–20 Dec 2018

The moon is full. I draw tarot cards for the first time in ages. *What is now complete*: ACE OF CUPS reversed. Withholding emotions for fear of being hurt—done. I thought the way forward was to become vulnerable and feel everything. But I like this better: being safe at home alone, enclosing myself in walls that are mine. I have not yet found another person to dissolve into, but I made my spirit bigger. Now I keep the fear close. Fear and love are not, as they say, opposites: fear is one kind of love in a violent place, keeping my spirit from getting eaten. It will cocoon me forever. *12-23-18*

ANDY: This is important, that cave painting in the office, I finally figured it out. *Twin Peaks*

COOPER: What's that?

ANDY: I knew I'd seen it someplace before. I know where it's telling us to go, it's not a puzzle at all. It's a map.

While I'm driving from Jersey back to Ohio, traffic slows nearly to a stop a few miles beyond the bridge over the Delaware River. Thousands of snow geese cover the hill to my right. They move together and apart. This seems like an omen, but I'm driving, so I can't ask the internet. I stop at Cabela's in West Virginia to visit some animals I like. The fish tank is still there. The taxidermy bear is still there. Everything is still there, really, but this time, *12-26-18*

I notice the jackrabbit against the wall, asking me to decipher its dead-eyed stare.

Twin Peaks, Log Lady intros

LOG LADY: So now the sadness comes. The revelation. There is a depression after an answer is given. It was almost fun not knowing. Yes, now we know. At least we know what we sought in the beginning. But there is still the question, why? And this question will go on and on until the final answer comes. Then the knowing is so full there is no room for questions.

12-28-18

I do not like this date. The man says he can get people to tell him things they normally wouldn't tell anyone. I pity him. I'll tell anyone anything. Maybe I'm trying to make them think they've gotten close to me. He says he likes dating lots of women because it feels taboo to be let into private spaces. Buddy, even *I* don't know my secret parts. There's no question you could ask that could make me give that up. He asks to make out in my car. I decline.

At home, I set up my new PlayStation, bought so I can find a way to relax and check out from the world. I bought two games; the first I try is *Friday the 13th*. In single-player mode, I can only play as Jason, even though I identify more with the campers. I barely kill anybody. Instead I wander. It's always night in this game. It's always summer. The people who made the game got the place exactly right: these could be the woods I grew up in, with saturated air, the roar of nocturnal insects, leaves veiling the sky, lake just beyond view. As I navigate my Jason from cabin to cabin, fumbling in the dark world, I begin to feel New Jersey summer, with its indescribable smell of warm microbial life flooding my cold, drafty living room. On my couch, it becomes another high school summer night, and all my crushes are miles away, all my plans years away, so I am looking into a screen and asking to be taken somewhere else.

Laura and Dale are in the lodge, still. They stare at each other, silent. Finally, in backward-speak, Laura says, "You can go out now."

Twin Peaks: The Return

In 2012, Melania Trump tweeted out a photo of a beluga whale with the text, *What is she thinking?* and even though there's no edit function, that tweet now has an image of a giraffe instead. Today, Twitter wonders about it. Twitter is saying goodbye to the whole year and getting ready to start over. A few minutes after noon, the Jung Foundation tweets a Jung quote: "Psychological truths are not metaphysical insights; they are habitual modes of thinking, feeling, and behaving which experience has proved appropriate and useful." A few minutes before midnight, while we are playing board games, my friend tells me the big bang might have made two universes, one a mirror of the other. In the other universe, time moves backward. I don't understand. Before I can make sense of backward, I need to figure out forward.

12-31-18

I'm typing this and the statements are undoing themselves. I have, of course, moved forward, although maybe also side to side, and up and down. What are all the items on the book-resolution checklist? Am I ready to go out now? I'll check later. Tonight, I'm losing at Monopoly and drinking nonalcoholic champagne. I'm just fine in Ohio, with no resolutions, no plans, nothing on my mind but cards and dice. I've got nothing for you. The year ends. I exit the timeline.

IN HIM WE HAVE REDEMPTION THROUGH HIS BLOOD

There will be signs in the sun, the moon, and the stars, and on earth nations will be in dismay, perplexed by the roaring of the sea and the waves. People will die of fright in anticipation of what is coming upon the world, for the powers of the heavens will be shaken. And then they will see the Son of Man coming in a cloud with power and great glory. But when these signs begin to happen, stand erect and raise your heads because your redemption is at hand.

—Luke 21:25–28

tcii'pɢam ɢanihimi'm' ɢuc-DꜪDi•nihω•'Du. anDω•'ʙi'.
    la'u'mDꜪ' DꜪni'ω•'Diha•t
ɢuc-anDω•'ʙi'. DꜪni'ni'cna, "SDω• ´-tcinDiDa•'tcit-wi•'.
    tcinDih ω•'Duʙutswu la'u'-
ma' '-tcꜪntcumi'nω•-yu' tcinDiDa•'tcit-wi•."

Long ago when the people saw the (new) moon then they spoke to the moon. They said to it, "We are still (alive) here yet. We see you now that you have come out again, (and) we are still (alive) here yet."

—John B. Hudson, as told to Melville Jacobs,
Kalapuya Texts

WHEN THE WORLD TURNED OVER into the new year, I departed from my festive friends and took to the couch in the house I still haven't furnished the echoes from. My friend Hanif has been tweeting about *Red Dead Redemption 2*, and he told me its world includes a magic show. My brother, Nate, said there's a reservation. This sounded like research. I bought a PlayStation. Since I last played console games, someone figured out how to make them real. Except when you see the faces. They give the falseness away because that's what faces do.

You play as this guy Arthur, an outlaw in a gang led by this guy Dutch. The year is 1899. Intro text says the West is mostly tamed, outlaws hunted. This gang just botched a job, and they're trying to get enough money to disappear into the West, even though the West is where they were undone.

The landscape is familiar and the US history is accurate enough, but the names and shapes of the five states are fake. That hardly matters. Borders are the flesh wounds of empire. On the map they look like stitches on a belly.

I spend nights on my imaginary horse, galloping for so long it feels like this is the real world and the one I'm avoiding is the fake one. Racing up snowy hills past near-black evergreen boughs, or easing up a crag from a green valley, I see my past more clearly than I remember it. A snow-coated graveyard in a Washington coal mining town, the mountain-foot settlement where the *Twin Peaks* diner sells real pie, the shining lake I saw on my last drive across Snoqualmie Pass—forcing them to stay clear was too painful after I chose to leave the West. Rustling snow off boughs while my old hands keep a controller well-wrangled and a horse on a path, I see a world more real than a movie, and movies always seem more real than my life.

I play for days. When I remember Twitter exists, I check on it, and it's glad to see me, has something to tell me, lines by Carolyn Forché: "The heart is the toughest part of the body. / Tenderness is in the hands." Mine become sore from the hours. The heart in my real body is resting. The heart in my satchel was carved from a wolf that nearly killed me. The game told me to collect perfect pelts from three jackrabbits, but I have no time. I cook the wolf. I become so thin I'm warned that this cannot continue.

The game's plodding pace forces endurance. I wash my limbs, ride my horse, chop wood. I walk the land, and my controller's rumbling tells me there's sage under my feet. I watch the other outlaws get wasted while I press R2 to raise my beer to my mouth. I am freed from the burden of narrative, allowed to waste my hours looking at birds, opening drawers, and greeting strangers who have nothing to say. This is what I came here for. And yet I don't want it. There are so many paid ladies to bathe me, so many wild horses to break, but I am skipping the sidetracking delights because I want to know what's going to happen.

I pass days and nights following Dutch's orders to rob and swindle the rich. We just need some money, he keeps saying. I'll do whatever he wants. I am happier than I have ever been, lone body collapsed on this couch, mind collapsed into someone else's make-believe land. This is the first time I've played a game and haven't had to suspend disbelief. Instead, I have to suspend my belief in its world when I step away and remember my flesh body needs food and my flesh friends need care. I haven't felt wonder lately, not for months, and I'm embarrassed by my enchanted obsession with this fake life.

After many hours on the couch, I find the magic show. The game invites me to sit and watch. What better way to set the tone for a year in which I intend to finish the job of divorcing myself from reality? The magician is going to catch a bullet between his teeth. A Reddit user wrote, "That show was a genuine experience for me. I booed him throughout his show. When he asked for a volunteer I went straight up with a smug smile on my face. Then I shot him . . . And he cought the damn bullet. My jaw dropped." I'm trying to remember how the bullet trick was explained in *The Prestige*. In *Red Dead*, the explanation from the magician Benjamin Lazarus is that death is only an illusion. I can do nothing with my controller but leave or react, cheer or boo, so I wait in this wonderland, not yet ready to accept the rational world and its mystery-erasing explanations.

I get good at killing. It soothes me to take out the bad men. Anyway, death is an illusion. Die in a mission and restart a million times. The outlaws talk of two kinds of killers: the ones who do it desperate and the ones who like the blood. They'd make you think that evil and need have the same means and ends. Over and over and over, I careen down hills after bad men, foolish men, brave men, flawed men who are going to change by the end of all this. I shoot a man in the hand to save him. A man shoots my horse and I cry—I, Elissa, cry—but then I find a horse

I like better because I saw her kick her man in the head and drop him. I tell an outlaw I'm not married because no one would have me. I rescue a lying magician—another one, not the one from the theater. I chase after yet another magician, who disappears in clouds of smoke before turning up holding a jackrabbit. I blow up a bridge. I meet a Tesla-type guy. I get pretty good at a game called *five finger fillet*, stabbing a knife into a table between spread fingers. I help out a circus master, keeper of farm animals costumed as zoo beasts, who tells me, "No one will pay for the truth. They will only pay for deception. The allure of the stage, dreams and reality . . . It's the difference between prose and poetry, it's alchemy. We're selling dreams, dear boy!"

In real life, I have given up spells. I am tired of trying to control this life. If people could make this game, an entire world of shops and garbage and roots and moonbeam mists, then I, person, must have more power of design than I know: maybe I did make the whole thing up, the thing about there being any cosmic plan. Slumped here, unmagicked by loss of hope, I wonder whether what feels mystical is just unadulterated reality, allowed to gleam with the alcohol haze removed. Maybe it's not synchronicity so much as it is sobriety and its unrelenting readiness to attention. I never check out, and the more I notice, the more my brain makes patterns so this mean existence might make sense. And yet I feel something following me. The synchronicities build.

I help a woman because if I don't, she says she'll be shipped off to live "somewhere awful, like . . . Ohio." Her beloved calls her a "woman from the future," says, "She's like tomorrow, if tomorrow turns out fine." It won't, actually. Tomorrow Dutch bashes his head and sees triple. Tomorrow he kills a woman for nothing and I ask if he'll strangle me too. Tomorrow men with machetes pour out of a cave where they keep a woman in a cage. Tomorrow I run through a coal mine like those where my real-life ancestors inhaled anthracite dust until their lungs were more black water than breath. Tomorrow we ride to die together, believing that's what it takes to be free. Tomorrow Dutch leads me to my death over and over. He says we're going to make a lot of smoke and then we're going to disappear. "*Real*," he says when his plans are questioned, when he's told his perception might be off. "Oh, how I detest that word. So devoid of imagination."

What is real is that my wrists and left elbow are killing me. My hands might harden into claws around my controller. Outside the video game I agree to pay eighty-six dollars a month for parking at work; inside the video game I'm rewarded for being nice to a horse. Outside, I am in Ohio, which is not awful. It's just real. Ohio is where I visited the Serpent Mound the game tries to replicate with the same name. That day, I was so listless with sweat and dread I could think of nothing to do but drive, which is not so different from Arthur's riding. In the game and in life, there is a tower to climb to see the effigy coil from above. In life but not in the game, the curves align with celestial bodies. In the game but not in life, there is a treasure map in a hole in the middle, there to be taken, so I do.

I don't want to go to bed; I want to be an outlaw. I forgot all about the planets, didn't even realize a solar eclipse came and went. The only moon I've seen in days shines on my blood-soaked shoulders while I ride. I am supposed to be relaxing so my life doesn't kill me, but I'm playing with urgency because

I have a feeling the ending will turn something like a key. But maybe I just can't relax. I can't shake the need to task myself with the work of controlling destiny; it's like Dutch says, "There simply isn't a reality in which we do nothing and get everything."

Everyone says to give it time. This is my training ground for patience. Time is what I feel when I'm on the horse, riding from town to town, looking for the end. The sun moves through the sky while I move across the land. I would like a portal. Eventually, I will get one, a map that will transport me to any place I've been before, but first I must put in my time on the paths, taking myself from point to point.

I've been playing for days when I get to the reservation. I like the Indians. I like their Indian wisdom. I like how Rains Fall, the chief, says things like, "See the wolves over there feasting on that horse? Brutality and beauty are both all around us, yet so often we're unable to see past our own grievances." I like that Arthur knows this situation is more complex than the white outlaws can understand and sees their intervention for what it is: interference. Most of all, I like riding to the fort where Rains Fall's son Eagle Flies is being held by the US Army to be hanged for treason, and I like breaking him out of his cell, and I like escaping through river rapids that remind me of the Cascades of the Columbia from the *Oregon Trail II* game, which remind me of the Cascades of the Columbia that broke through what my real ancestors knew as the Bridge of the Gods. Swimming away from weapons of the government that has always wanted to kill us—us, me, my family, my ancestors—I feel I'm saving Tumulth, held at Fort Vancouver before his hanging. Is it a spoiler to say it doesn't matter, a white man can't save Eagle Flies, only give him brief reprieve before he has to die? Anyway, saving him doesn't change the real-life timeline. My ancestor was still hanged.

Along a different river, animals show up mangy. Bewitched villagers say demons come in darkness. The water pools orange—from the mine, it turns out. Nobody says *sulfur creek*, but I know. The demons are dogs. The possession is slow poisoning. The mine rots the land, and even in this fantasy, nothing can be done. The mission ends when I find the source and make a capitalist swindler drink the water. Nothing heals the villagers because knowing the problem doesn't fix it. The mine never closes, the water never clears, and still I have inherited something I can't understand.

I don't want to go outside with these feelings: I think about Dutch when he's not around. By that I guess I mean I think about an imaginary man in a video game when I'm not playing it. This began when we robbed a train station and the frame lingered on Dutch, masked up with his red bandanna covering half his face, his gun drawn, all of which, unfortunately, I found incredibly hot. Maybe I only want a dangerous man. Maybe it's just that these conjured men are the only people I've seen in days. Certainly, Dutch wants a mess and I love him. A nature photographer says, "This is America, after all. We hold a love for killers that borders on macabre. Loving killers is part of our makeup."

For the first time in memory, I do not have a man in my romantic sights. What does a real man have that an imaginary one doesn't? There may be a good answer to consider, but right now, I have to rob this train. Dutch yells at me to have some goddamn faith. He has a plan and I need to trust him. He says, "We need to move towards a conclusion. Now." I think he says something about how it all comes down to the fact that we outlaws love each other, but I don't think to write it down, so maybe I just wanted to hear it.

I have to leave the house and go to therapy, so I explain the entire plot of the game to my therapist, and yet we come no closer to understanding why I'm this way. I tell her about Dutch. How I became attracted to the fake man when he masked up for that robbery. It takes me considerable nerve to say so, but it seems like the key to understanding my whole life. She only says, "So you like the bad boys," and when she puts it that way, it almost seems like what I want might not kill me. So I go back to my house-cave and talk to no real men until I can resolve these competing desires in me: to be loved by a dangerous man and to live.

Every man in this game could lead a woman to her death if he hasn't already. Some of the women look like me. Arthur's ex writes him a letter and says, "I see clearly that your world is not one from which one can escape." I begin to dream about Billy and his knife and his lies. My men never change, only I do when they leave me, but Arthur becomes a new man. A nun suggests, "Do a loving act," and he does. I can't figure out which character I am because I'm most of them, and so are my lost loves. I pause the game to cry because I don't know a loving act when I see it, could feel nothing but scorn for the mercy of their disappearances.

I ride my horse through lands that look just like Billy's mother's ranch, where I spent those days alone, patting the horses, studying the creep of a line of vultures down the sun-hot hill, watching the jackrabbit stand still in the field at dawn and wondering what it was going to mean. I like the game better. I like the meaning already made. I like how Arthur teaches a widow to skin a jackrabbit and says, "Just hold the legs tight and pull the skin away quickly. Should come right off," and like magic, it does. I like to collect pretend carcasses instead of spending all my time having realizations. I would rather die and restart missions a thousand times than keep orchestrating the death of part of my soul so I can transform and reset myself.

I'm racing through the narrative, trying to choke the meaning out of it. "It is mutually beneficial to draw attention to one problem and a veil over another," Dutch says, and isn't that a message? "We are dreamers in an ever duller world of facts," he says, and isn't that one too? A video game, what is it but a dream, and who is the dreamer? I am studying the fit of his brocade vest. The hinge of his hips. His anthracite eyes. My soot-souled king on a white horse grows cold. I am hurting—me, Elissa, I am hurting—when he shows he doesn't love me like he said. One last job, he says. One last big score. One paradise we will reach at the end of all this. I keep noticing the way Dutch won't look his woman in the eye, and I hear them in their tent at night, him asking what she wants from him, her saying she just wants some affection, just wants to be touched. Dutch van der Linde is no less real than any man I've ever loved. My long line of difficulties. My huckster beloveds.

In the swamp, in an empty house fit for a séance, a painting of a strange top-hatted man completes itself. Messages on the walls are hardly readable in the candlelight: THE MOON WILL SHINE ON IN THE DARKNESS. THE WATER IS BLACK WITH VENOM. HIS FINAL TOLL WILL SOUND MY GREATEST COMING. I GAVE EVERYTHING FOR ART AND I LEARNED TOO MUCH AND NOTHING AT ALL. I hear that when every other game task is done, the strange man's features will come into focus and he will appear behind me in the mirror. But now it's just me, this dark little house, these paintings of animals, this man without a face.

I begin sleeping through the night. I dream stories about men I used to think I understood. I read trauma rewires the brain. They say the same about video games. My brain is like an old Nintendo console, and I'm blowing on it hard and shoving it back in the slot. I want to make a mess of what's in my head, pull it all apart and start over.

Maybe I will spend the rest of my days in this world, starting and ending the game over and over. Maybe I will resolve America, which Dutch says is an apathy maker and Rains Fall says is a thing we cannot endure but must.

Spoiler alert: at the end we are changed. We feel foolish or sad. Any narrative is a magic trick: the unfolding happens where you're not looking. I wanted this narrative—this one, this story, this riddle, this experiment, this trick, this device—to teach me to love right, but all I know is that I'm not sure I can love a man who wouldn't let me die. And maybe that means I can't love a man if I want to live.

I have to keep cycling through the game's end and beginning over and over until I've beaten something. "We will disappear," Dutch said. "Be reborn." I have to lie under my weighted blanket, controller resting on my belly, until I learn to give up my strangulation hold on the narrative for just a little while. Living inside narratives means becoming an insight machine, and I am tired of *realizing*—that word is a lie. Conjuring up epiphanies doesn't make anything real. Mostly, realizing is how I lie. I met a stranger on the side of the road who told me, "You keep hidden all that matters, sir, maybe even from yourself." This is where I find myself stuck: at the edge of a dark lake whose bottom I can't see or even imagine, trying to reason my way in from the shore.

After the story ends and the credits roll, the game continues, and in a forest overtaken by torturers, a writer stands on a cliff and tells me the land is God and dreams. He says, "Wonderment is our morphine, I suppose." His books used to sit in Dutch's tent: *An American Eden*, *The American Inferno*. Now he's writing one he thinks will be different. He's calling it *America*. He shuts himself in his cabin, refusing to leave, eat, or drink liquor until the manuscript is complete. He dies at his desk, his face in a notebook where he's written, "When I'm done, just burn me," so I set the little house aflame.

I am nearing my cue for the epilogue I will not write because nobody likes that part of the game. I will exit while I still have something at stake, something still to be gained or lost, because resolution has gone out of fashion. I'm more interested in looking back to my curious and hopeful beginning, before I knew I would cry. I will start over. Do it better this time. Identify every animal. Craft every garment from their pelts. I'm going to listen to what Dutch said about love, and I'll find out whether he meant it at all, or whether he just wanted something and got confused, or whether any of his act was real. Maybe it doesn't matter, because the empire doesn't want us to love. It was built to break our reaching hands. Dutch once said, "This is America, you can always make a deal," and sometimes I think I made mine with the devil, agreeing to this pretty incarnation in exchange for life as a wanted woman. That's not what Dutch meant. He thinks he has a plan to outrun empire, but we who dreamed of escape were born with bounties on our heads. Is a plan the same as intuition? It might be the opposite. I collapsed into the universe's plan and followed the map of its signs, but I feel a change coming: soon, I'm going to ask myself what *I* want. Magic, but then what? The super blood wolf eclipse of the moon is coming soon. I hear that out in the woods, on a peak in the snow, among the evergreens, there's a fast white horse you can coax into your arms. After I restart, I will look for it in the unmapped thin place where the universe and I meet, not at a single point, but consuming each other in a dimension beyond plotting. Dutch says, *Ride with me*. We die. We ride. I restart again and again because the worst part of the story is the end.

ACKNOWLEDGMENTS

White Magic is a Creative Capital Project, supported in part by an award from the National Endowment for the Arts. "White City" and "Centerless Universe" were drafted as part of the Fremont Bridge Artist-in-Residence funded by Seattle's Department of Transportation's 1% for Art Funds and administered by the Office of Arts & Culture. I'm not sure this book would exist without the cash and affirmation of the Artist Trust Arts Innovator Award. Non-monetary support from Hugo House (the Made at Hugo House Fellowship) and Hedgebrook kept me moving toward this book.

"White Witchery" originally appeared at *Guernica*. An early version of "White City" appeared at *The Offing*, published as an excerpt from the anthology *Ghosts of Seattle Past* (Chin Music Press, ed. Jaimee Garbacik). An early version of part of "My Heartbreak Workbook" was published in *Pie & Whiskey: Writers under the Influence of Butter & Booze* (Sasquatch Books, eds. Kate Lebo and Samuel Ligon).

I wrote the first words of this book in 2012, but I didn't know that this book was what I was writing until five years later. I was already fully living inside the book by the time I saw what it was. My gratitude extends far beyond this too-brief list.

For reading drafts of this book or its parts, and for the encouragement and/or suggestions I needed to hear, I thank Kirsten Reach, Melissa Febos, Raena Shirali, Ruth Awad, Brian McGackin, Michelle Herman, Kathy Fagan Grandinetti, Lee Martin, Jaimee Garbacik, Cali Kopczick, Kristen Ramirez, Kristen Arnett, Byron Aspaas, Sasha LaPointe, Trevino Brings Plenty, Andrea Rogers, and Hillary Brenhouse. I am especially grateful to Julie Allain, Ken Workman, and Edith Loyer Nelson.

Many of these readers suggested source material and research avenues, as have other friends and colleagues; I've also had countless conversations that got me to the insights at the heart of this book. For these contributions and influences, I thank Theresa Warburton, Nick

White, Marcus Jackson, Kristen Millares Young, Eloisa Amezcua, Elizabeth Dark, Shaawano Chad Uran, Mattilda Bernstein Sycamore, Cynthia Updegrave, Elissa Ball, Emily Wittenhagen, Laura Scott, Hanif Abdurraqib, Colin McNamara, Travis Askew, Richard Chiem, Becca Schuh, Tommy Pico, Paullette Gaudet, Nate Washuta, and all the other friends, relatives, and colleagues who have made this world and work make some sense. I thank Leslie Ciechanowski for helping me find myself in the chaos so that I could write this.

For their help with the important but tedious parts of book compilation and promotion, I thank Max Delsohn and David Grandouiller.

The faculty and staff of American Indian Studies at the University of Washington taught me new ways of knowing. My brilliant, caring colleagues and students at the Ohio State University have created a space of support and inspiration where this book was immediately able to turn from a mess into a narrative. To Coven, Small Twitter, and Kenny Group, I'm grateful for your friendship, for meeting my dread spirals with your good sense, and for being writers and artists I aspire to impress.

My agent, Monika Woods, believed I could make this real when I wasn't sure, handles the crises in my anxious heart, and makes my dreams become realities. My editor, Tony Perez, approached this book on its own terms, located the flaws I was trying not to see, and guided me toward that moment when I put the final piece into this 107,703-piece jigsaw puzzle. Tin House is bringing this book into the world with incredible care. I'm deeply grateful to those who have worked on the book and its production and launch: Molly Templeton, Yashwina Canter, Jakob Vala, Becky Kraemer, Masie Cochran, Elizabeth DeMeo, Alyssa Ogi, Spencer Ruchti, Meg Storey, Allison Dubinsky, Craig Popelars, Nanci McCloskey, and everyone else who has worked to make this book beautiful and loved.

My family's support is unwavering, and I love them with all my heart.

I'll end as I began, by thanking Weston Morrow, my true love and best reader, whose support has changed everything. He was in the middle of this story long before I found him there.

BIBLIOGRAPHY

NOTE: Many of the sources used in the writing of *White Magic* were found online between 2012 and 2020. As we've already discussed, Online is a state of flux and the internet a mutable medium. Some of these links have already broken, and more will break. During the writing process, many were captured using the Internet Archive's Wayback Machine. Interested readers can visit archive.org/web and enter URLs to check.

WHITE WITCHERY

Atkin, Emily. "Do You Know Where Your Healing Crystals Come From?" *New Republic*, May 11, 2018. newrepublic.com/article/148190 /know-healing-crystals-come-from.

Phillip, Abby. "The bizarre ESP experiments conducted on aboriginal children without parental consent." *Washington Post*, January 16, 2015. washingtonpost.com/news/morning-mix/wp/2015/01/16 /the-bizarre-esp-experiments-conducted-on-aboriginal-children -in-canada-without-parental-consent.

Silko, Leslie Marmon. *Storyteller*. New York: Henry Holt, 1981.

Simpson, Leanne Betasamosake. *As We Have Always Done: Indigenous Freedom through Radical Resistance*. Minneapolis: University of Minnesota Press, 2017.

LITTLE LIES

Altringer, Ida Williams. "Indian Mary." *Skamania County Heritage* 16, no. 4 (March 1988): 2–8.

Blistein, Jon. "Lindsey Buckingham on Stevie Nicks: There's a Subtext of Love Between Us." *Rolling Stone*, March 22, 2013. rollingstone .com/music/news/lindsey-buckingham-on-stevie-nicks-theres-a -subtext-of-love-between-us-20130322.

"Cascade Resident Passes." *Skamania County Pioneer.* Volume XXIX, no. 21. May 27, 1921.

Cult Mania. "Phil Collins Interview 2016, (Writing In The Air Tonight)." YouTube video, 5.34. January 1, 2016. youtu.be/JuatAtEe9FQ.

Cunningham, James K., Teshia A. Solomon, and Myra L. Muramoto. "Alcohol use among Native Americans compared to whites: Examining the veracity of the 'Native American elevated alcohol consumption' belief." *Drug and Alcohol Dependence* 160 (March 1, 2016): 65–75.

Derickson, Alan. *Black Lung: Anatomy of a Public Health Disaster.* Ithaca: Cornell University Press, 1998.

Destiny Rules. Directed by Matt Baumann and Kyle Einhorn. New York: VH1 Television, 2004.

Fisher, Andrew H. *Shadow Tribe: The Making of Columbia River Indian Identity.* Seattle: University of Washington Press, 2010.

Frank, John W., Roland S. Moore, and Genevieve M. Ames. "Historical and cultural roots of drinking problems among American Indians." *American Journal of Public Health* 90, no. 3 (2000): 344–51. doi:10.2105/ajph.90.3.344.

Jonze, Tim. "Fleetwood Mac's Stevie and Christine: 'We were like rock'n'roll nuns.'" *Guardian,* December 12, 2013. theguardian.com/music/2013/dec/12/fleetwood-mac-stevie-nicks-christine-mcvie-nuns.

Kessler, Tom. "NOT JUST secondhand news; Going solo suits former Fleetwood Mac member Lindsey Buckingham." *Dallas Morning News,* April 2, 1993.

McLean, Craig. "Fleetwood Mac's Stevie Nicks on addiction, Botox and the burying of hatchets - interview." *Telegraph,* September 15, 2013. telegraph.co.uk/culture/music/rockandpopfeatures/10305143/Fleetwood-Macs-Stevie-Nicks-on-addiction-Botox-and-the-burying-of-hatchets-interview.html.

———. "Stevie Nicks: The men, the music, the menopause." *Guardian,* March 25, 2011. theguardian.com/music/2011/mar/25/stevie-nicks-interview.

Mikkelson, David. "In the Air Tonight." Snopes. September 12, 2000. snopes.com/fact-check/in-the-air-tonight.

"Phil Collins – In the Air Tonight." Genius. genius.com/Phil-collins-in-the-air-tonight-lyrics.

Savage, Mark. "Phil Collins: Back from the brink after alcohol battle." BBC News, October 22, 2016. bbc.com/news/entertainment-arts-37714459.

Spanos, Brittany. "'Silver Springs': Inside Fleetwood Mac's Great Lost Breakup Anthem." *Rolling Stone*, August 17, 2017. rollingstone.com/music/features/silver-springs-inside-fleetwood-macs-lost-breakup-anthem-w497060.

Spiller, Jan. *Astrology for the Soul*. New York: Bantam, 1997.

"Stevie Nicks Reveals 'I Was the Worst Drug Addict.'" Yahoo! Music. January 16, 2015. yahoo.com/music/stevie-nicks-reveals-i-was-the-worst-drug-addict-108281329281.html.

Stolz, Kim. "Fleetwood Mac's Stevie Nicks Dishes On Her Relationship With Lindsey Buckingam" [*sic*]. MTV News. April 10, 2009. mtv.com/news/1609042/fleetwood-macs-stevie-nicks-dishes-on-her-relationship-with-lindsey-buckingam.

Treaty with the Kalapuya, etc., 1855. Signed January 22, 1855. fws.gov/pacific/ea/tribal/treaties/kalapuya_1855.pdf.

White, Timothy. "Stevie Nicks' Magic Act." *Rolling Stone*, September 3, 1981. rollingstone.com/music/news/stevie-nicks-magic-act-19810903.

Williams, Chuck. *Bridge of the Gods, Mountains of Fire: A Return to the Columbia Gorge*. San Francisco: Friends of the Earth, 1980.

———. "Kalliah Tumulth (Indian Mary) (1854–1906)." Oregon Encyclopedia, Portland State University and the Oregon Historical Society. oregonencyclopedia.org/articles/indian_mary.

THE SPIRIT CORRIDOR

The Adventures of Mark Twain. Directed by Will Vinton. Los Angeles: Clubhouse Pictures, 1985.

Base, Graeme. *The Eleventh Hour: A Curious Mystery*. New York: Abrams, 1993.

Bible Hub, s.v. "3466. mustérion." biblehub.com/greek/3466.htm.

Carroll, Lewis. *Alice's Adventures in Wonderland and Through the Looking Glass*. 1865, 1871. New York: Penguin Clothbound Classics, 2010.

———. "Life Is but a Dream." Poetry Archive. poetry-archive.com/c/life_is_but_a_dream.html.

Corbett, William John. "Did Shakespeare Invent the Knock, Knock Joke?" *Master of the Ceremonies* (blog), October 5, 2012. masteroftheceremonies.wordpress.com/2012/10/05/did-shakespeare-invent-the-knock-knock-joke.

"Crystal Cave." Roadside America. roadsideamerica.com/story/12021.

DeKok, David. *Fire Underground: The Ongoing Tragedy of the Centralia Mine Fire*. Guilford, CT: Globe Pequot Press, 2009.

Driscoll, J. T. "Miracle." In *The Catholic Encyclopedia*. Volume 10. New York: Robert Appleton Company, 1911. newadvent.org/cathen/10338a.htm.

"FAQ." The Satanic Temple. thesatanictemple.com/pages/faq.

Games, Alison. *Witchcraft in Early North America*. Lanham, MD: Rowman Littlefield, 2010.

Hammer, Jill. "Lilith: Lady Flying in Darkness." My Jewish Learning, October 17, 2008. myjewishlearning.com/article/lilith-lady-flying-in-darkness.

Hill, Lynda. "The Sabian Symbols Story." Sabian Symbols. sabiansymbols.com/the-sabian-symbols-story.

Hontheim, Joseph. "Hell." In *The Catholic Encyclopedia*. Volume 7. New York: Robert Appleton Company, 1910. newadvent.org/cathen/07207a.htm.

Hunter, M. Kelley. "The Dark Goddess Lilith." *Mountain Astrologer*, April/May 1999. mountainastrologer.com/standards/editor's%20choice/articles/lilith_hunter/lilith.html.

"Inana's descent to the nether world: translation." Electronic Text Corpus of Sumerian Literature. etcsl.orinst.ox.ac.uk/section1/tr141.htm.

Jacobs, Melville. "Part I: Santiam Kalapuya Ethnologic Texts." *Kalapuya Texts*. University of Washington Publications in Anthropology 11 (June 1945). https://digitalcollections.lib.washington.edu/digital/collection/lctext/id/1590/rec/1.

———. *Northwest Sahaptin Texts*, 1. University of Washington Publications in Anthropology 2.6 (June 1929): 243. digitalcollections.lib.washington.edu/digital/collection/lctext/id/7620/rec/1.

Jung, C. G. *Two Essays on Analytical Psychology*. Translated by H. G. Baynes and C. F. Baynes. London: Baillière, Tindall Cox, 1928.

Kent, William. "Devil." In *The Catholic Encyclopedia*. Volume 4. New York: Robert Appleton Company, 1908. newadvent.org/cathen/04764a.htm.

Korson, George. *Black Rock: Mining Folklore of the Pennsylvania Dutch*. Baltimore: Johns Hopkins University Press, 1960.

L'Engle, Madeleine. *A Wrinkle in Time*. 1962. New York: Dell Yearling, 1984.

Lindbergh, Anne. *Travel Far, Pay No Fare*. New York: HarperCollins, 1992.

"List of Sabian Symbols." Sabian Mysteries. jamesburgess.com/list-of-sabians.html.

Mark, Joshua J. "Inanna's Descent: A Sumerian Tale of Injustice." *Ancient History Encyclopedia*, February 23, 2011. ancient.eu/article/215/inannas-descent-a-sumerian-tale-of-injustice.

Meridian, Bill. "Working with Natal Eclipse Paths." Microsoft PowerPoint, New Orleans, 2012. billmeridian.com/2012UACWORKSHOP.pdf.

Miller, Donald L. and Richard E. Sharpless. *The Kingdom of Coal: Work, Enterprise, and Ethnic Communities in the Mine Fields*. Philadelphia: University of Pennsylvania Press, 1985.

Milton, John. *Paradise Lost*. 2.621–627. Translated by Merritt Yerkes Hughes. Indianapolis: Hackett, 2003.

Mishkov, Aleksandar. "Mark Twain and the Halley's Comet - Writer Predicting Own Death." DocumentaryTube, April 29, 2016. documentarytube.com/articles/mark-twain-and-the-halley-s-comet -writer-predicting-own-death.

The New American Bible Revised Edition. United States Conference of Catholic Bishops. usccb.org/bible/books-of-the-bible/index.cfm.

Newell, William H. "Legends and Traditions of Schuylkill Co." *Publications of the Historical Society of Schuylkill County*. Volume IV. Pottsville, PA: Daily Republican Print, 1914.

Nick. "Lewis Carroll On Eternal Punishment." *Skeptical Eye* (blog), February 7, 2008. skepticaleye.com/2008/01/lewis-carrol-on-eternal -punishment.html.

"Religion." The Lewis Carroll Society of North America. lewiscarroll .org/carroll/study/religion.

Shakespeare, William. *Macbeth*. Edited by Barbara Mowat and Paul Werstine. Folger Shakespeare Library. Washington: Folger Shakespeare Library, 2013.

"Should We Fear Satan the Devil?" *The Watchtower*, November 2014. jw.org/en/publications/magazines/wp20141101/fear-satan-the-devil.

Symon, Evan V. "I Live In Centralia, PA: It's America's Creepiest Ghost Town." Cracked, October 23, 2017. cracked.com/personal -experiences-2537-i-live-in-centralia-pa-its-americas-creepiest-ghost -town.html.

Twain, Mark. "Mental Telegraphy. A Manuscript with a History." *Harper's*, December 1891.

———. "Mental Telegraphy Again." *Harper's*, September 1895.

ROCKS, CAVES, LAKES, FENS, BOGS, DENS, AND SHADES OF DEATH

Barlow, Bill. "Bears awaken to ongoing debate about their place in N.J." WHYY, April 19, 2019. whyy.org/articles/bears-awaken-to-ongoing -debate-about-their-place-in-n-j.

"Black Bear Biology and Behavior." New Jersey Division of Fish Wildlife. state.nj.us/dep/fgw/bearfacts_biology.htm.

Burns, Ashley and Chloe Schildhause. "The Art Of Murdering Kevin Bacon: An Oral History Of How 'Friday The 13th' Became A Horror Classic." UPROXX, June 3, 2015. uproxx.com/movies/friday-the-13th-oral-history.

"Bushkill Park." PAranormal (and TrueCrime) (blog), August 9, 2016. pennsylvaniaparanormal.tumblr.com/post/148690442738/bushkill-park-this-worn-and-torn-former-amusement.

Ellwood, Lisa J. "Ramapough Lenape and Powhatan Renape Nations of New Jersey have state recognition reaffirmed." *Indian Country Today*, March 27, 2019. indiancountrytoday.com/news/ramapough-lenape-and-powhatan-renape-nations-of-new-jersey-have-state-recognition-reaffirmed-NUHKiCDZSU6qBoZZyJp1fg.

Fear. Season 1, episode 5. "Camp Spirit Lake." MTV, 2000.

Friday the 13th. Directed by Sean S. Cunningham. Los Angeles: Paramount, 1980.

"Friday the 13th (1980)." IMDb. imdb.com/title/tt0080761.

"Friday the 13th, Part 1 Filming Location Tour." Crystal Lake Tours. crystallaketours.com.

Getlin, Larry. "This man wrote a small book for his family — and it became a bestseller." *New York Post*, December 25, 2016. nypost.com/2016/12/25/this-man-wrote-a-small-book-for-his-family-and-it-became-a-best-seller.

Heath, Chris. "18 Tigers, 17 Lions, 8 Bears, 3 Cougars, 2 Wolves, 1 Baboon, 1 Macaque, and 1 Man Dead in Ohio." *GQ*, February 6, 2012. https://www.gq.com/story/terry-thompson-ohio-zoo-massacre-chris-heath-gq-february-2012.

Johnson, Tom. "The List: NJ Locales with the Highest Amount of Toxic Chemical Releases." NJ Spotlight, November 2, 2015. njspotlight.com/stories/15/11/01/the-list-nj-locales-with-the-highest-amount-of-toxic-chemical-releases.

"Lt. Eric Kranz in the production of Friday the 13th?" Answers
.com, September 13, 2011. answers.com/Q/Lt._Eric_Kranz_in_the
_production_of_Friday_the_13th.

Martinelli, Patricia A. and Charles A. Stansfield, Jr. *Haunted New
Jersey: Ghosts and Strange Phenomena of the Garden State.* Mechanics-
burg, PA: Stackpole, 2004.

McArdle, Kevin. "NJ Black Bears Don't Hibernate: What That
Means for You." New Jersey 101.5. Townsquare Media, Inc., October
25, 2015. nj1015.com/nj-black-bears-dont-hibernate.

Meslow, Scott. "How Friday the 13th accidentally perfected the
slasher movie." *The Week*, June 13, 2014. theweek.com/articles/446191
/how-friday-13th-accidentally-perfected-slasher-movie.

Michallon, Clemence. "It doesn't look very fun! Inside the spooky,
century-old abandoned amusement park left frozen in time that once
was home to the oldest funhouse in America." *Daily Mail*, April 12, 2016.
dailymail.co.uk/news/article-3537025/Seph-Lawless-pictures-Bushkill
-Park-abandoned-amusement-park-near-Easton-Pennsylvania-oldest
-funhouse-America.html.

Miller, Rudy. "Another flood, another comeback for Bushkill
Park." Lehigh Valley Live, August 6, 2018. lehighvalleylive.com
/easton/2018/08/another_flood_another_comeback.html.

"Mountain Lake Bog Preserve." New Jersey Natural Lands Trust.
nj.gov/dep/njnlt/mountainlakebog.htm.

"Ohio sheriff: Only one monkey remains missing." CBS News.
CBS Interactive, October 19, 2011. cbsnews.com/news/ohio-sheriff
-only-one-monkey-remains-missing.

Orlean, Susan. "The Lady and the Tigers." *New Yorker*, February
18, 2002.

———. "Wild Animals Don't Want to Be Owned." *New Yorker*,
October 20, 2011.

Pinedo, Isabel. "Recreational Terror: Postmodern Elements of the
Contemporary Horror Film." *Journal of Film and Video* 48, no. 1/2
(Spring–Summer 1996): 17–31. jstor.org/stable/20688091.

"Princess Doe Case Details." Princess Doe Site. princessdoe.org /details.html.

Shonduras. "JENNY FELL OFF THE TRAIL.. scary moment for our family." YouTube Video, 19:44. May 23, 2019. https://web .archive.org/save/https://www.youtube.com/watch?v=vnR4KKBvzS0 feature=youtu.be.

Smothers, Ronald. "After Escaped Tiger Is Shot, Town Finds It Has a Lot More." *New York Times*, January 29, 1999.

Tatu, Christina. "Renovations to Bushkill Park's 'Barl of Fun' reveal new clues about its past." *Morning Call*, May 21, 2019. mcall .com/news/local/easton/mc-nws-easton-bushkill-park-renovations -20190521-3l7723pswrb7paolbszwksa724-story.html.

Young, William P. *The Shack*. Newbury Park, CA: Windblown Media. Kindle Edition, 2008.

WHITE CITY

Adamson, Thelma, ed. *Folk-Tales of the Coast Salish*. Lincoln: University of Nebraska Press, 2009.

Arrowsmith, William. "Indian Speeches The Deathsong Of Red Bird." *American Poetry Review* 2, no 1. (January/February 1973): 10–13. jstor.org/stable/40742749.

———. "Speech of Chief Seattle." *Arion: A Journal of Humanities and the Classics* 8, no. 4 (Winter 1969): 461–64. jstor.com/stable/20163221.

Bressan, David. "Ancient Stories Provided An Early Warning About Potential Seattle Earthquakes." *Forbes*, July 27, 2015. forbes .com/sites/davidbressan/2015/07/27/ancient-stories-provided-an -early-warning-about-potential-seattle-earthquakes/#2d91fd76546b.

Curtis, Edward S. Wishham. MS GC 1143 Box B #B115, Seaver Center for Western History Research, Natural History Museums of Los Angeles County. 113–20.

Davis, Margaret Bryan. "Pollen Evidence of Changing Land Use around the Shores of Lake Washington." *Northwest Science* 47, no. 3 (1973): 133–48.

Furtwangler, Albert. *Answering Chief Seattle*. Seattle: University of Washington Press, 1997.

Ludwin, Ruth S., Robert Dennis, Deborah Carver, Alan D. McMillan, Robert Losey, John Clague, Chris Jonientz-Trisler, Janine Bowechop, Jacilee Wray, and Karen James. "Dating the 1700 Cascadia Earthquake: Great Coastal Earthquakes in Native Stories." *Seismological Research Letters* 76, no. 2 (March/April 2005): 140–8.

Ludwin, R. S., C. P. Thrush, K. James, D. Buerge, C. Jonientz-Trisler, J. Rasmussen, K. Troost, and A. de los Angeles. "Serpent Spirit-power Stories along the Seattle Fault." *Seismological Research Letters* 76, no. 4 (July/August 2005): 426–31.

Miller, Jay and Astrida R. Blukis Onat. *Winds, Waterways, and Weirs: Ethnographic Study of the Central Link Light Rail Corridor.* BOAS Project No. 20005.D. BOAS, Inc. Seattle: 2004.

"One Of Kurt Cobain's Last Meals Was At Cactus—48 Hours Before His Death." *Cactus Restaurant Blog*, September 18, 2017. cactusrestaurants.com/2017/09/one-of-kurt-cobains-last-meals-was-at-cactus-48-hours-before-his-death.

Peretti, Jacques. "Where did you sleep last night?" *Guardian*, November 3, 2006. theguardian.com/music/2006/nov/04/popandrock.nirvana.

Schulz, Kathryn. "The Really Big One." *New Yorker*, July 13, 2015. newyorker.com/magazine/2015/07/20/the-really-big-one.

Tagas, Bryan. "Dredging ends, beavers return." *Madison Park Blogger.* madisonparkblogger.blogspot.com/2010/05/dredging-ends-beavers-return.html.

Thomas, Jane Powell. *Madison Park Remembered*. Seattle: J. P. Thomas, 2004.

Thrush, Coll. *Native Seattle: Histories from the Crossing-Over Place*. Seattle: University of Washington Press, 2007.

OREGON TRAIL II FOR WINDOWS 95/98/ME MACINTOSH: CHALLENGE THE UNPREDICTABLE FRONTIER

"Biography of Narcissa Whitman." Whitman Mission National Historic Site, National Park Service. nps.gov/whmi/learn/historyculture /narcissa-biography.htm.

Bull, Brian. "Sex and the Lewis and Clark Expedition." National Association of Tribal Historic Preservation Officers. nathpo.org/Many _Nations/mn_news12.html.

Clark, William and Meriwether Lewis. "April 18, 1806." Journals of the Lewis and Clark Expedition Online. lewisandclarkjournals.unl .edu/item/lc.jrn.1806-04-18#ln32041803.

Minnesota Educational Computing Consortium. *Oregon Trail II*. Minnesota Educational Computing Consortium, 1995, Windows 95.

The Revenant. Directed by Alejandro González Iñárritu. Los Angeles: 20th Century Fox, 2015.

"Sacagawea." PBS. pbs.org/lewisandclark/inside/saca.html.

Tunzelmann, Alex von. "How historically accurate is The Revenant?" *Guardian*, January 20, 2016. theguardian.com/film/2016/jan/20 /reel-history-the-revenant-leonardo-dicaprio.

CENTERLESS UNIVERSE

Adamson, Thelma, ed. *Folk-Tales of the Coast Salish*. Lincoln: University of Nebraska Press, 2009.

"All You Need to Know About Duane Hagadone, his Net Worth, His House, Private Jet and Lady Lola Yacht." Superyacht Fan. superyachtfan .com/superyacht_lady_lola.html.

Ball, Elissa. Hit the Deck Tarot. "#August 2016 may feel like you're wrapping up major life lessons in The Underworld . . ." Facebook, August 5, 2016. facebook.com/htdtarot/photos/a.464290037104770 /504189566448150.

Beason, Tyrone. "Central District's shrinking black community wonders what's next." *Seattle Times*, May 28, 2016. seattletimes.com /seattle-news/central-districts-shrinking-black-community-wonders -whats-next.

———. "Seattle's gritty bridges are built for function, not beauty." *Seattle Times*, November 25, 2015. seattletimes.com/pacific-nw-magazine /seattles-gritty-bridges-are-built-for-function-not-beauty.

Boyd, Colleen E. and Coll Thrush, eds. *Phantom Past, Indigenous Presence: Native Ghosts in North American Culture and History*. Lincoln: University of Nebraska Press, 2011.

Central Puget Sound Regional Transit Authority. East Link Project Draft Environmental Impact Statement, December 2008. soundtransit .org/sites/default/files/documents/pdf/projects/eastlink/deis/h4 _historic_and_archaeological_resources_technical_report.pdf.

"Culture Today." Duwamish Tribe. duwamishtribe.org/culture -today.

Davila, Vianna. "Native Americans, Seattle's original residents, are homeless at highest rate." *Seattle Times*, February 8, 2018. seattletimes.com /seattle-news/homeless/native-americans-are-this-regions-original -residents-and-they-are-its-most-likely-to-be-homeless.

———. "Nearly every Native American woman in Seattle survey said she was raped or coerced into sex." *Seattle Times*, August 23, 2018. seattletimes.com/seattle-news/homeless/survey-reveals-high-rates -of-sexual-assault-among-native-american-women-many-of-them -homeless.

"Dougsley's a Dud?" Volunteer Park Conservatory. volunteerpark conservatory.org/dougsley-a-dud.

Gregory, James N. "Remember Seattle's segregated history." *Seattle Post-Intelligencer*, December 11, 2006. seattlepi.com/local/opinion /article/Remember-Seattle-s-segregated-history-1222098.php.

Grundhauser, Eric. "Fremont Bridge." Atlas Obscura. atlasobscura .com/places/fremont-bridge.

Guydelkon, Sherry. "Point Elliott Treaty's 150th Birthday: A Cause for Celebration." *Tulalip syəcəb*, January 19, 2005. Reprinted on January 14, 2014. tulalipnews.com/wp/2014/01/19/point-elliott-treaty-159-years-later.

Heffter, Emily. "Human remains found in Eastlake neighborhood." *Seattle Times*, December 10, 2011. seattletimes.com/seattle-news/human-remains-found-in-eastlake-neighborhood.

Henderson, Jamala. "Why is Seattle so racially segregated." KUOW, September 20, 2016. kuow.org/stories/why-seattle-so-racially-segregated.

Gargas, Jane. "Columbia River petroglyphs show beauty of ancient art." *Everett Herald*, November 4, 2012. heraldnet.com/news/columbia-river-petroglyphs-show-beauty-of-ancient-art.

Irfan, Umair. "The human feet that routinely wash ashore in the Pacific Northwest, explained." Vox, February 11, 2019. vox.com/science-and-health/2017/12/18/16777724/human-feet-beach-pacific-northwest-seattle-vancouver.

Ishisaka, Naomi. "An epic battle against gentrification." Crosscut, April 2, 2018. crosscut.com/2018/04/epic-battle-against-gentrification.

Klingle, Matthew. *Emerald City: An Environmental History of Seattle.* New Haven, CT: Yale University Press, 2007.

Lewis, David. "The Man Who Burned Down Chief Seattle's Lodge." *Seattle Weekly*, August 25, 2016. seattleweekly.com/news/the-man-who-burned-down-old-man-house.

Long, Priscilla. "Duwamish Tribe wins federal recognition on January 19, 2001, but loses it again two days later." HistoryLink, January 20, 2001. historylink.org/File/2951.

"Lucky Lady." Superyachts.com. superyachts.com/motor-yacht-3050/lucky-lady.htm.

Madej, Patricia. "Harborview uses 'Pokémon Go' in patient recovery." *Seattle Times*, July 18, 2016. seattletimes.com/seattle-news/health/harborview-uses-pokmon-go-in-patient-recovery.

Mah, Norm. "How do the Fremont and Ballard Bridge Openings work?" *SDOT Blog*. Seattle Department of Transportation, September 28, 2016. sdotblog.seattle.gov/2016/09/28/how-do-the-fremont-and-ballard-bridge-openings-work.

Miller, Jay and Astrida R. Blukis Onat. *Winds, Waterways, and Weirs: Ethnographic Study of the Central Link Light Rail Corridor.* BOAS Project No. 20005.D. BOAS, Inc. Seattle: 2004.

Miller, Jay. *Lushootseed Culture and the Shamanic Odyssey: An Anchored Radiance.* Illustrated ed. Lincoln: University of Nebraska Press, 1999.

Ott, Jennifer. "Lake Union Lumber and Manufacturing is incorporated on March 9, 1882." HistoryLink, January 4, 2013. historylink.org/File/10218.

———. "Seattle Board of Trustees passes ordinance, calling for removal of Indians from the town, on Feb. 7, 1865." HistoryLink, December 7, 2014. historylink.org/File/10979.

Parrish, Susan. "Aboriginal art comes with a view." *Columbian*, August 16, 2014. columbian.com/news/2014/aug/16/she-who-watches-horsethief-lake-aboriginal-art.

Payne, Patti. "Bay-Area media mogul's super yacht 'Invader' – one of America's largest – moors in Lake Union." *Puget Sound Business Journal*, June 24, 2015. bizjournals.com/seattle/blog/2015/06/bay-area-media-moguls-super-yacht-invader-one-of.html.

Phelps, Myra L., Leslie Blanchard, James R. Robertson, and Claude E. Buckner. *Public Works in Seattle: A Narrative History [of] the Engineering Department, 1875–1975.* Seattle, WA: Seattle Engineering Dept., 1978.

Pitt, Lillian. "She Who Watches." Website for Lillian Pitt. lillianpitt.com/she-who-watches.

Poncavage, Joanna, compiled from work by George P. Donehoo, 1928, and the New Jersey Writers Project, 1938. "Lenape language LEGACY **In towns; creeks and more, Indian nation left its mark on our region." *Morning Call*, November 14, 2008, mcall.com/news/mc -xpm-2008-11-14-4242347-story.html.

Rosay, André B. "Violence Against American Indian and Alaska Native Women and Men: 2010 Findings From the National Intimate Partner and Sexual Violence Survey." US Department of Justice: Office of Justice Programs, National Institute of Justice, May 2016. https://www.ncjrs.gov/pdffiles1/nij/249736.pdf.

Seattle FRIENDS. seattlefriends.org.

"Shoreline Foster Island." University of Washington Botanic Gardens. botanicgardens.uw.edu/washington-park-arboretum/gardens /shoreline-foster-island.

Simpson, Audra. "The State is a Man: Theresa Spence, Loretta Saunders and the Gender of Settler Sovereignty." *Theory Event* 19, no. 4 (2016). muse.jhu.edu/article/633280.

Stark, Virginia Carraway. "The Mystery of the Salish Sea Disembodied Feet." National Paranormal Society. national-paranormal-society .org/the-mystery-of-the-salish-sea-disembodied-feet-2.

Thrush, Coll. *Native Seattle: Histories from the Crossing-Over Place*. Seattle: University of Washington Press, 2007.

"Treaty of Point Elliott." Duwamish Tribe. duwamishtribe.org /treaty-of-point-elliott.

"Treaty of Point Elliott, 1855." Governor's Office of Indian Affairs, State of Washington. goia.wa.gov/tribal-government/treaty-point-elliott -1855.

"Visit the Longhouse." Duwamish Tribe. duwamishtribe.org /longhouse.

Wikipedia. "Amorphophallus Titanum." Last modified July 4, 2020. en.wikipedia.org/wiki/Amorphophallus_titanum.

Willingham, William F. "Cascade Locks." Oregon Encyclopedia, Portland State University and the Oregon Historical Society. oregonencyclopedia.org/articles/cascade_locks.

Wilma, David. "Straightening of Duwamish River begins on October 14, 1913." HistoryLink, February 16, 2001. historylink.org/File/2986.

"Yacht INVADER, Codecasa." CharterWorld. charterworld.com /?sub=yacht-charter charter=invader-2649.

MY HEARTBREAK WORKBOOK

Hendrix, Harville. *Keeping the Love You Find: A Personal Guide*. New York: Atria, 1992.

THE SPIRIT CABINET

Abdurraqib, Hanif. "It's Not Like Nikola Tesla Knew All of Those People Were Going to Die." Produced by Katie Klocksin. *PoetryNow*, September 24, 2018. Podcast, 4:01. https://www.poetryfoundation .org/podcasts/147973/it39s-not-like-nikola-tesla-knew-all-of-those -people-were-going-to-die.

Acher, Frater. "On the Dweller on the Threshold." Theomagica. theomagica.com/the-dweller-on-the-threshold.

Blaine, David. *Mysterious Stranger*. New York: Villard, 2002.

Boulègue, Franck. *Twin Peaks: Unwrapping the Plastic*. Chicago: University of Chicago Press, 2016.

Bullwinkel, Rita. *Belly Up*. Austin: A Strange Object, 2016.

Bush, Evan. "New report highlights flaws in police data on missing, murdered indigenous women and girls." *Seattle Times*, November 14, 2018. seattletimes.com/seattle-news/new-report-highlights-flaws-in -police-data-on-missing-murdered-indigenous-women-and-girls.

Clifton, Lucille. "the light that came to lucille clifton." *The Collected Poems of Lucille Clifton 1965–2010*. Rochester: BOA Editions, Ltd., 2012.

Cramer, Stuart. *Germain the Wizard*. Seattle: Miracle Factory, 2002.

———. *Germain the Wizard and His Legerdemain*. Goleta, CA: Buffum Publishing Corporation, 1966.

———. *The Secrets of Karl Germain*. Cleveland Heights, OH: Mr. Meriweather and Company, 1962.

Crew, Bec. "Scientists Propose a 'Mirror Universe' Where Time Moves Backwards." Science Alert, January 25, 2016. sciencealert.com /scientists-propose-a-mirror-universe-where-time-moves-backwards.

Davila, Vianna. "Nearly every Native American woman in Seattle survey said she was raped or coerced into sex." *Seattle Times*, June 10, 2019. seattletimes.com/seattle-news/homeless/survey-reveals-high -rates-of-sexual-assault-among-native-american-women-many-of -them-homeless.

Fimrite, Peter. "Mysterious great white shark lair discovered in Pacific Ocean." *San Francisco Chronicle*, September 16, 2018. sfchronicle .com/news/article/Mysterious-great-white-shark-lair-discovered-in -13234068.php.

Gíslason, Gunnar Karl and Jody Eddy. *North: The New Nordic Cuisine of Iceland*. Berkeley, CA: Ten Speed Press, 2014.

Granrose, John. "The Archetype of the Magician." Diploma thesis, C. G. Jung Institute, Zürich 1996. granrose.com/main/articles/thesis2 .html.

Jung, C. G. *Psychology and Alchemy*. 2nd edition. Translated by R. F. C. Hull. New York: Pantheon, 1968.

———. "Lecture I." In *The Symbolic Life*. Translated by R. F. C. Hull. 5–35. Princeton: Princeton University Press, 1976.

Levith, Will. "10 Real-Life 'Twin Peaks' Locations You Can Visit Today." *Condé Nast Traveler*, June 1, 2017. cntraveler.com/galleries /2015-03-16/10-real-life-twin-peaks-locations-you-can-visit-today.

Magness, Josh. "Boy bit by shark in video is 'so lucky that happened' and hopes to swim with them again." *Miami Herald*, December 3, 2018. miamiherald.com/news/nation-world/national/article222543725.html.

Meder, Amanda Linette. "Doorways To The Other Side: Am I A Portal? Is My House A Portal?" *Intuitive Lifestyle Blog*, September 15, 2014. amandalinettemeder.com/blog/2014/9/9/doorways-to-the-other-side-am-i-a-portal-is-my-house-a-portal.

Ouspensky, P. D. *In Search of the Miraculous: Fragments of an Unknown Teaching*. 1949. New York: Harcourt, 1977.

Pollari, Niina. *Dead Horse*. Austin, Minneapolis, New York, Raleigh: Birds LLC, 2015.

The Prestige. Directed by Christopher Nolan. Buena Vista Pictures, 2006.

"Selket: Large Scorpion Ring with Labradorite." BloodMilk. bloodmilkjewels.com/products/selket-large-scorpion-ring-with-labradorite.

"Shark attack survivor says he's more grateful than ever." NBC4 WCMH-TV, November 25, 2018. nbc4i.com/news/u-s-world/shark-attack-survivor-says-hes-more-grateful-than-ever.

Siken, Richard. "Snow and Dirty Rain." *Crush*. New Haven: Yale University Press, 2005.

Staniforth, Nate. *Here Is Real Magic: A Magician's Search for Wonder in the Modern World*. New York: Bloomsbury, 2018.

Twain, Mark. *The Mysterious Stranger*.

Twin Peaks. Created by Mark Frost and David Lynch. New York: CBS, 1990–91.

Twin Peaks: The Return. Created by Mark Frost and David Lynch. New York: Showtime, 2017.

Urban, Eusebio. "The Dweller of the Threshold." Blavatsky.net, Theosophy Foundation. blavatsky.net/index.php/dweller-of-the-threshold.

"The White Pilgrim and the Dark of the Moon." Weird NJ. weirdnj.com/stories/garden-state-ghosts/the-white-pilgrim.

Wyler, Grace. "The Beluga Whale Image In That Popular Melania Trump Tweet Mysteriously Turned Into A Giraffe." BuzzFeed News, December 30, 2018. buzzfeednews.com/article/gracewyler/melania-trump-whale-giraffe-tweet.

IN HIM WE HAVE REDEMPTION THROUGH HIS BLOOD

Forché, Carolyn. "Because One Is Always Forgotten." *Iowa Review* 12, no. 2 (Spring/Summer 1981): 85. ir.uiowa.edu/cgi/viewcontent .cgi?article=2698 context=iowareview.

"I wonder how many people here have watched the show in Saint Denis because its actually pretty decent." [*sic*] Reddit, November 22, 2018. reddit.com/r/reddeadredemption/comments/9zjgf2/i_wonder _how_many_people_here_have_watched_the.

Jacobs, Melville. "Part I: Santiam Kalapuya Ethnologic Texts." *Kalupuya Texts*. University of Washington Publications in Anthropology 11 (June 1945): 34. https://digitalcollections.lib.washington.edu/digital /collection/lctext/id/1590/rec/1.

The New American Bible Revised Edition. United States Conference of Catholic Bishops. usccb.org/bible/books-of-the-bible/index.cfm.

Rockstar Games. *Red Dead Redemption 2.* Rockstar Games, 2018, PlayStation 4.

ELISSA WASHUTA is a member of the Cowlitz Indian Tribe and a nonfiction writer. She is the author of *Starvation Mode* and *My Body Is a Book of Rules*, named a finalist for the Washington State Book Award. With Theresa Warburton, she is co-editor of the anthology *Shapes of Native Nonfiction: Collected Essays by Contemporary Writers*. She is an assistant professor of creative writing at the Ohio State University.